THE FUTURE OF THE FAMILY

THE FUTURE OF THE FAMILY

Daniel P. Moynihan,
Timothy M. Smeeding,
and Lee Rainwater
EDITORS

Russell Sage Foundation ◆ New York

The Russell Sage Foundation

The Russell Sage Foundation, one of the oldest of America's general purpose foundations, was established in 1907 by Mrs. Margaret Olivia Sage for "the improvement of social and living conditions in the United States." The Foundation seeks to fulfill this mandate by fostering the development and dissemination of knowledge about the country's political, social, and economic problems. While the Foundation endeavors to assure the accuracy and objectivity of each book it publishes, the conclusions and interpretations in Russell Sage Foundation publications are those of the authors and not of the Foundation, its Trustees, or its staff. Publication by Russell Sage, therefore, does not imply Foundation endorsement.

Library of Congress Cataloging-in-Publication Data
The future of the family / Daniel Patrick Moynihan, Timothy M. Smeeding, and Lee Rainwater, editors.
   p.   cm.
  Includes bibliographical references and index.
  ISBN 0-87154-625-6
    1. Family—United States.   2. Family policy—United States.   3. Child welfare—United States.   4. United States—Social conditions—1945–
I. Moynihan, Daniel P. (Daniel Patrick), 1927–2003   II. Rainwater, Lee.
III. Smeeding, Timothy M.
HQ536.F98   2004
306.85'0973—dc22   2004056670

Text design by Genna Patacsil.

RUSSELL SAGE FOUNDATION
112 East 64th Street, New York, New York 10021
10 9 8 7 6 5 4 3 2 1

For Liz, Mary Ann, Carol,
and all our families and children

CONTENTS

CONTRIBUTORS

Daniel P. Moynihan was university professor at Syracuse University until his untimely death in March 2003, as well as a former United States senator and ambassador to India and the United Nations.

Lee Rainwater is professor of sociology emeritus at Harvard University and research director of the Luxembourg Income Study.

Timothy M. Smeeding is the Maxwell Professor of Public Policy at the Maxwell School of Syracuse University and overall director of the Luxembourg Income Study.

P. Lindsay Chase-Lansdale is professor of human development and social policy in the School of Education and Social Policy and faculty fellow in the Institute for Policy Research of Northwestern University.

David T. Ellwood is Scott M. Black Professor of Political Economy and dean of the John F. Kennedy School of Government at Harvard University.

Nancy Folbre is professor of economics at the University of Massachusetts, Amherst.

Frank F. Furstenberg is Zellerbach Family Professor of Sociology at the University of Pennsylvania.

Irwin Garfinkel is Mitchell I. Ginsberg Professor of Contemporary Urban Problems at Columbia University School of Social Work.

Janet C. Gornick is associate professor of political science at the Graduate Center and Baruch College at the City University of New York and associate director of the Luxembourg Income Study.

Wade F. Horn is assistant secretary of the Administration on Children and Families in the United States Department of Health and Human Services. From 1994 until assuming his present position, he was president of the National Fatherhood Initiative (NFI). From 1989 to 1993, he was commissioner of the Administration on Children, Youth and Families and chief of the Children's Bureau within the United States Department of Health and Human Services.

Christopher Jencks is Malcolm Wiener Professor of Social Policy in the John F. Kennedy School of Government at Harvard University.

Kathleen Kiernan is professor of social policy and demography at the University of York and codirector of the ESRC Centre for Analysis of Social Exclusion at the London School of Economics.

Will Marshall is president and founder of the Progressive Policy Institute (PPI) in Washington, D.C.

Sara McLanahan is professor of sociology and public affairs at Princeton University and director of the Bendheim-Thoman Center for Research on Child Wellbeing.

Samuel H. Preston is Fredrick J. Warren Professor of Demography and dean of the School of Arts and Sciences at the University of Pennsylvania.

Isabel V. Sawhill is vice-president and director of Economic Studies at the Brookings Institution and serves as president of the National Campaign to Prevent Teen Pregnancy.

Wendy Sigle-Rushton is lecturer in the Department of Social Policy at the London School of Economics and associate of the ESRC Centre for Analysis of Social Exclusion.

Douglas A. Wolf is Gerald B. Cramer Professor of Aging Studies and professor of public administration at Syracuse University's Maxwell School of Citizenship and Public Affairs.

FOREWORD

ON MARCH 26, 2003, the United States lost one of its most eminent and visionary public servants, the social sciences lost one of their most astute and prolific practitioners, and the Maxwell School lost one of its most celebrated and distinguished faculty members. I am writing, of course, about the death of Daniel Patrick Moynihan, which has left so very many holes in the fabric of our common life.

Much has been written about Moynihan's accomplishments, and much more, no doubt, will be forthcoming. This volume, however, may well be the last book that will ever be published under his name and containing, in print, his singular voice. And since that voice will be so profoundly missed, in so many different forums, this seems an appropriate place to reflect for a moment on what made the voice so distinctive.

The voice was frequently and combatively prophetic. Who else, at the height of the civil rights and sexual liberation agitation, could have predicted so accurately the social costs of family dissolution, particularly among blacks? And who else, some twenty-five years ago in the grip of cold war tension, could have predicted the demise of the Soviet Union? Pat Moynihan valued truth more than the semblance of collegiality, and he was not often thanked for it. I thank him here.

The voice was always well, and astonishingly widely, informed. Who else could quote from memory whole stanzas of W. H. Auden on the subject of the lead-up to World War II and then turn around and give you a detailed disquisition on the development of the women's rights movement in upstate New York? For those who wanted an education, he was a walking university. I thank him for that too.

The voice was always human. Who else, in a volume like this, filled with graphs and statistics, could write the sentence: "The 'present-oriented,' in Edward C. Banfield's term, seems ever more present." That he always held on to the human and never yielded to the temptation to disappear behind a mask of expertise—though expertise, God knows, he had—made him a wonderfully entertaining and exhilarating person to work with, and I thank him most personally for that.

We have lost something irreplaceable in Moynihan's voice, and we can only be grateful for what is preserved in this volume.

John L. Palmer
University Professor and former dean
Maxwell School of Citizenship and Public Affairs
Syracuse University

PREFACE

A Dahrendorf Inversion and the Twilight of the Family: The Challenge to the Conference

Daniel P. Moynihan, edited and amended by Timothy M. Smeeding

A WHILE BACK I had something of a start coming upon a reference in *The New Yorker* magazine to an article I had written "in the middle of the last century." "Epidemic on the Highways" (Moynihan 1959) was perhaps the first comprehensive statement on the medical trauma associated with the automobile. Anyone who has ever buckled a seatbelt or watched a television advertisement of an automobile crashing into a brick wall is engaging the subject as it has evolved in the decades since.

The beginning of the 1960s was a creative moment. All manner of new subjects were being explored, not least at Syracuse University's Maxwell School, where I was a professor in 1960–1961. During this period I wrote my portion of *Beyond the Melting Pot*, a project conceived and for the most part executed by Nathan Glazer (Glazer and Moynihan 1963/1970). The subject was "The Negroes, Puerto Ricans, Jews, Italians, and Irish of New York City." The preface to the first edition in 1963 opens with these words:

> This is a beginning book. It is an effort to trace the role of ethnicity in the tumultuous, varied, endlessly complex life of New York City. It is time,

we believe, that such an effort be made, albeit doomed inevitably to approx-
imation and to inaccuracy, and although it cannot but on occasion give
offense to those very persons for whom we have the strongest feeling of
fellowship and common purpose. The notion that the intense and unprecedented mixture of ethnic and religious groups in American life was soon to
blend into a homogeneous end product has outlived its usefulness, and also
its credibility. In the meanwhile the persisting facts of ethnicity demand
attention, understanding, and accommodation. (Glazer and Moynihan 1963/
1970, v)

But the point about the melting pot, hinted at above, is that it did not
happen. At that time much of the academic world was still in thrall to the
nineteenth-century notion of class as the defining subject of social structure
and, by extension, of politics. By this I mean that the "workers of the
world would unite," and so on. Many of us suspected otherwise, but were
circumspect. We were less so in the introduction to the second edition
(Glazer and Moynihan 1963/1970, xxxiv), where we wrote:

First: ethnic identities have taken over some of the task in self-definition
and in definition by others that occupational identities, particularly working-
class occupational identities, have generally played. The status of the worker
has been downgraded; as a result, apparently, the status of being an ethnic,
a member of an ethnic group, has been upgraded.

The book was fairly candid about matters such as family, education,
occupation, and politics. We had feared we might give offense, and we
did. We had written, "This is a beginning book," in the first edition. Alas,
by the second edition the subject of minorities had come to be seen as
ruinous to one's reputation. But a few fine spirits pursued the subject, and
after nearly a half-century the *Melting Pot* is still in print.

In 1964 the book received the Anisfield-Wolf Book Award for inquiry
into race relations. But this peace was not to last. In 1961 I had joined the
Kennedy administration as assistant secretary of labor for policy planning
and research. In an oft-told tale (see especially Rainwater 1970), I had
begun to worry that the issue of full employment, so central to social policy
of that time, was fading a bit as economic growth resumed after an earlier
recession. Would it help if we could associate unemployment with social
issues that were not, strictly speaking, economic—for instance, out-of-
wedlock births or single parenthood?

Figure P.1   Moynihan's Scissors: Unemployment Versus Welfare, 1948 to 1969

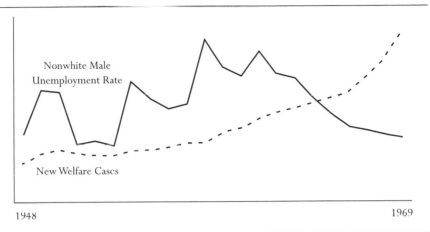

Source: U.S. Census Bureau (1976, 135 [table series D87–101], 356 [table series H346–67]).

BLACK MALE UNEMPLOYMENT AND OUT-OF-WEDLOCK CHILDREN

The policy planning staff in the Labor Department, led by Paul Barton, found a stunning correlation between black male unemployment and various social indicators, notably new welfare cases. At this juncture in history, the topic was just emerging as a subject of concern. From the late 1940s to the early 1960s, the correlation between the two was as near as nature gets to perfect, with a 1948 to 1962 correlation coefficient of .91. But then it weakened, and in an instant it became negative as unemployment went down but welfare receipt went up (figure P.1). I wrote this up in a report for the DOL called "The Negro Family: The Case for National Action" (Moynihan 1965). After reading the report, the political scientist James Q. Wilson labeled this widening gap "Moynihan's Scissors."

FAMILY BREAKDOWN: THE EARTHQUAKE

In June 1965, President Lyndon Johnson gave the commencement address, which I partly wrote, at Howard University.[1] Family would become an issue of national policy, in the president's words, at "the next and more profound stage of the battle for civil rights." Johnson said:

Perhaps most important—its influence radiating to every part of life—is the breakdown of the Negro family structure. For this, most of all, white America must accept responsibility. It flows from centuries of oppression and persecution of the Negro man. It flows from the long years of degradation and discrimination, which have attacked his dignity and assaulted his ability to produce for his family.

This, too, is not pleasant to look upon. But it must be faced by those whose serious intent is to improve the life of all Americans.

Only a minority—less than half—of all Negro children reach the age of 18 having lived all their lives with both of their parents. At this moment, tonight, little less than two-thirds are at home with both of their parents. Probably a majority of all Negro children receive federally aided public assistance sometime during their childhood.

The family is the cornerstone of our society. More than any other force it shapes the attitude, the hopes, the ambitions, and the values of the child. And when the family collapses it is the children that are usually damaged. When it happens on a massive scale the community itself is crippled.

So, unless we work to strengthen the family, to create conditions under which most parents will stay together—all the rest: schools, and playgrounds, and public assistance, and private concern, will never be enough to cut completely the circle of despair and deprivation. (Johnson 1966; quoted in Rainwater and Yancey 1967, 130)

Everyone was thrilled. Two months later the Voting Rights Act was signed. But scarcely a week after that, riots broke out in the Watts section of Los Angeles, and thirty-four people were killed, nearly all of them black. This experience was disorienting. I found myself asking whether the sudden disconnect between employment and family structure that we had encountered (and we had *not* been looking for it) might help explain the seemingly inexplicable outbreak of rioting. I gave one of my few copies of "The Negro Family" to the fabled political columnist Robert Novak, who got it right off. The next day his column, written with Rowland Evans (1965), was titled "The Moynihan Report." Fury broke out on the left; there was not, at that time, much of a "right."

In the Howard University address, Johnson had called for a White House conference "to fulfill these rights," which met the following year. White House aide Berl Bernhard commenced the proceedings with the reassuring pronouncement, "I want you to know that I have been reliably informed that no such person as Daniel Patrick Moynihan exists" (quoted in Rainwater and Yancey 1967, 248). The subject of family change was stricken from the conference. I was charged with "blaming the victim."

The conference came to nothing, and the topic virtually disappeared from public discourse for a decade or more.

Life went on. But the trends we had picked up kept going. The fraction of black out-of-wedlock births had been 24 percent in 1960, but by the beginning of the twenty-first century it was 69 percent. The white ratio had been 3 percent at that time; it reached 23 percent in 2002. Overall, one-third of the births in the nation were outside of marriage by 2002 (Child Trends 2003). In the early 1980s, Harold A. Richman, founding director of the Chapin Hall Center for Children at the University of Chicago, told a House committee that single parenthood is now a fact of life for all classes and for all races.

In the 1984 presidential address to the Population Association of America, Samuel H. Preston (1984, 451) spoke of "the earthquake that shuddered through the American family in the past twenty years," referring in large part to the sudden sustained rise in single parenthood and out-of-wedlock births since the mid-1960s, when our data series had ended with that scissors. Even as Preston spoke, the estimable Eleanor Holmes Norton, whom Jimmy Carter had named as the first woman to chair the Equal Employment Opportunity Commission, observed that the repair of the black family was central to any serious strategy to improve the black condition. But nothing much seemed to work to reverse this trend. The American sociologist Peter Rossi (1987, 4) had already laid down his "Iron Law of Evaluation: The expected value of any net impact assessment of any large scale social program is zero." The optimism of the 1960s gave way to an almost painful silence, even as "activists" went on about investigating "root causes."

WHAT HAPPENED?

Again, the larger question is whether in 1964–1965, quite by accident, we had picked up the first tremors of the earthquake Preston wrote about two decades later. This was indeed a seismic event, as it persisted across the North Atlantic and down under to Australia. Are such things possible? Do the new 2000 census data conceal some other set of facts? I surely don't think so, but it is plain to me that while the subject has attracted increasing interest, academics for a long time have been unwilling to write about the racial dimensions of this issue. In three decades since out-of-wedlock childbearing has exploded, there has not, to my knowledge, been a single book, book review, paper, whatever, that has definitively addressed the racial dimensions of this change. Has the subject become too sensitive or even dangerous? Some thirty-five years ago I gave the commencement address at the New School in which I suggested that "the training of any social scientist in years to come should include something equivalent to the processes by which psychiatrists are taught to anticipate and accept hostility" (Moynihan 1968, n.p.). Perhaps that training has not occurred.

We must, of course, entertain the null hypothesis that nothing happened, or nothing much. This turns on the rise of cohabitation, a matter that the economist Barbara Boyle Torrey is pursuing with energy and range (Torrey and Haub 2003). As we go up the social scale, increased cohabitation will surely account for some of the change in marriage patterns, assuming the former has replaced the latter to some extent in this and other rich countries. (For an examination of the breadth and plethora of cohabitation forms in rich countries, see Kiernan, chapter 3, this volume.) But of what consequence is that where it matters most—in lower-income and "at risk" families? Here it seems that cohabitation is neither stable nor long-term.

In September 2000, I was commanded by James Q. Wilson to present a paper at the annual meeting of the American Political Science Association on "Government Work: Forty Years of National Politics" (Moynihan 2000). My central theme was that in those forty years we seemed to have resolved the economic problem of unemployment that John Maynard Keynes described in his classic book *The General Theory of Employment, Interest, and Money* (1936), and which he thought we might resolve in about that time frame. The nagging unemployment that had so bothered us in government in the early 1960s had given way to generally low rates accompanied by extraordinary economic growth in the late 1990s. Gross domestic product, in real dollars, grew tenfold in forty years. And so I asked: "If everything is going so well, why are we not happier?" I suggested that "the Economic Problem" had been succeeded by what Francis Fukuyama (1999, 4–5) had recently termed "the Great Disruption." Fukuyama wrote:

This period, from roughly the mid-1960s to the early 1990s, was also marked by seriously deteriorating social conditions in most of the industrialized world. Crime and social disorder began to rise, making inner-city areas of the wealthiest societies on earth almost uninhabitable. The decline of kinship as a social institution, which has been going on for more than two hundred years, accelerated sharply in the last half of the twentieth century. Fertility in most European countries and Japan fell to such low levels that these societies will depopulate themselves in the next century, absent substantial immigration; marriages and births became fewer; divorce soared; and out-of-wedlock childbearing came to affect one out of

Table P.1   Nonmarital Birth Ratios

Country	1960	Recent
United States	5.3%	33.0% (1999)
Canada	4.3	30.0 (1999)
United Kingdom	5.4	38.0 (1998)
Ireland	1.6	32.0 (2000)
Australia	4.8	28.0 (1997)
New Zealand	5.3	42.0 (1997)
France	6.1	40.0 (1997)

Source: Council of Europe (2003); Bradshaw and Finch (2002).

every three children born in the United States and over half of all children born in Scandinavia. . . .

These changes were dramatic, they occurred over a wide range of similar countries, and they all appeared at roughly the same period in history. As such, they constituted a Great Disruption in the social values that prevailed in the industrial age society of the mid-twentieth century. . . . It is highly unusual for social indicators to move together so rapidly; even without knowing why they did so, we have reason to suspect that they might be related to one another. Although conservatives . . . are often attacked for harping on the theme of moral decline, they are essentially correct: the breakdown of social order is not a matter of nostalgia, poor memory, or ignorance about the hypocrisies of earlier ages. The decline is readily measurable in statistics on crime, fatherless children, reduced educational outcomes and opportunities, broken trust, and the like.

Next, in my speech, I recorded the trend in nonmarital ratios, surely a leading indicator of this disruption; a partial list of my findings and sources are shown in table P.1.

What happened? Did some cosmic deity decree that as of an instant, the world would so rapidly become so different in such disparate places as the multicultural United States and the homogeneous Ireland? The upending can be stunning in other ways as well: in 1980 out-of-wedlock births in the largely Catholic province of Quebec came to 14 percent; by 1994 it was 48 percent (Torrey and Haub 2003). Obviously, Roman Catholicism has little to do with this outcome.

WHAT DO WE KNOW?

As I told the political scientists in 2000, we don't know much about the exact causes of out-of-wedlock births, despite the growing literature on the consequences (see, for example, McLanahan and Sandefur 1994). The impact of fatherlessness on children is abundantly documented. As far back as 1982, the sociologist James S. Coleman (1982, 144), that giant of his age, observed that the process of making human beings human is breaking down in American society. He went on to ask if ours could be "the first species to forget how to appropriately raise its young."

Racial sensitivity is also a difficulty. In 1965 Martin Luther King Jr. delivered a speech in which he referred to a "recent study" and declared that the breakdown of the Negro family was a "social catastrophe" (King 1965; Rainwater and Yancey 1967, 404).[3] King remained supportive in the years left to him. Not that long afterward, however, the columnist Carl Rowan accused public figures who raised the subject of unmarried births of spreading "subtle demagogic racism." Public figures presumably seek public approval, and thus the subject submerged for a long time. For example, not until 2003 did the Washington-based organization Child Trends, a nonpartisan, nonprofit research group of the first quality, supported by the best foundations and working closely with federal statistical agencies, begin to report the trend in out-of-wedlock childbirth, broken down by race and ethnicity, into its social indicators website, the Child Trends DataBank (Child Trends 2003).[4]

There are indeed some contrary trends in recent research. The 1998 Morehouse College Conference on African American Fathers observed:

> Although the proportion of children with absent fathers is growing fastest among whites, the problem of father absence is especially acute in the African American community. Of all Black babies born in 1996, approximately 70 percent were born to unmarried mothers. On average, a Black child born in the early 1950s would eventually spend about four years (or about 22 percent of childhood) living in a one-parent home. But for Black children born in the early 1980s, that figure, according to one estimate, would nearly triple, to almost 11 years or about 60 percent of childhood. (Morehouse Research Institute 1999, 8)

And in an address to a September 2001 conference sponsored by the Department of Health and Human Services, Reverend Walter Fauntroy, president of the National Black Leadership Roundtable and a close associate of Dr. King, declared that the fatherless family was the final item on the civil rights agenda. He was speaking by now to conservatives, but he was speaking.

Liberal default invited conservative initiative in research and commentary on the black family. Columbia University professor Ronald B. Mincy (2002) has commented: "The whole subject of the black family was aban-

doned by liberal scholars . . . leaving what we know about families and
. . . the policy recommendations about how to respond to them to conservatives." In 1994, in the House Republican "Contract with America,"
the term "illegitimacy" all of a sudden reappeared. This became "the fifth
horseman of the Apocalypse" in the view of influential Republicans, as
related by Ron Haskins, a senior research fellow at the Brookings Institution and George W. Bush's senior adviser for welfare policy (personal
communication, 2001). In the early 1990s a range of state governments
took up the cause of moving clients from "welfare to work," an explosive
proposition unmentionable in the turbulent 1970s. In 1996 a Republican
Congress enacted the Personal Responsibility and Work Opportunity
Reconciliation Act, which outright abolished AFDC and included monetary incentives to states to achieve decreases in out-of-wedlock childbirths. President William J. Clinton signed the bill in a ceremony pro-
claiming, "A New Beginning: Welfare to Work." This was the end of an
era, but it was not the end to Rossi's Law, since out-of-wedlock childbirth still rose after welfare reform.[5]

A saving remnant of analysis has stayed with the issue of dependency.
Jonathan Rauch (2001, 1471) asks whether "America's families and children may be splitting into two increasingly divergent and self-perpetuating
streams—two social classes, in other words—with marriages as the dividing
line." He notes Isabel Sawhill's finding that "the proliferation of single-
parent households accounts for virtually all of the increase in child poverty since the early 1970s." And with that, is there not a corresponding
loss of social capital such that the ever-widening division deepens?

DAHRENDORF REVISITED

We are nowhere near a general theory of family change. When such
efforts begin, they will give multivariate analysis a whole new meaning.
In the tradition, if scarcely the authority, of Keynes, I would think we
will have a fix on it by, say, 2075. But then again, in the analytic model
laid out by Ralf Dahrendorf (1968), we may yet see a wholesale upturn-
ing of present social values. In his luminous essay "On the Origin of
Inequality Among Men," given as the inaugural lecture at the University
of Tübingen, Dahrendorf shows that inequality is inevitable, inasmuch as
all societies have norms and within a society some will achieve them
better than others, whether they be headhunters in a jungle or monks in
a monastery:

Human society always means that people's behavior is being removed
from the randomness of chance and regulated by established and inescap-

able expectations. The compulsory character of these expectations or norms is based on the operation of sanctions, i.e., of rewards or punishments for conformist or deviant behavior. *If every society is in this sense a moral community, it follows that there must always be at least that inequality of rank which results from the necessity of sanctioning behavior according to whether it does or does not conform to established norms.* (Dahrendorf 1968, 158, emphasis added)

But then comes, or may come, what I shall call a "Dahrendorf Inversion."[6] Those of unequal rank rise up and change the rules so as to reward their own behavior. This could well happen in the Western world as regards marriage, and American culture resonates with signals that something such as this is being attempted. The historian Gertrude Himmelfarb (1999) sees it as a struggle between competing elites. I have observed the processes of "defining deviancy down" (Moynihan 1992). Charles Murray (2001) has gone from there to "add a third voice to the mix, that of that late historian Arnold Toynbee, who would find our recent history no mystery at all: We are witnessing the proletarianization of the dominant minority." Well, something is happening. The "present oriented," in Edward C. Banfield's (1970) term, seems ever more present as social scientists seem to compare the magnitude of the change we are undergoing. James Q. Wilson has now given us a magisterial summation of his take on the issue, *The Marriage Problem: How Our Culture Has Weakened Families* (2002, 197). He writes: "For two nations to become one again, marriage must become more common. Many Americans wish this, but despite some encouraging trends, history is marching in a different direction."

A pretty certain sign of the misdirection in the policy circles is the proposed "Family Amendment" recently introduced in the House by three Republican and three Democratic members. It would prevent any court from granting homosexual unions the same legal status as marriage. *The Weekly Standard* (Teti 2003) commented that a growing number of lawmakers and religious leaders are coming to believe in the need for a constitutional amendment to protect the definition of marriage as a union of man and woman. When all else fails, amend the Constitution.

In the late 1930s the Carnegie Corporation brought Gunnar and Alva Myrdal to the United States to inquire into *The American Dilemma* (Myrdal 1944), as his work would be titled, and into *Nation and Family* (1941/1968), her title. Alva's work got lost in the chaos of the Second World War, but it was republished by MIT Press in 1968. In a foreword, I summarized her argument:

The theme of *Nation and Family* is that in the nature of modern industrial society no government, however firm might be its wish, can avoid having policies that profoundly influence family relationships. This is not to be avoided. The only option is whether these will be purposeful, intended policies or whether they will be residual, derivative, in a sense concealed ones. (Myrdal 1941/1968, vi–vii)

Myrdal's concerns, brought over from Sweden, were of another era. But surely the proposition stands.

In 1984 I gave the Godkin Lectures at Harvard on the same subject, published as *Family and Nation* (Moynihan 1986, 190). I concluded: "The central conservative truth is that it is culture, not politics, which determines the success of a society. The central liberal truth is that politics can change a culture and save it from itself." The case for one (policy) overruling the other (culture) is yet to be made (for an elaboration of this point, see Harrison and Huntington 2000).

MOST RECENTLY

Following the conference to which this address by Moynihan served as a call to arms, Christopher Jencks (personal communication to Daniel Patrick Moynihan and Timothy M. Smeeding, October 30, 2003) offered some thoughts in reaction to the lecture on which this preface is based by offering some answers to the central question: what happened to the family?

> I think this question is the right one, and . . . I obviously don't know the answer, but . . . if I have to answer I would say the biggest factor was more widespread cultural acceptance of two ideals: "tolerance" and "personal freedom." These ideals made most Americans and Western Europeans less willing to treat sex, childbearing, and marriage as matters of right and wrong. I think that was probably progress, though I sometimes have my doubts. Still, progress is seldom a free lunch.

My colleague Tim Smeeding reminds me that prison policy may have something to do with why the black family especially has changed to such an extent (see Raphael 2004). And for the moment I agree that one of the most pervasive "anti-family" policies in the United States during the last two decades would seem to have been prison policy. From 1980 to 1997, the number of adults on probation, in jail, or in prison more than tripled, rising from 1.6 million to 5.7 million (Pettit and Western, forthcoming). But few have noticed or commented upon the effect of this increase on family life, parenthood, employment, and earnings.

My former staff leader, Paul Barton (2002, personal communication), also responded and offers the following:

My suspects would be the following:

- The decline of religious participation

- Growing wealth in general, which permits more choices

- Gender equality with its concomitant increase in earnings opportunities for women (women have alternatives to marriage, and they have the option of leaving a husband and supporting the children)

- The decline of community and neighborhood, where social opinion of marital and family behavior was the enforcer of the social code

- A more compassionate society, with the means and the desire to step in and support children when they are not claimed by the father

- And last but not least, the pill, which cut down on shotgun marriages

As I read Fukuyama, we could still turn around. He describes the Victorian era as a reaction to the excesses of the middle of the nineteenth century. And he seems optimistic that a similar process has started now, a century later. And there we shall leave it, the question still standing: who indeed can tell us what happened to the American family?

This preface is based on Daniel Patrick Moynihan's address, which opened the conference. After his death, Timothy M. Smeeding edited and expanded the text, based on his many conversations with Moynihan on the subject. Our thanks to the editors and to the two anonymous reviewers for several clarifying comments and suggestions.

NOTES

1. Johnson's speech is reprinted in its entirety in Rainwater and Yancey (1967, 125–32).

2. The Irish experience is striking: as recently as the midtwentieth century single parents could be treated as felons.

3. King's speech of October 29, 1965 is reprinted in its entirety in Rainwater and Yancey (1967, 402–9).

4. Shortly before his death, Pat Moynihan thanked Brett Brown, area director for social indicators research, for this addition to the Child Trends website.

5. However, out-of-wedlock childbirth dropped in the late 1990s. See figure 1.1 on this trend.

6. A bemused but tolerant Dahrendorf withholds assent but encourages inquiry.

REFERENCES

Banfield, Edward C. 1970. *The Unheavenly City: The Nature and Future of Our Urban Crisis*. Boston: Little, Brown.

Bradshaw, Jonathan, and Naomi Finch. 2002. "A Comparison of Child Benefit Packages in 22 Countries." Report 174. London: Department for Work and Pensions. Available at: http://www.dwp.gov.uk/asd/asd5/174summ.pdf (accessed May 21, 2004).

Child Trends. 2003. "Percentage of Births to Unmarried Women." Washington, D.C.: Child Trends. Available at: http://www.childtrendsdatabank.org/indicators/75UnmarriedBirths.cfm (accessed May 21, 2004).

Coleman, James S. 1982. *The Asymmetric Society*. Syracuse, N.Y.: Syracuse University Press.

Council of Europe. 2003. *Recent Demographic Developments in Europe 2002*. Strasbourg: Council of Europe Publishing Division.

Dahrendorf, Ralf. 1968. "On the Origin of Inequality Among Men." In *Essays in the Theory of Society*. Stanford, Calif.: Stanford University Press.

Fukuyama, Francis. 1999. *The Great Disruption: Human Nature and the Reconstitution of Social Order*. New York: Free Press.

Glazer, Nathan, and Daniel Patrick Moynihan. 1963/1970. *Beyond the Melting Pot: The Negroes, Puerto Ricans, Jews, Italians, and Irish of New York City*. Cambridge, Mass.: MIT Press.

Harrison, Lawrence E., and Samuel P. Huntington. 2000. *Culture Matters: How Values Shape Human Progress*. New York: Basic Books.

Himmelfarb, Gertrude. 1999. *One Nation, Two Cultures*. New York: Alfred A. Knopf.

Johnson, Lyndon B. 1966. "To Fulfill These Rights: Commencement Address at Howard University, June 4, 1965." In *Public Papers of the Presidents of the United States: Lyndon B. Johnson, 1965*, Vol. II, entry 301. Washington: U.S. Government Printing Office. Available at: http://

www.lbjlib.utexas.edu/johnson/archives.hom/speeches.hom/650604. asp (accessed May 21, 2004).

Keynes, John Maynard. 1936. *The General Theory of Employment, Interest and Money.* New York: Harcourt, Brace.

King, Martin Luther, Jr. 1965. "The Dignity of Family Life." Address at the Abbott House, Westchester County, N.Y., October 29, 1965. Document ID 651029–001. The Martin Luther King Jr. Papers Project. Stanford, Calif.: Stanford University.

McLanahan, Sara, and Gary Sandefur. 1994. *Growing Up with a Single Parent: What Hurts, What Helps.* Cambridge, Mass.: Harvard University Press.

Mincy, Ronald B. 2002. Interview for PBS *Frontline*, "Let's Get Married." Broadcast November 14. Boston: PBS/WGBH. Available at http://www.pbs.org/wgbh/pages/frontline/shows/marriage/interviews/mincy.html (accessed May 21, 2004).

Morehouse Research Institute. 1999. *Turning the Corner on Father Absence in Black America: A Statement from the Morehouse Conference on African American Fathers.* Atlanta: Morehouse College. Available at: http://www.americanvalues.org/turning_the_corner.pdf (accessed May 21, 2004).

Moynihan, Daniel Patrick. 1959. "Epidemic on the Highways." *The Reporter* (April 30).

———. 1965. "The Negro Family: The Case for National Action." Report issued by the Office of Policy Planning and Research, U.S. Department of Labor, GPO no. O-794–628. Washington: U.S. Government Printing Office. Reproduced in its original format in Rainwater and Yancey 1967, 41–124.

———. 1968. "The New Racialism." Commencement address, New School for Social Research, New York, June 4, 1968. *Atlantic Monthly* 222(2, August): 35–40. Available at: http://www.theatlantic.com/politics/race/moynihan.htm (accessed on May 10, 2004).

———. 1986. *Family and Nation.* New York: Harcourt Brace Jovanovich.

———. 1992. "Defining Deviancy Down: How We've Become Accustomed to Alarming Levels of Crime and Destructive Behavior." *The American Scholar* 62(1, Winter): 17–30.

———. 2000. "Government Work: Forty Years of National Politics." Paper presented to the American Political Science Association. Washington (September 2).

Murray, Charles. 2001. "America's Elites Take Their Cues from the Underclass." Available from "AEI Online: On the Issues," http://www.aei.org/publications/pubID.12513/pub_detail.asp.

Myrdal, Alva. 1941/1968. *Nation and Family.* Cambridge, Mass.: MIT Press.

Myrdal, Gunnar, with the assistance of Richard Sterner and Arnold Rose. 1944. *An American Dilemma: The Negro Problem and Modern Democracy.* New York: Pantheon.

Novak, Robert, and Rowland Evans. 1965. "Inside Report: The Moynihan Report." *New York Herald Tribune*, May 15, 1965. Reprinted in its entirety in Rainwater and Yancey 1967, 375–77.

Pettit, Becky, and Bruce Western. Forthcoming. "Mass Imprisonment and the Life Course: Race and Class Inequality in Lifetime Risks of Imprisonment." *American Sociological Review.*

Preston, Samuel. 1984. "Children and the Elderly: Divergent Paths for America's Dependents." *Demography* 21(4, November): 435–57.

Rainwater, Lee. 1970. *Behind Ghetto Walls: Black Families in a Federal Slum.* Chicago: Aldine.

Rainwater, Lee, and William L. Yancey, eds. 1967. *The Moynihan Report and the Politics of Controversy.* Cambridge, Mass.: MIT Press.

Raphael, Steven. 2004. "The Socioeconomic Status of Black Males: The Increasing Importance of Incarceration." Unpublished paper. Berkeley: University of California, Goldman School of Public Policy (March).

Rauch, Jonathan. 2001. "The Widening Marriage Gap: America's New Class Divide." *National Journal* 33(20, May 19): 1471.

Rossi, Peter. 1987. "The Iron Law of Evaluation and Other Metallic Roles." In *Research in Social Problems and Public Policy*, vol. 4, edited by Joann I. Miller and Michael Lewis. Greenwich, Conn.: JAI Press.

Teti, Daniel. 2003. "The Federal Marriage Amendment Is Hopeless: But Federal Law Can Succeed in Protecting Marriage Where a Constitutional Amendment Is Destined to Fail." *The Weekly Standard*, November 19. Available at: http://www.weeklystandard.com/Content/Public/Articles/000/000/003/395zmzjc.asp (accessed May 21, 2004).

Torrey, Barbara, and Carl Haub. 2003. "Death in North America." Paper presented to the Statistics Canada Economic Conference. Unpublished paper. Washington, D.C.: Population Reference Bureau (May 12).

U.S. Census Bureau. 1976. *The Statistical History of the United States from Colonial Times to the Present [1970].* With an introduction and user's guide by Ben J. Wattenberg. New York: Basic Books.

U.S. Congress. House of Representatives. 1994. "Republican Contract with America." Available at: http://www.house.gov/house/Contract/CONTRACT.html (accessed May 21, 2004).

Wilson, James Q. 2002. *The Marriage Problem: How Our Culture Has Weakened Families.* New York: HarperCollins.

———. 2003. Interview for PBS, "First Measured Century." "Broken Windows" segment. Available at: http://www.pbs.org/fmc/interviews/jwilson.htm (accessed May 21, 2004).

ACKNOWLEDGMENTS

THE EDITORS and authors would like to thank the Center for Policy Research, especially Mary Santy, Martha Bonney, and Kim Desmond, for their support, help, and expertise in arranging the original October 2002 conference on the Future of the Family and also in producing this volume. Special thanks also go to the John and Catherine T. MacArthur Foundation's Network on the Family and the Economy and the Maxwell School for their financial and intellectual support of the conference, and to the two anonymous referees and the editors at the Russell Sage Foundation press, who also greatly improved the manuscript.

CHAPTER ONE

The Challenge of Family System
Changes for Research and Policy

Timothy M. Smeeding, Daniel P. Moynihan,
and Lee Rainwater

IN 1963, THE Policy Planning Staff at the U.S. Department of Labor, led by Daniel Patrick Moynihan, first observed that out-of-wedlock childbirth was on the rise. Some forty years later, after a period of denial, we have finally acknowledged it and are as a nation beginning to address it head-on. Moynihan has noted that this 1960s sighting was just the beginning of "the earthquake that shuddered through the American family" (Preston 1984, 451) and still rumbles. It has shaken many nations, ours included, and has led to nearly forty years of demographic statistics, but not to a complete understanding of the structural changes to the family or even serious academic debate of the issues. Here we address Moynihan's question of what happened, and two others: why it happened and what we ought to do about it.

In addressing the rise in out-of-wedlock childbirth, we also examine a closely related phenomenon, the rise of single-parent families and households. While the term *single parenthood* still needs to be carefully defined, the number of children living either exclusively or primarily with one person has increased dramatically in almost all Western countries, especially in the Anglo-Saxon ones.

What could have caused this trend in so many countries with such different socioeconomic systems at roughly the same time? And it persists, despite the fact that at the same time more effective and more acceptable forms of birth control have become increasingly available. Was it caused by low wages or poor work opportunities compared to generous income support for single parents, by lack of education, or by the gender revolution and women's growing economic independence?

This issue also has a racial dimension. The level and trend is much more pronounced among African Americans, 22 percent of families with children in 1960 and 53 percent in 2000, than whites, 7 percent in 1960 and 22 percent in 2000. By 1995, the percentage of black women aged fifteen to forty-four who had experienced at least one unmarried birth was 45 percent, compared to 10 percent for whites and 22 percent for Hispanics (Child Trends 2002, 2003).[1] Could higher rates among blacks be caused by culture (Patterson 2000), or by low wages, high joblessness, and low incomes (Rainwater 1970), leading to unmarriageable mates (Wilson 1987)? Could low wages and high joblessness among African American men combined with increased incarceration (Pettit and Western, forthcoming; Raphael 2004) and poor job prospects afterwards (Pager 2003; Raphael 2004) be behind the large and growing numbers of fatherless African American families?

Our goal is to assess this trend, pinpointing, as much as possible, what changed, how it changed, and—most important—why it changed. These changes have negative consequences for children who face long periods of fatherlessness and the economic insecurity inherent in single parenthood; their specific effects must also be documented. We also ask, what should public policy do in the face of uncertain causes but much more definitive poor outcomes for the children? We begin by better framing the issues.

THE ISSUES

As many people, experts and nonexperts alike, are aware and readily acknowledge in one way or another, there have been profound changes over the past half century in American family roles, family relations, and living arrangements. Parallel changes seem to have occurred in most European societies. In this volume a number of well-known authors review the evidence of these changes and consider some of the consequences. Experts in child development, demography and gender, and comparative political economy present additional perspectives. We then assess how American public policy addresses and might address the issue of family formation, living arrangements, marriage, and family relations more generally. Some would argue that these are not a government matter, but rather the domain of churches or communities. Others point out that by its overarching nature government action affects citizens' decisions about family relations. For them the question is whether and how existing family policies and related tax and transfer policies affect, directly and indirectly, mothers, fathers, and children. For example, family subsidies like the Earned Income Tax Credit and prison policy may have strong, if unintended, effects on family formation.[2]

The chapters that follow chart statistical changes, examine causal relations, and consider actual and proposed government actions—all abstracted from the complex patterns and meanings of daily life. In the course of these discussions, however, we must not forget that these somewhat dry demographics abstract from often intense and emotional realities. And, probably for this reason, we find that discussions of the values underlying family formation and family policy are often contentious in ways researchers and analysts do not always recognize. But "when research and values collide, values will always win. Analysts who ignore this fact are wasting their time" (Sawhill 1995, 12).

This volume addresses these issues head-on. First, we document the changes in the family more fully and review the current research on the causes and effects of out-of-wedlock childbirth and single parenting (chapters 2 through 5: Ellwood and Jencks; Kiernan; Rainwater and Smeeding; Sigle-Rushton and McLanahan) and put this into perspective (chapters 6 through 8: Gornick; Chase-Lansdale; Wolf). Faced with incomplete knowledge of the determinants of family change, policymakers and policy analysts still advocate agendas in response to these changes that fit their preferences. We therefore then discuss how marriage, childbirth, and children can and should be affected by public policy (chapters 9 through 11: Horn; Marshall and Sawhill; Folbre). Finally, drawing on decades of experience in studying family formation and change, we reflect on what we do and do not know about family change, and how policy has and might affect the family process (chapters 12 through 14: Preston; Furstenberg; Garfinkel).

First, however, using some of these perspectives, we describe how changes in the family system challenge the family and public policy. We begin with Belgian demographer Ron J. Lesthaeghe (2002, n.p.), who observed recently that:

Western European, and consequently also North American, demographic systems of the past were characterized by long celibacy, late marriage and the dominance of the nuclear family. New households were neolocal and could only be established if economic independence was obtained. This "Malthusian" system with "prudent marriage" is an alien form of social organization to other societies and cultures.

Lesthaeghe goes on to suggest that this system was strengthened by the adoption of family limitation as the key to the first "demographic transition" of declining family size. Now, he argues, we are seeing a second transition characterized by "increased divorce, again later marriage but insertion of periods of premarital cohabitation, marked postponement of parenthood, procreation within cohabiting unions, declining remarriage but increasing post-marital cohabitation or other forms of living arrangements, and persistence of sub-replacement fertility." While Lesthaeghe's model of the broad sweep of changes from the sixteenth century to the twenty-first, and particularly in recent decades, is based primarily on West European data, many of the changes described also can be found in the United States, either at the same level or lagging a bit. And America (also Australia, Britain, and Canada) has added the issue of increased births to young unmarried women to the contentious mix.

An unsystematic catalogue of changes over the last century, especially from 1950 to 2000, that affect adult sexual roles, marriage, and what goes on in marriage, and changes in nontraditional family relationships would include the following:

- People moved to the cities to find work as agrarian society declined, increasing the possibilities for intimate contact at younger ages.

- Many upper-class children delayed work to extend their schooling and older workers retired at an increasingly earlier age, even as life expectancy at older ages grew enormously.

- Older people lived increasingly alone but, when possible, near children and grandchildren.

- After the baby boom of the 1950s families decided to have fewer children, but, on average, increased the time and money spent on those they had.

- Women, and especially wives with children, increased their participation in the labor force during the twentieth century; but their earnings remained at about 20 percent of family income until the 1980s, when they increased to about 30 percent.

- Until the 1970s and 1980s there was little relation between husbands' and wives' earnings, but that correlation began to rise as well-educated women entered the marketplace. Coupled with "assortive mating" along education lines, a wide gulf arose in measured parental incomes between rich and poor parents.

- Divorce rates increased, especially during the 1960s and 1970s, but leveled off afterward as cohabitation and consensual unions became more common.

- Patterns of family formation, fertility, and change have varied across racial and ethnic groups for some time, with both out-of-wedlock childbearing and single parenthood being highest among blacks (see preface).

- Sexual relations among teenagers grew more common, and to varying degrees more normative, over the past twenty years.

- In most European countries, family planning among teenagers increased so that unplanned teen pregnancies did not rise as rapidly as they otherwise might have. In the United States, family planning and contraceptive use were and are less prevalent, and birthrates among teens thus substantially higher than in other Western countries.

- Despite increasingly effective contraceptives and legalized abortion, the birthrate among unmarried women increased.

These facts suggest that family change in the United States was not limited to out-of-wedlock childbirth and single parenthood (see Wolf, chapter 8).

This century of change has in the main improved people's lives. Certainly the elderly have benefited from increased leisure, independence, and health, and these changes reflect better and more reliable incomes, especially higher Social Security benefits.[3] Most adults have been able to pursue more independent and creative lives. But not everyone has benefited equally, in particular, children and, to a lesser extent, their mothers. Public concern about many of these changes is fundamentally concern about how out-of-wedlock childbirth and the weakening of the family affect children's lives.

THE NUMBERS

We now consider the differences in family living arrangements among children across countries and over time. These patterns are what need to be explained and interpreted.

Single Parenthood

Most children in the United States traditionally grew up in a two-parent family (see figure 1.1). But what has been taken for granted no longer

Figure 1.1   U.S. Children Not Living with Both Parents,
                1880 to 2000

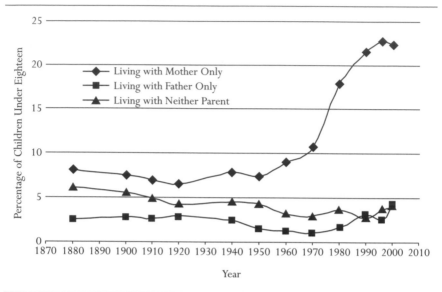

Source: For 1880 to 1996, U.S. Census Bureau (2001). For 2001, U.S. Census Bureau (2003).

can be. From 1880 to 1970 that figure was between 83 percent and 87 percent. By 1990 it dropped to about 73 percent, and by 2000 to 69 percent. Most single parents continue to be the mother. Initially they accounted for about 50 percent of single-parent families, and by the 1990s about 75 percent. Most of the increase in the number of children living in single-parent households was therefore in those living with their mother—from 7 or 8 percent through 1950 to 22 percent in the 1990s. While in the late 1990s the number of children living with single mothers fell a bit, it rose for those living with either the father or neither parent (see O'Hare 2001 and, for more on children living with neither parent, Bitler, Gelbach, and Hoynes 2002). The recent declines in children living with one parent belie a disturbing long-term trend, however. The number of children not living with both biological parents continues to increase.

If this pattern were unique to the United States, and unfortunately much scholarly and public discussion often implies that it is, analysis might proceed without attention to other countries. But, in fact, sharp increases in single-parent households seem to have occurred between 1970 and 1995 in most European nations and in Canada and Australia

Figure 1.2   Children in Single-Parent Households in Ten Countries, 1960 to 1997

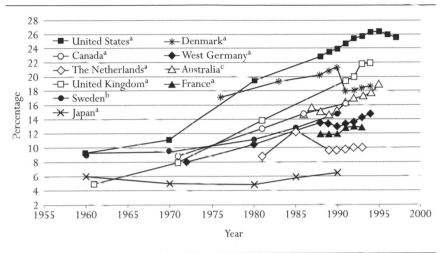

Source: Federal Interagency Forum on Child and Family Statistics (2001).
[a]Under age eighteen.
[b]Under age sixteen.
[c]Under age fifteen.

(see figure 1.2). In 1970 all countries had single-parent rates of less than 12 percent. By the mid-1990s a large majority had rates higher than that, with the United States, the United Kingdom, and Australia at or above 20 percent. But there is a wide range in the rate. Adding nine countries from a Council of Europe study (2003) to the ten in figure 1.2 we find certain clusters of single-parenthood rates:

- 6 percent or less: Greece, Italy, Japan, Portugal, Spain;

- 7 to 10 percent: Luxembourg, Ireland, Switzerland, Belgium, the Netherlands;

- 11 to 16 percent: Finland, France, Sweden, Germany, Canada;

- 19 to 26 percent: Australia, Denmark, United Kingdom, United States.

We can hypothesize that several factors account for the sharp increases—rising divorce rates; rises in consensual unions, which sometimes are not counted as two-parent families and in any case have a higher

Figure 1.3   Births to Unmarried Mothers

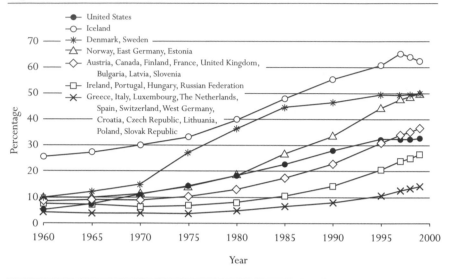

Sources: Council of Europe (2000) and Federal Interagency Forum on Child and Family Statistics (2002).

rate of dissolution than legal marriage; and rises in births to unmarried mothers. The last may in turn be a product of increases in unprotected sexual relations, particularly by teenagers. The rising proportion of children born to unmarried mothers is, of course, also a product of declining fertility in married women and the increasing age at marriage, which puts women at risk for out-of-wedlock births for more of their most fertile years.[4]

Out-of-Wedlock Births

Perhaps the most dramatic of the trends is the increase in births to unmarried women (Wu and Wolfe 2001). In the United States the rise is from about 5 percent in 1960 to over 30 percent in the 1990s, with most of it between 1970 and 1990. As before, we profit by comparison. Figure 1.3 summarizes the increasing rates of some thirty countries. We have used cluster analysis to group those with similar patterns for 1960 to 2000, and find six clusters, fairly homogeneous trends, and systematic differences. It is readily apparent that the American rise is not the most extreme. In Iceland the increase was from an already high 25 percent to over 60 percent. Denmark and Sweden moved from about 10 percent in

1960 to 50 percent. Norway, the former East Germany, and Estonia end up at the same 50 percent, but got there only by accelerating greatly during the 1980s and early 1990s.

A large group of countries have rates and growth paths similar to America's: Austria, Canada, Finland, France, and United Kingdom in the West, and Bulgaria, Latvia, and Slovenia in the East. Four countries—Ireland, Portugal, Hungary, Russia—start with rates not too different from the United States, but do not increase as rapidly until the mid-1980s. A very large group of countries show only a slight increase in out-of-wedlock births. These include seven in the West—Greece, Italy, Luxembourg, Netherlands, Spain, Switzerland, and West Germany—and five in the East—Croatia, the Czech Republic, Lithuania, Poland, and the Slovak Republic.

The phenomenon, then, is common among Western countries. By the turn of the twenty-first century fourteen had rates either nearly as high as or considerably higher than the United States, and four others were not far behind.

Cohabitation

One issue that must be considered, though it is difficult to resolve the trend with current data, is cohabitation. We need to know whether the babies born to unmarried mothers are also the children of mothers who do not have a partner and who are not cohabiting. We know that there has been a rapid rise in consensual rather than legal unions. If the vital statistics offices that assemble data have continued to count mothers in consensual unions as single, then the conclusions we draw could be quite misleading.

In fact, according to the international data recently released from the Fertility and Family Surveys (FFS) in several European nations, large proportions of out-of-wedlock births occur to mothers in consensual unions (table 1.1). More children are born to consensual unions than to single mothers in every country except the United States, from 1989 to 1995, and the former East Germany, from 1984 to 1989. Moreover, Gunnar Andersson (2002) goes on to show that the cumulative percent of children ever living with only one parent is highest in the United States, reaching almost 50 percent by the time a child is fifteen years old (figure 1.4). Excluding the former East Germany, the next highest is in West Germany and in France, each about 30 percent.

To further explore this issue we have graphed the proportion of young couples, age sixteen to twenty-nine, in consensual unions by the percent of births to unmarried mothers in eighteen countries for which we can find both numbers (figure 1.5). Overall the correlation of the two per-

Table 1.1   Relative Distribution of Births (Percentage)

Country	Period	To Lone Mother	In Marriage	In Consensual Union
Sweden	1987 to 1993	5	51	45
Norway	1983 to 1989	7	71	22
Finland	1983 to 1989	3	85	13
France	1988 to 1994	10	68	23
United States	1989 to 1995	17	72	11
Austria	1990 to 1996	10	70	19
West Germany	1986 to 1992	6	83	11
Democratic Republic of Germany	1984 to 1989	18	67	15
Flanders[a]	1985 to 1992	1	94	4
Italy	1990 to 1995	2	94	4
Spain	1989 to 1995	2	93	4
Hungary	1988 to 1993	3	90	6
Czech Republic	1992 to 1997	4	89	7
Slovenia	1989 to 1995	6	78	16
Latvia	1989 to 1995	11	79	11
Lithuania	1989 to 1995	5	93	2
Poland	1986 to 1991	9	89	2

Source: Andersson (2002, table 2).
[a]The Belgian Fertility and Family Survey (FFS) only covers the Flemish-speaking parts of the country (Andersson 2002, 361n4).

centages is quite high (almost 0.8) also suggesting that some of the countries with high out-of-wedlock birth rates may have much lower single-mother birth rates (see table 1.1). This is surely the case for the Nordic countries, where there is strong ideological and traditional support for consensual unions. Even in countries with more traditional Western cultures, the range of acceptable options for coupling and parenting has expanded greatly over the last generation (see also Kiernan, chapter 3).

One telling example of acceptability comes from the 2002 election campaign in Germany. The aspiring chancellor, Edmund Stoiber of the very catholic Christian Socialist party, chose as his family expert for the election campaign a twenty-nine-year-old single mother of two, who then told journalists she may some day marry. The appointment was regarded as a valuable political gesture to the growing number of younger and nontraditional Germans (Wosnitza 2002).

Figure 1.4   Percentage Ever out of Union, by Age of Child

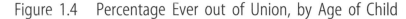

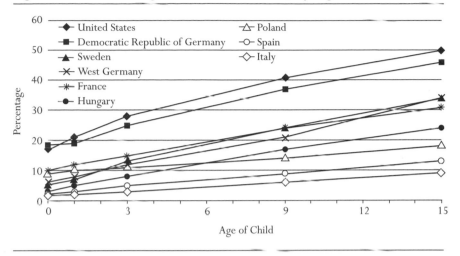

Source: Authors' compilation of data from Andersson (2002).

Figure 1.5   Consensual Unions by Births to Unmarried Mothers

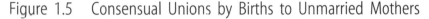

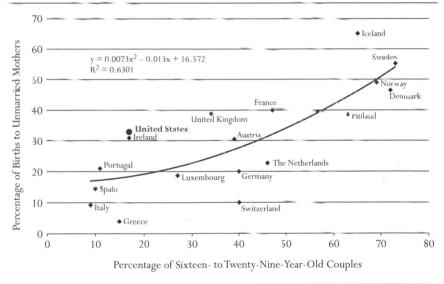

Source: Authors' compilation of data from Andersson (2002); Council of Europe (2000); and Federal Interagency Forum on Child and Family Statistics (2004).

CAUSES AND CONSEQUENCES

Explanations for what could have caused this common outcome and its consequences for children are explored in the next four chapters. Ellwood and Jencks (chapter 2) begin by systematically addressing the possible causes of single parenthood in the United States over the past fifty years, noting similarities and differences by race, education, and other relevant covariates. They find no one explanation to fit all the facts, but do establish a number of very interesting correlations.

Declining age at menarche combined with a longer period of active childbirth at older ages (and increasing age of menopause), increasing sexual activity at younger ages, and increasing age at marriage have increased the share of the lifespan over which women are exposed to the risk of pregnancy and childbirth. At the same time, better and more available forms of birth control have become increasingly available, but have not affected the trends. It could be that the availability of the pill increased the acceptability of sex outside of marriage.

What about women's rising presence in the labor force, which is occurring over roughly the same period in each of these countries, and how is it related to family change and the decline of marriage? Could the continued increase in women's economic independence, comingled with their valuing children much more than they do men, or at least much more than they do marriage, mean that the decision to have a child is becoming increasingly independent of the decision to marry?

In sum, social science has so far done a poor job in explaining why family structure in the United States and other nations has changed both in terms of marriage and childbearing over the past forty or fifty years, as our next three authors have earlier claimed (Ellwood and Jencks 2001; Kiernan 2001a, 2001b). David Ellwood describes this lack of explanation as "perhaps the greatest embarrassment of social science in recent times." Kathleen Kiernan's contribution (chapter 3) is to show that many different bands of union formations exist in the rich countries of the world, where in some cases cohabitation and consensual union are present for long periods, but in others not. Thus, the crossnational picture is also multivaried. Her findings corroborate those quoted in Andersson (2002; and table 1.1 and figure 1.4).

Lee Rainwater and Timothy Smeeding (chapter 4) document the economic disadvantages of single parenthood and their variance across rich countries. In all nations, single parents do economically less well than two-parent families. Policy, then, can do much to keep single parents and their children from abject poverty. But there seems to be no single solution: the political will to keep children from poverty finds different ways to reach this goal in each successful country. In some, almost universal low-cost child care allows single mothers to effectively combine part-time work with other subsidies (Sweden, France). In others, child allowances and income-tested benefits, supplemented by guaranteed child support ("advance maintenance") do the trick (Denmark, Netherlands). In others, income tested benefits alone help keep single mothers with children at acceptable levels of well-being, while earnings supplements and other programs help single mothers combine work and "welfare" (Canada, United Kingdom). Unfortunately, the United States is not as successful at similar efforts.

Wendy Sigle-Rushton and Sara McLanahan look at some of the consequences of these demographic trends for children (chapter 5). Earlier research in the United States (McLanahan and Sandefur 1994; McLanahan 2001; Haveman and Wolfe 1995) and more recently in Britain (Ermisch and Francesconi 2001) suggests that children who grow up in "broken" families, especially in single-parent families, including those with unmarried mothers on their own, grow up at a distinct disadvantage, in part because of the lower incomes of single-mother families. They suffer other disadvantages, however, even after "income" effects are taken account of: less education, more economic inactivity, more distress, and more smoking and drinking. While there is evidence that there may be offsetting influences, for example, increased supervision by grandparents (DeLeire and Kalil 2002), by and large single parenthood is hard on children. While there is some evidence that marriage, even following pregnancy, improves children's economic circumstances (Lerman 2002; *American Experiment Quarterly* 2001) there is less evidence that the same can also be said for child outcomes. In fact, research on how to promote strong, low-conflict marriages is thin at best (Moore, Jekielek, and Emig 2002). Sigle-Rushton and McLanahan add to this literature and corroborate most of these arguments. While the case for single parenthood producing poor outcomes is yet to be proved, their paper does show us how the two are related in systematic ways.

Chapters 6 through 8 present a series of shorter reactions that broaden and strengthen the developmental, demographic, and gender specific arguments made in the previous five, and extend them in different ways. P. Lindsay Chase-Lansdale's (chapter 7) comments argue for greater attention to the developmental effects of parent absence on children and the nurturing effects of a good marriage, underpinning Wade Horn's policy recommendations (chapter 9). Douglas Wolf (chapter 8) suggests that other types of family change are also relevant to the one we consider here. And Janet Gornick (chapter 6) reminds us that marriage is a contract between two consenting adults, with women doing most of the "heavy lifting" in regard to children.

Summary

We believe that these changes in the family are now so deeply set there is no turning back, and that policy will need to proceed without a complete explanation of the causes behind them. Public policy institutions have to some extent adapted to them, but by and large not explicitly encouraged them. Indeed, public institutions are often ignorant of secular changes until they are well underway. And in most countries public policy and institutions are slow to change in any case, particularly on issues as emotionally and culturally volatile as family change and out-of-wedlock births. It is also apparent that social institutions and policies created in one era do not always fare well in another. This is certainly the case, for example, with the Old Age and Survivors Insurance benefits program (Social Security) in the United States of the 1930s (see Steuerle, Favreault, and Sammartino 2002). The next set of essays addresses these issues head-on.

THE POLICY CHALLENGE

If marriage and childbearing have in fact become disconnected in the United States and elsewhere how should public policy react? Is marriage policy a legitimate explicit realm of government activity? What role do moral issues play? Can we treat the patterns of change in family structure from a purely positivist position, as many analysts do, or is it a normative and moral issue as well? As we see it, the question for policy is this: what is the most constructive response to parents sharing responsibility for their children but not in a shared household and not at the same time?

From a policy perspective, one must first ask if we first need to understand why we find these changes, or can policy proceed in any case? The answer seems to depend both on what type of policies we contemplate and on the social legitimacy of public action in each realm. For instance, if we find that growing up with a single parent is bad for children, and assuming that the well-being of children is a legitimate issue for policy action, how can and should we design policies to address the adverse consequences of that situation?

On the other hand, if we want to promote policies to preserve and encourage marriage, or to reduce out-of-wedlock births, or to increase fathers' involvement with their children, a greater understanding of the causes seems to be called for before a response is formulated (assuming that public policy can and should intervene in these decisions). For example, recent studies suggest that among unmarried couples with children in the United States, about half of those parents are biologically tied to at least one other child who lives in a different family unit (Carlson, McLanahan, and England 2004; Mincy 2002). Depending on the relationship with the unmarried mother, 33 to 39 percent of unmarried fathers have a child by another woman (Carlson, McLanahan, and England 2004). This produces divided loyalty—fathers spend money and time on both and confounds policies designed to involve fathers in supporting their children (Manning, Stewart, and Smock 2001). In fact, in households with unmarried couples each of whom already has a child or children, partners are far less likely to marry than those who have a child in common (Mincy 2002). Marriage promotion policy might be better targeted at this second group, or at mothers and fathers giving birth for the first time.

Clearly, welfare reform has been successful in reducing single parents' dependence on social programs alone for economic well-being and in promoting self-reliance through work. However, not all who have left welfare have done well economically. Moynihan observed about the 1996 Welfare Reform Act that "the premise of this legislation is that the behavior of certain adults can be changed by making the lives of their children as wretched as possible" (1996). For some, work behavior, incomes, and children's lives changed for the good. But for others the outcome is less certain and the effects on the children more mixed (Brooks, Hair, and Zaslow 2001; Gennetian et al. 2002; Chase-Lansdale et al. 2003). To what extent should welfare reform take account of these differences and offer more financial help to the working poor and their children?

The obstacles to stable unions are high for low-income single parents. Incomplete education, irregular employment, low income (whether personal or partner), and poor health all contribute to fewer marriages and less cohabitation among young single parents (Sigle-Rushton and McLanahan 2002; Carlson, McLanahan, and England 2004). It therefore seems that we have to provide financial help to overcome these barriers if we are to promote stable marriages among low-income single parents over and above anything accomplished by welfare reform (Furstenberg 2002). Developing skills to help couples better communicate and understand each other is an important component of a successful relationship, but it works best where there is also a solid and tangible financial basis.

Chapters 7, 8, and 9 cover this territory and more. Wade Horn (chapter 9) passionately argues that we should consider the benefits of marriage to children and use public policy to encourage healthy marriage and better parent-child relations. Most people at the conference were in general agreement with this statement. Relationship training can be used to both strengthen existing marriages (preventing divorce) and at the same time encourage marriage among cohabiters.

Will Marshall and Isabel Sawhill (chapter 10) endorse Horn's policy prescriptions but would be more proactive, would add systematically to family support in a myriad of other ways, including more child care, more child support, and better family leave (see also Sawhill 2003).

Nancy Folbre (chapter 11) offers a fresh and different look at policy, taking "caring" (for children) as the core value. The value of caregiving to children and to the nation, and the cost to mothers, especially, is well documented. When recent policy changes (for example, welfare reform, family leave, child support enforcement) are viewed in this light, they do not perform well. Folbre thus advocates a redesign for American family policy that is based on reinforcing the moral value of "caring."

Rapporteurs

The final chapters add the wisdom of three longtime researchers of family policy (chapters 12 through 14). In his singularly effective way, Samuel Preston reminds us that children are beneficial to society and that policy needs to better adapt to the "earthquake," rather than trying to tame it. In terse terms, Preston makes the case for supporting families with children regardless of their family structure. Frank Furstenberg reviews the simple models of family, child, and society links found in these chapters and makes the important point that, in his estimation, a good marriage needs to be supported by a broad set of social policies if we are to be more successful as a society in fostering children. Finally, Irwin Garfinkel quickly reviews the chapters and then suggests that much greater attention be placed on studying the ways that policy affects marriage in both tax and transfer systems. He also suggests combinations of policies from Marshall-Sawhill and Folbre that would increase family income security, but not "welfare reliance."

CONCLUSIONS

We have raised many questions both of understanding and for policy that many of the chapters here have answered, though not completely. Nations are judged by the way they treat their children. Certainly, the well-being of American children who live with single parents does not measure up very well in crossnational comparison. Slogans like "Leave No Child Behind" ring hollow in the face of the evidence (Smeeding 2002; Rainwater and Smeeding 2004). We can and should do better at improving the economic and social lives of children who are subject to varied family living circumstances, while promoting more stable unions and better parenting by those who supervise these kids. The participants and commentators at the conference and in this volume have helped show us the way, and in so doing, have begun to answer Daniel Patrick Moynihan's enduring questions about family change: what happened, why did it happen, and what can we as a nation do in response?

The authors would like to thank the Maxwell School, the Woodrow Wilson Center, MacArthur Foundation Network in the Family and the Economy, and the Russell Sage Foundation for their support of this paper and conference. The authors would also like to thank especially Christopher Jencks, two anonymous reviewers, and other participants at the conference for excellent comments. Also we are grateful to Kati Foley, Mary Santy, and Kim Desmond for their help in preparing this chapter.

NOTES

1. Child Trends (2002, 73, figure 4.1). Child Trends has recently added a set of racial breakdowns for each of these categories. Find them at http://www.childtrendsdatabank.org/indicators/75UnmarriedBirths.cfm.

2. The Earned Income Tax Credit (EITC) is not thought of as "family" policy. However, the decision to marry and/or to have children has large effects on the value of the EITC and therefore possibly large effects on "family" formation (Ellwood and Liebman 2000). Similarly, the movement to imprison increasingly larger fractions of the young adult male population, especially African Americans, many of whom are fathers, has had a lasting effect on family formation (Pettit and Western, forthcoming; Pager 2003; Raphael 2004).

3. See McGarry and Schoeni (2000), Wolf (1995), and Engelhardt, Gruber, and Perry (2002).

4. A recent paper by Smith, Philip, and Koropeckyj-Cox (1996) finds that this latter factor plays a surprisingly important role in out-of-wedlock childbirths.

REFERENCES

American Experiment Quarterly. 2001. "An Issue Devoted to the Theme of Strengthening Marriage and Children." 2001. American Experiment Quarterly 4(2, Summer): entire issue. Available at: http://www.amexp. org/aeqpdf/AEQv4/aeqv4n2/acqv4n2.pdf. (accessed May 21, 2004).

Andersson, Gunnar. 2002. "Children's Experience of Family Disruption and Family Formation: Evidence from 16 FFS Countries." Demographic Research 7(7, August 14): 343–63. Available at: http://www.demographic-research.org/Volumes/Vol7/7/7-7.pdf (accessed May 21, 2004).

Bitler, Marianne P., Jonah B. Gelbach, and Hilary Hoynes. 2002 (revised September 2003). "The Impact of Welfare Reform on Living Arrangements." Unpublished paper. Department of Economics, University of California, Davis.

Brooks, Jennifer L., Elizabeth C. Hair, and Martha J. Zaslow. 2001. "Welfare Reform's Impact on Adolescents: Early Warning Signs." Child Trends Research Brief. Washington, D.C.: Child Trends. Available at: http://www.childtrends.org/PDF/WelfareEditBrief.pdf (accessed May 21, 2004).

Carlson, Marcia, Sara McLanahan, and Paula England. 2004. "Union Formation and Stability in Fragile Families." Center for Research on Child Wellbeing Paper No. 2001-06-FF. Princeton, N.J.: Princeton University (January). Available at: http://crcw.princeton.edu/workingpapers/WP01-06-FF-Carlson.pdf (accessed May 21, 2004).

Chase-Lansdale, P. Lindsay, Robert A. Moffitt, Brenda J. Lohman, Andrew J. Cherlin, Rebekah Levine Coley, Laura D. Pittman, Jennifer Roff, and Elizabeth Votruba-Drzal. 2003. "Mothers' Transitions from Welfare to Work and the Well-Being of Preschoolers and Adolescents." Science 299 (5612): 1548–52.

Child Trends. 2002. "Charting Parenthood: A Statistical Portrait of Fathers and Mothers in America." Washington, D.C.: Child Trends. Available at: http://12.109.133.224/Files/ParenthoodRpt2002.pdf (accessed May 21, 2004).

———. 2003. "Percentage of Births to Unmarried Women." Washington, D.C.: Child Trends. Available at: http://www/childtrendsdatabank.org/indicators/75UnmarriedBirths.cfm (accessed May 21, 2004).

Council of Europe. 2000. Recent Demographic Developments in Europe 2000. Strasbourg: Council of Europe Publishing Division.

———. 2003. Recent Demographic Developments in Europe 2002. Strasbourg: Council of Europe Publishing Division.

DeLeire, Thomas, and Ariel Kalil. 2002. "Good Things Come in Threes: Single-Parent Multigenerational Family Structure and Adolescent Adjustment." Demography 39 (2, May): 393–413.

Ellwood, David, and Christopher Jencks. 2001. "The Growing Differences in Family Structure: What Do We Know? Where Do We Look for Answers?" Unpublished paper. Kennedy School of Government. Harvard University, Cambridge, Mass. (August).

Ellwood, David T., and Jeffrey B. Liebman. 2000. "The Middle Class Parent Penalty: Child Benefits in the U.S. Tax Code." NBER Working Paper W8031. Cambridge, Mass.: National Bureau of Economic Research (December).

Engelhardt, Gary, Jonathan Gruber, and Cynthia D. Perry. 2002. "Social Security and Elderly Living Arrangements." NBER Working Paper W8911. Cambridge, Mass.: National Bureau of Economic Research (April).

Ermisch, John F., and Marco Francesconi. 2001. "Family Structure and Children's Achievements." *Journal of Population Economics* 14 (2): 249–70.

Federal Interagency Forum on Child and Family Statistics. 2001. *POP3: Family Households with Children and Single-Parent Households.* Washington: U.S. Government Printing Office. Available at: http://www.childstats.gov/data/xls/pop3.xls (accessed May 19, 2004).

———. 2002. *America's Children: Key National Indicators of Well-Being, 2002* (Part 1). Washington, D.C.: U.S. Government Printing Office. Available at: http://www.childstats.gov/ac2002/pdf/pop.pdf (accessed May 19, 2004).

———. 2004. *POP4b: Percent of Births to Unmarried Women (U.S.).* Washington: U.S. Government Printing Office. Available at: http://www.childstats.gov/ac2003/tbl.asp?id=1&iid=105 (accessed May 19, 2004).

Furstenberg, Frank. 2002. "What a Good Marriage Can't Do [Op-Ed]." *New York Times*, August 13, p. A19.

Gennetian, Lisa A., Greg J. Duncan, Virginia W. Knox, Wanda G. Vargas, Elizabeth Clark-Kauffman, and Andrew S. London. 2002. "How Welfare and Work Policies for Parents Affect Adolescents: A Synthesis of Research." New York: Manpower Demonstration Corporation (May).

Haveman, Robert H., and Barbara L. Wolfe. 1995. "The Determinants of Children's Attainments: A Review of Methods and Findings." *Journal of Economic Literature* 33(4): 1829–78.

Kiernan, Kathleen. 2001a. "European Perspective on Union Formation." Unpublished paper. London School of Economics (June).

———. 2001b. "Partnership Behavior across Nations and Generations: Continents, Discontinuities and Interrelations." Paper presented at Jacob Foundation Conference on Well-Being and Dysfunction across the Generations: Change and Continuity, Marbach, Germany (October 25–27).

Lerman, Robert I. 2002. "How Do Marriage, Cohabitation and Single Parenthood Affect the Material Hardship of Families with Children?" Research Report. Washington, D.C.: Urban Institute (July 1). Available at: http://www.urban.org/UploadedPDF/410539_SippPaper.pdf (accessed May 21, 2004).

Lesthaeghe, Ron J. 2002. "From the Reformation to Multiculturalism: A Political and Cultural Reading of the Demography of the Low Countries" (The Erasmus Lectures, Harvard University, Cambridge, Mass., April 8, 15, and 29, 2002).

Manning, Wendy D., Susan D. Stewart, and Pamela J. Smock. 2001. "The Complexity of Fathers' Parenting Responsibilities and Involvement with Nonresident Children." Research Report No. 01-478. University of Michigan, Institute for Social Research, Population Studies

Center (June). Available at: http://fatherfamilylink.gse.upenn.edu/research/recent/2107.htm (accessed May 21, 2004).

McGarry, Kathleen, and Robert F. Schoeni. 2000. "Social Security, Economic Growth, and the Rise in Elderly Widows' Independence in the Twentieth Century." *Demography* 37(2, May): 221–36.

McLanahan, Sara. 2001. "Life Without Father: What Happens to the Children?" Unpublished paper. Princeton University.

McLanahan, Sara, and Gary Sandfur. 1994. *Growing Up with a Single Parent: What Hurts, What Helps.* Cambridge, Mass.: Harvard University Press.

Mincy, Ronald B. 2002. "Who Should Marry Whom? Multiple Partner Fertility Among New Parents." Paper No. 2002-03-FF. Princeton, N.J.: Center for Research on Child Wellbeing, Princeton University (February). Available at: http://crcw.princeton.edu/workingpapers/WP02-03-FF-Mincy.pdf (accessed May 21, 2004).

Moore, Kristin Anderson, Susan M. Jekielek, and Carol Emig. 2002. "Marriage from a Child's Perspective: How Does Family Structure Affect Children and What Can We Do About It?" Child Trends Research Brief. Washington, D.C.: Child Trends (June). Available at: http://www.childtrends.org/pdf/MarriageRB602.pdf (accessed May 21, 2004).

Moynihan, Daniel Patrick. 1996. "Opinion: When Principle Is at Issue." *The Washington Post*, Sunday, August 4, p. C07. Available at: http://www.washingtonpost.com/wp-srv/politics/special/welfare/stories/op080496.htm (accessed May 21, 2004).

O'Hare, William. 2001. "The Rise—and Fall?—of Single-Parent Families." *Population Today* 29(5): 1–2.

Pager, Devah. 2003. "The Mark of a Criminal Record." *American Journal of Sociology* 108(5, March): 937–75.

Patterson, Orlando. 2000. "Taking Culture Seriously: A Framework and an Afro-American Illustration." In *Culture Matters: How Values Shape Human Progress*, edited by Lawrence E. Harison and Samuel P. Huntington. New York: Basic Books.

Pettit, Becky, and Bruce Western. Forthcoming. "Mass Imprisonment and the Life Course: Race and Class Inequality in Lifetime Risks of Imprisonment." *American Sociological Review*.

Preston, Samuel H. 1984. "Children and the Elderly: Divergent Paths for America's Dependents." *Demography* 21(4, November): 435–57.

Rainwater, Lee. 1970. *Behind Ghetto Walls: Black Families in a Federal Slum.* Chicago: Aldine.

Rainwater, Lee, and Timothy M. Smeeding. 2004. *Poor Kids in a Rich Country: America's Children in Comparative Perspective.* New York: Russell Sage Foundation.

Raphael, Steven. 2004. "The Socioecononic Status of Black Males: The Increasing Importance of Incarceration." Unpublished paper. Berkeley,

Calif.: Goldman School of Public Policy. University of California, Berkeley (December).

Sawhill, Isabel V. 1995. "Distinguished Lecture on Economics in Government: The Economist vs. Madmen in Authority." *Journal of Economic Perspectives* 9(3, Summer): 3–13.

―――. 2003. *One Percent for the Kids: New Policies, Brighter Futures for America's Children*. Washington, D.C.: Brookings Institution.

Sigle-Rushton, Wendy, and Sara McLanahan. 2002. "For Richer or Poorer?" JCPR Working Paper 264. Evanston, Ill.: Joint Center for Poverty Research, Northwestern University (January 8). Available at: http://www.jcpr.org/wp/wpdownload.cfm?pdflink=wpfiles/siglerushton_mclanahan_2.pdf (accessed May 21, 2004).

Smeeding, Timothy M. 2002. "No Child Left Behind?" *Indicators* 1(3): 6–30.

Smith, Herbert L., Jr., Morgan S. Philip, and Tanya Koropeckyj-Cox. 1996. "A Decomposition of Trends in the Nonmarital Fertility Ratios of Blacks and Whites in the United States, 1960–1992." *Demography* 33(May): 141–51.

Steuerle, C. Eugene, Melissa Favreault, and Frank J. Sammartino, eds. 2002. *Social Security and the Family: Addressing Unmet Needs in an Underfunded System*. Washington, D.C.: Urban Institute.

U.S. Census Bureau. 2001. "Internet Table 2. Historical Living Arrangements of Children." Washington: U.S. Government Printing Office. Available at: http://www.census.gov/population/socdemo/child/p70-74/tab02.pdf (accessed May 19, 2004).

―――. 2003. "Table C2. Household Relationship and Living Arrangements of Children Under 18 Years, by Age, Sex, Race, Hispanic Origin, and Metropolitan Residents: March 2001." Washington: U.S. Government Printing Office. Available at: http://www.census.gov/population/socdemo/hh-fam/cps2001/tabC2-all.pdf (accessed May 19, 2004).

Wilson, William J. 1987. *The Truly Disadvantaged: The Inner City, the Underclass and Public Policy*. Chicago: University of Chicago Press.

Wolf, Douglas A. 1995. "Changes in the Living Arrangements of Older Women: An International Study." *The Gerontologist* 35(December): 724–31.

Wosnitza, Regine. 2002. "A Clash of Family Values: Katherina Reiche's Appointment as Stoiber's Campaign Family Expert Raised Eyebrows—Not Least in His Own Party." *Time Magazine [Europe]*, September 23. Available at: http://www.time.com/time/europe/magazine/2002/0923/germanelex/reiche.html (accessed May 21, 2004).

Wu, Lawrence L., and Barbara Wolfe, eds. 2001. *Out of Wedlock: Causes and Consequences of Nonmarital Fertility*. New York: Russell Sage Foundation.

vorce, separation, death, or imprisonment, and nearly half of all out-of-wedlock births are now to cohabiting fathers and mothers. These facts suggest that we need to be more precise about which changes worry us. Americans worry about family change for at least three kinds of reasons, which we will label economic, developmental, and moral. Each of these concerns implies a different definition of "the problem."

The Economic Problem

From an economic perspective, the most troubling feature of family change has been the spread of families headed by a single mother who is not living with another adult who helps support her and her children. Single mothers seldom command high wages. They also find it unusually difficult to work long hours, since they must also care for their children. Many get very little child support from the absent father, and even generous child support payments provide less money than a resident father with the same income would normally provide. While single mothers are eligible for various forms of public assistance, neither legislators nor voters have wanted to make such assistance at all generous, lest generosity encourage still more women to raise children on their own. The spread of single-mother families has therefore played a major role in the persistence of poverty in the United States. In 1964, when Lyndon Johnson declared a war on poverty, only 30 percent of poor families with children were headed by single mothers. Since the late 1970s the figure has been about 60 percent.[1]

Not all children from disrupted families live with what the English call a lone mother, but other living arrangements are less likely to leave children in poverty. Mothers who divorce and remarry tend to be about as well off economically as mothers who remain married to their children's biological father (McLanahan and Sandefur 1994). Unmarried mothers who cohabit with a boyfriend also tend to have significantly higher household incomes than those who live on their own, although it is not clear how much of the typical boyfriend's income is available to support the mother's children. And when unmarried mothers live with their parents or other relatives, they too face fewer economic problems than when they live alone. If we are mainly concerned with reducing child poverty, all these alternatives reduce its incidence. Unfortunately, however, these alternatives to lone motherhood often have noneconomic costs that make lone mothers reject them. Nor would marrying the father of her children solve every single mother's economic problems. Marrying a chronically unemployed man, for example, is likely to exacerbate a mother's economic problems rather than reduce them. Nonetheless, if our basic

PART I

What Do We Know?

CHAPTER TWO

The Spread of Single-Parent Families in the United States Since 196

David T. Ellwood and Christopher Jenc

THE SPREAD OF single-parent families has been both an intellectual ch
lenge and a source of persistent frustration for social scientists. Some
the nation's most influential social theorists, including Gary Becker (1
and William Julius Wilson (1987), have sought to explain the char
These theories have led to a large body of empirical research, but th
is still no consensus about why single parenthood spread, much less ab
why it spread faster in some populations than in others. The most wi
cited empirical papers seem to be those that disprove various hypothe
Indeed, it is only a slight exaggeration to say that quantitative social so
tists' main contribution to our understanding of this change has bee
show that *nothing* caused single-parent families to become more comm
Nonetheless, they did.

WHAT CHANGES SHOULD WORRY US?

When legislators, policy analysts, and opinion leaders discuss fa
change they usually focus on two issues: out-of-wedlock births and fa
less families. In many cases they discuss these two issues as if they
identical. Yet more than half of all fatherless families are created b

PART I

What Do We Know?

CHAPTER TWO

The Spread of Single-Parent Families in the United States Since 1960

David T. Ellwood and Christopher Jencks

THE SPREAD OF single-parent families has been both an intellectual challenge and a source of persistent frustration for social scientists. Some of the nation's most influential social theorists, including Gary Becker (1991) and William Julius Wilson (1987), have sought to explain the change. These theories have led to a large body of empirical research, but there is still no consensus about why single parenthood spread, much less about why it spread faster in some populations than in others. The most widely cited empirical papers seem to be those that disprove various hypotheses. Indeed, it is only a slight exaggeration to say that quantitative social scientists' main contribution to our understanding of this change has been to show that *nothing* caused single-parent families to become more common. Nonetheless, they did.

WHAT CHANGES SHOULD WORRY US?

When legislators, policy analysts, and opinion leaders discuss family change they usually focus on two issues: out-of-wedlock births and fatherless families. In many cases they discuss these two issues as if they were identical. Yet more than half of all fatherless families are created by divorce, separation, death, or imprisonment, and nearly half of all out-of-wedlock births are now to cohabiting fathers and mothers. These facts suggest that we need to be more precise about which changes worry us. Americans worry about family change for at least three kinds of reasons, which we will label economic, developmental, and moral. Each of these concerns implies a different definition of "the problem."

The Economic Problem

From an economic perspective, the most troubling feature of family change has been the spread of families headed by a single mother who is not living with another adult who helps support her and her children. Single mothers seldom command high wages. They also find it unusually difficult to work long hours, since they must also care for their children. Many get very little child support from the absent father, and even generous child support payments provide less money than a resident father with the same income would normally provide. While single mothers are eligible for various forms of public assistance, neither legislators nor voters have wanted to make such assistance at all generous, lest generosity encourage still more women to raise children on their own. The spread of single-mother families has therefore played a major role in the persistence of poverty in the United States. In 1964, when Lyndon Johnson declared a war on poverty, only 30 percent of poor families with children were headed by single mothers. Since the late 1970s the figure has been about 60 percent.[1]

Not all children from disrupted families live with what the English call a lone mother, but other living arrangements are less likely to leave children in poverty. Mothers who divorce and remarry tend to be about as well off economically as mothers who remain married to their children's biological father (McLanahan and Sandefur 1994). Unmarried mothers who cohabit with a boyfriend also tend to have significantly higher household incomes than those who live on their own, although it is not clear how much of the typical boyfriend's income is available to support the mother's children. And when unmarried mothers live with their parents or other relatives, they too face fewer economic problems than when they live alone. If we are mainly concerned with reducing child poverty, all these alternatives reduce its incidence. Unfortunately, however, these alternatives to lone motherhood often have noneconomic costs that make lone mothers reject them. Nor would marrying the father of her children solve every single mother's economic problems. Marrying a chronically unemployed man, for example, is likely to exacerbate a mother's economic problems rather than reduce them. Nonetheless, if our basic concern is with economic hardship, lone mothers are the group at greatest risk.

The Child Development Problem

Most Americans believe that growing up in a single-parent family is likely to harm children even if the family's income remains ample. Indeed, the idea that two loving parents can raise children better than one seems self-evident to most couples who get along reasonably well. But when parents do *not* get along, the assumption that their children will always fare better if the parents remain together becomes problematic. Much is likely to depend on what form the parents' incompatibility takes. Getting a violent parent out of a household may often be good for the children. Getting an unfaithful parent out of a household may benefit the other parent more than the children.

Determining what proportion of divorces and decisions not to marry harm children and what proportion benefit children is currently beyond the powers of social science. Given such uncertainty, leaving the choice to parents themselves has obvious advantages, but from a policy viewpoint this strategy runs two major risks. First, adults tend to make marital choices aimed at maximizing their own individual welfare. If one parent wants to marry while the other does not, no marriage is likely to occur, even if the couple's mean well-being would be higher if it did. Second, while parents considering marriage or divorce usually put some weight on what they think would be good for their children, they may not give their children's welfare as much weight as the rest of society thinks they should. Children's long-term welfare might, for example, be optimized when 80 percent of couples who conceived children stayed together until their children were grown. At least one of the two parents might, however, be better off if only 40 percent of all couples stayed together until their children were grown. If this were the case, a laissez faire system that allows each parent to do what he or she wants, giving some weight to children's interests but more weight to the least satisfied parent's interests, might mean that half of all biological parents split up. Such a system would not serve children very well.

Those who worry about the noneconomic effects of lone parenthood on children express concern about the lack of male role models, the potential for reduced discipline and control over children, the legitimation of "dependency" on the government, and the quality of single parents' relationships with their children. Of course, not all single-parent families suffer from any of these problems, and having two resident parents does not always solve any of them. Still, the correlational evidence is suggestive.

Sara McLanahan and Gary Sandefur (1994) used data from a variety of American surveys to compare young people who had grown up with both of their biological parents to those who had grown up with a single biological parent or a biological parent plus a stepparent. After taking account of differences in parental education, number of siblings, race, and region, late adolescents and young adults who had grown up with both biological parents performed better on school achievement tests, had fewer children as teenagers, finished high school more often, attended college more often, and were more likely to be employed in early adulthood than those who had grown up with a single parent or a stepparent. The reasons for these disparities seemed to vary depending on who the children lived with.

Most children raised by a single parent are raised by their mother, and families headed by a single mother tend to have less income than two-parent families. McLanahan and Sandefur found that about half the disadvantage associated with growing up in a single-parent family was explained by this income difference.[2] Children living with a stepparent, in contrast, were almost as well off economically as children living with two biological parents. Nonetheless, children who lived with a stepparent in adolescence were at least as likely as children who had lived with a single parent to drop out of high school or to have a baby before they turned twenty. For adolescents, the economic advantages of having a stepparent seemed to be offset by psychological disadvantages. Presumably most children find it harder to deal with a new parent than one who has been there for as long as they can remember, and presumably most adults find it easier to parent their own children than somebody else's children.

For our purposes McLanahan and Sandefur's key finding is that children raised by two biological parents fare better than children raised either by an unmarried parent or a biological parent plus a stepparent. This may be partly because children need stability, and not living with both biological parents is associated with changes in household composition that children find upsetting. In principle, one could test this hypothesis by looking at children raised by single mothers who never cohabited or married while their children were growing up, but we have not seen evidence of this kind. We note, however, that in McLanahan and Sandefur's surveys children raised by a widowed parent fared better than children raised by a parent who had never married, had divorced, or had divorced and remarried, so instability is not the only factor at work. The sampling errors for some of McLanahan and Sandefur's estimates are also fairly large, so it would be premature to conclude that the disadvantages associated with having a single parent and a stepparent are strictly equivalent. There are also complex methodological issues associated with determining whether the differences between children living in different kinds of families are really causal, since the adults in these families proba-bly differ in ways that surveys do not measure.

Nonetheless, if children's social and psychological outcomes depend on whether their biological parents stay together, the trend that should worry us is not the percentage of children living with a lone mother but the percentage not living with both of their biological parents—a group we refer to as living in "disrupted" families. As we shall see, the percent-age of children from disrupted biological families is much larger than the percentage living with a single mother, and it has risen more since 1960.

The Moral Problem

When American politicians and citizens talk about changes in the family, they often focus explicitly on moral issues. When social scientists talk about these changes, in contrast, they usually try to avoid making explic-itly moral judgments. Even those social scientists who deplore the spread of single parenthood prefer to argue that single parenthood has costly social consequences rather than arguing that it is wrong. Sociologists do discuss changes in social norms and attitudes, many of which involve moral judgments, but they seldom endorse these judgments and often write as if all moral judgments were automatically suspect. Even the late Daniel Patrick Moynihan, who never shrank from moral judgments, made a more prudential argument when he delivered the Godkin lectures at Harvard, declaring:

> The institution of the family is decisive in determining not only if a person has the capacity to love another individual but in the larger social sense whether he is capable of loving his fellow men collectively. The whole of society rests on this foundation for stability, understanding and social peace. (Moynihan 1986, n.p.)

When Americans talk about the breakdown in traditional moral norms, they usually emphasize three forms of behavior: premarital sex, out-of-wedlock births, and divorce. Those who see such behavior as immoral often claim that it has costly social consequences, but their moral judg-ments seldom depend on claims about consequences. Most people who think premarital sex is morally wrong regard it as wrong even when couples contracept effectively, do not spread AIDS, and eventually marry. Likewise, among those who think that divorce violates immutable reli-gious principles, its moral status does not change when it makes both partners in a particular marriage happier or when it makes particular children better off. The proportion of Americans who view premarital sex, divorce, and out-of-wedlock births in moral terms has clearly declined over the past generation. But among those who continue to see such choices in moral terms, growing public permissiveness serves as further evidence that the nation faces a moral crisis.

Divorce   In the early twentieth century most Americans took wedding vows literally and saw marriage as a lifetime commitment. Indeed, official statistics suggest that divorces were almost as rare as nonmarital births. But between 1960 and 1980 the divorce rate more than doubled, and it has remained high ever since. Arland Thornton (1989) demonstrates that attitudes toward divorce changed dramatically between the early 1960s and the mid-1970s. In 1962, only half of all respondents disagreed with a statement suggesting that parents who don't get along should stay together for the children. By 1977, over 80 percent disagreed. Attitudes towards divorce do not seem to have changed appreciably since the 1970s.

Premarital Sex   In the early 1960s roughly half of all twenty-five-year-old women had had sexual intercourse before they married. By the late 1980s five out of six had done so. This change in behavior has been accompanied by a parallel change in the way people talk about premarital sex. In early 1960s roughly three-quarters of American adults said that premarital sex was wrong. By the 1980s only one-third of adults said that premarital sex was "always" or "almost always" wrong.[3]

Out-of-Wedlock Births   In 1960 most men and women who engaged in premarital sex assumed that if the woman became pregnant they would marry and raise the child together. As a result, premarital pregnancies were fairly common, but premarital births were rare. By the 1990s roughly one baby in three was born to an unmarried couple. Here again moral norms have changed along with behavior, but apparently not as much. In 1994 three-quarters of all adults interviewed by the General Social Survey (GSS) agreed with the proposition that "people who want children ought to get married." For many respondents, however, this judgment may have been prudential rather than moral.

TRENDS IN FAMILY DISRUPTION

We now turn to an examination of trends in disrupted families, divorce, out-of-wedlock childbearing, and single parenthood.

Disrupted Families   Traditional moral arguments all suggest that biological parents have an obligation to raise their children together if this is at all possible. The child development literature also suggests that this moral injunction may serve a practical purpose. We therefore begin by examining changes in children's chances of growing up with both of their biological parents. Unfortunately, the U.S. Census Bureau, which is our main source of data on long-term trends in living arrangements, seldom distinguishes between biological parents and stepparents.[4] This omission probably reflects the fact that federal policy has been mainly concerned with the spread of single-parent families, which tend to be poor, not with the spread of stepparent families, which are not especially poor. The dearth of data has made research on trends in the proportion of children living with their biological parents quite scarce.

One can, however, get some information on such trends using the General Social Survey. Since 1972 the GSS has been asking American adults if they were living with both their own mother and father around the time they were sixteen. Most respondents presumably interpret this question as referring to their biological parents, although some adopted children may well have said they lived with their "own mother and father," especially since children adopted before 1960 were often not told that they had been adopted.

Figure 2.1 shows that from 1900 until around 1970 about a quarter of American sixteen-year-olds did not live with both of their own parents. By the 1990s the proportion had risen to almost half. The estimate for the 1990s is roughly consistent with other sources.[5]

Figure 2.1 also shows the fraction of children whose parent(s) died before they reached sixteen and the fraction that split up for all other reasons. In the early part of the twentieth century family disruptions due to the death of a parent affected about one child in six, while other sources of disruption affected about half that number. By the end of the century the pattern was reversed. Just 5 percent of those who turned sixteen in the 1990s reported that one of their parents had died, while 39 percent reported that they did not live with both of their parents for some other reason.[6] Unfortunately, the GSS does not distinguish respondents whose parents divorced from those whose parents never married.

Similar changes have occurred in most other affluent nations, but none experiences as much family disruption as the United States (see figure 2.2). It is true that out-of-wedlock births are as common in many European countries as in the United States. But the estimated percentage of fifteen-year-olds living with both of their biological parents is far lower in the United States that in Western Europe.[7] Even in Sweden, where nonmarital births are almost twice as common as in the United States, most unmarried parents raise their children together. As a result, two-thirds of all Swedish fifteen-year-olds are expected to live with both of their biological parents at age fifteen—a figure comparable to that in Germany and France.

Figure 2.1   Sixteen-Year-Olds Not Living with Both Parents

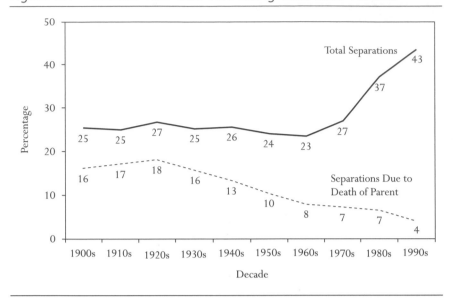

Source: Retrospective reports from 40,090 surviving adults interviewed by the General Social Survey between 1972 and 2000 (tabulations by Zoua Vang).

Note: The question is, "Were you living with both your own mother and father around the time you were 16?" If not, "With whom were you living around that time?" If respondents had married or left home by age sixteen, the interviewer asked with whom the respondent lived, "Before that." If respondents were not living with both their own mother and father, they were asked, "What happened?" Aside from a parent dying, the most common answer was that the respondent's parents, "Were divorced or separated." There is no separate category for respondents whose parents never lived together. Some of these respondents may have described their parents as "separated." Others may have given answers that were tabulated as "other."

Divorce   Figure 2.3 shows both divorce rates and the fraction of children whose parents will divorce by age eighteen. Until the 1940s divorce was rare. It shot up briefly after World War II, but quickly returned to roughly the prewar level, which persisted until the 1960s, when it began to rise again. The divorce rate peaked around 1980 and has fallen slightly since that time.

Nonmarital Births   Figure 2.4 shows that nonmarital childbearing was also unusual until the 1960s. But whereas divorce leveled off around 1980, the fraction of children born out of wedlock continued to rise until

Figure 2.2   Children Not Living with Both Biological Parents at
Age Fifteen, Projected

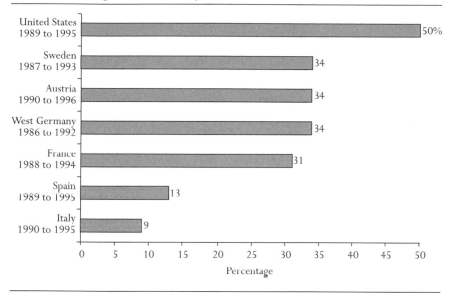

Source: Authors' compilation calculated from Andersson (2001).

the 1990s. Since then the increase has slowed dramatically. Figure 2.4
also shows the percentage of children under the age of one who were
not living with married parents. Between 1940 and 1970 this figure
matched the percentage of births to unmarried parents quite closely.
Since 1970 the two sets of numbers have diverged dramatically. This
divergence is not well understood.[8] As we noted earlier, the fact that
nonmarital births were rare before the 1960s does not mean that nonmarital *pregnancies* were rare, only that prospective parents nearly always
married before the baby was born.

Another important change since 1980 is the increasing probability that
unmarried parents are living together when their baby is born. Larry
Bumpass and Hsien-Hen Lu (2000) argue that cohabitors accounted for
the entire increase in nonmarital births among white women between the
early 1980s and the early 1990s. No consensus has emerged about how
we should think about such families. Gunnar Andersson (2001) has calculated that if the patterns that prevailed in the United States between 1989
and 1995 were to persist, 65 percent of parents who were married when
they had a child would still be married when their child was fifteen.
Among parents who were cohabiting when their child was born, only 22

Figure 2.3   Divorce Rates

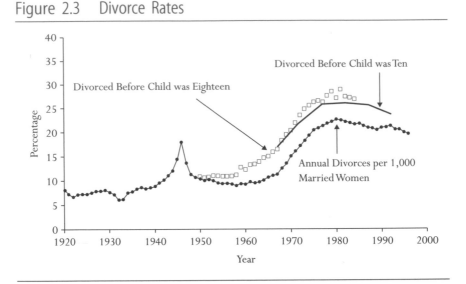

Sources: Divorces per 1,000 married women are annual estimates from U.S. Census Bureau, *Historical Statistics of the United States*, series B-217, and U.S. Census Bureau (various years). Percentages of children whose parents will divorce before the child is eighteen are based on the percentage of children whose parents divorced in the year shown, taken from London (1989, table 1). We converted the annual risks that a child's parents would divorce (P_{DI}) to a cumulative eighteen year risk (P_{D18}) by assuming $P_{D18} = 1 - (1 - P_{DI})^{18}$. Percentages of firstborn children actually experiencing a divorce within ten years of birth are for children from first marriages and are based on hazard models for five-year birth cohorts in the June Current Population Survey. We are indebted to Steve Martin for these estimates. We used linear interpolation to estimate probabilities for one-year birth cohorts. Each cohort's probability of experiencing a divorce before age ten is shown for the midpoint of the interval during which it was at risk, namely the year in which the cohort was five years old.

percent would still be together when their child was fifteen. Furthermore, the cohabiting parents who stay together mostly marry within a few years of their child's birth. In the United States, therefore, parental cohabitation is seldom a stable arrangement. Most cohabiting parents split up, and most of the rest marry.

TRENDS IN SINGLE PARENTHOOD

For a child, living with a lone mother is often a temporary situation. The fraction of children living with a single mother in any given year depends

Figure 2.4   Out-of-Wedlock Births

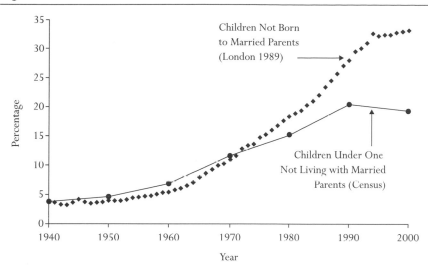

Sources: The pre-1970 percentages of nonmarital births are from U.S. Census Bureau, *Historical Statistics of the United States, Colonial Times to the Present*, Series B-1 and B-28. The post-1970 percentages are from London (1989). Pre-1980 estimates have been multiplied by 1.034 to make them consistent with post 1980 estimates. The percentages of children under age one not living with a married parent are from the Integrated Public Use Microsamples of the decennial Censuses for 1940 to 2000 and were calculated by Andrew Clarkwest. Definitions, methods, and coverage change slightly from year to year in both series.

on how many mothers have divorced in the past and how old their children were, how many remarried and how long they waited, how many mothers who had children out of wedlock subsequently married, whether they stayed married, how many cohabited, and so on.

The proportion of children under eighteen living in single-parent families rose from about 10 percent in 1965 to 29 percent in 1997 but had fallen back to 27 percent by 2001 (see figure 2.5). The reasons for this decline are still uncertain, but welfare reform and an extraordinarily tight labor market are the most obvious candidates. Figure 2.5 also shows that most of the rise during the 1960s and 1970s can be traced to rising divorce rates. In the 1980s and 1990s nearly the entire rise was traceable to out-of-wedlock births.

The data in figure 2.5, which come from the Current Population Survey (CPS), do not allow us to distinguish children who live with a step-

Figure 2.5   Children Living with One Parent, By Marital Status

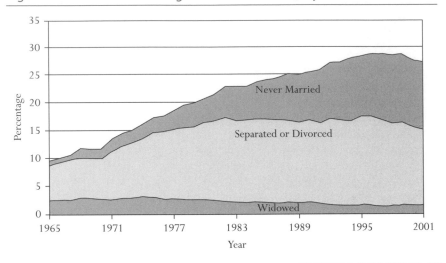

Source: Authors' tabulations from the March Current Population Survey.

parent from children who live with both of their biological parents. Figure 2.5 therefore understates the fraction of all children not living with both biological parents, the fraction who have experienced the death or divorce of a parent, and the fraction whose parents have never been married to one another.

Figure 2.6 shows the same information for African American children only. Vastly more black children live in single parent families (note the change of scale). And for black children, never-married motherhood became the primary source of change much earlier. Here too rates have fallen slightly in recent years. The reasons for the difference between blacks and non-blacks remain controversial and poorly understood.

In her comprehensive review of trends in the well-being of American women, Francine Blau (1998) demonstrated that trends in single parenthood differed considerably by education between 1970 and 1995. Figure 2.7 looks only at children living with their mother and asks how the mother's education relates to the probability that she is married. Trends for college graduates are strikingly different from trends for less-educated mothers. Among children whose mothers had college degrees, the fraction living in single-parent households rose from 6 percent in 1965 to 10 percent in 1980 and then leveled off. Among children whose mothers had not finished high school, the fraction living in single-parent house-

Figure 2.6 Black Children Living with One Parent

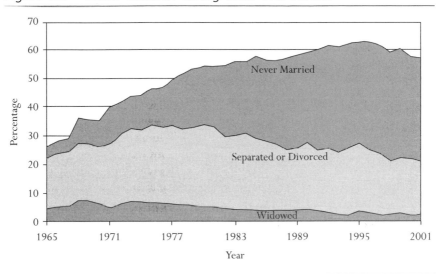

Source: Authors' tabulations from the March Current Population Survey.

Figure 2.7 Children in Single Mother Homes by Education

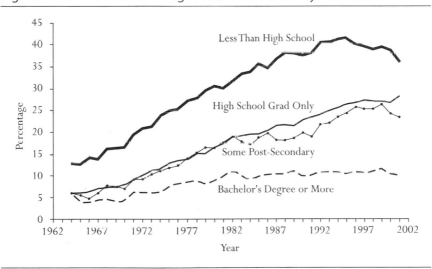

Source: Authors' tabulations from the March Current Population Survey.

holds rose from 13 percent in 1965 to over 40 percent in the mid-1990s, although there has been some decline since then.

If the growth of single motherhood had been largely confined to college-educated women with high earning power, it would not pose a major economic problem. But figure 2.7 shows precisely the opposite trend. Single motherhood has spread faster among women with lower potential earnings. The trend is not confined to the least educated, however. The increase has been almost as steep among women with twelve to fifteen years of school as among those with less.[9] Only college graduates seem largely exempt. The obvious question is why. The social science literature is rich with models and hypotheses that seek to explain these changes in family structure, but the empirical literature has not found that they explained much of the change. As a result, no explanation has won general acceptance. But there are some partial explanations in the literature and some pretty clear implications about where we should search for better answers.

THE CHANGING ROLES OF DIVORCE AND NONMARITAL CHILDBEARING

Until now we have focused on trends among children, since the discussion of family change has often focused on their well-being. But if we want to understand the causes of family change, we need to understand the choices made by adults—men and women making complicated and often joint decisions regarding whether and when to have sexual relations, use contraception, have abortions, live together, marry, divorce, and re-marry. Since 92 percent of children under eighteen live with their mother, most social scientists have found it convenient to focus on explaining women's behavior. We largely adopt that convention here, while conceding that this approach could obscure crucial elements of the story.

The rising correlation between a mother's marital status and her education can be traced primarily to the fact that nonmarital childbearing rose far more rapidly among the less educated. In 1965, hardly any mothers at any education level reported that they had never been married. This does not mean there were no nonmarital births. Some unmarried mothers placed their children with adoption agencies. Some mothers married after their child's birth. Some had been married and divorced before their child's birth. Still, nonmarital births were rare. That is still true among mothers who have finished college, all but 3 percent of whom have also been married. Among mothers without high school diplomas, in contrast, 25 percent now say that they have never been married. This pattern persists when we look at blacks, whites, and Hispanics separately.

Table 2.1   Change in Age at First Marriage and First Birth by Race

Birth Year	Percentage with First Marriage by a Given Age			Percentage with First Birth by a Given Age		
	Age Twenty-Five	Age Thirty	Age Forty[a]	Age Twenty-Five	Age Thirty	Age Forty[a]
All women						
1940 to 1944	84	91	94	71	84	88
1960 to 1964	64	78	86	52	70	81
Difference	−20	−13	−07	−19	−14	−07
White women						
1940 to 1944	86	92	95	71	84	88
1960 to 1964	68	82	89	49	69	80
Difference	−18	−10	−06	−22	−15	−08
Black women						
1940 to 1944	72	82	87	77	86	88
1960 to 1964	42	55	68	68	76	85
Difference	−30	−27	−19	−09	−10	−04

Source: Authors' tabulation of June and March CPS data.
[a]For women born between 1960 and 1964 estimates at age forty are extrapolated by combining percentages married or with children at ages thirty to thirty-five with the fraction of unmarried or childless thirty- to thirty-five-year-olds in the 1955 to 1959 cohorts who had a child within the next ten years.

Nonetheless, it is also true that blacks are more likely than whites with the same amount of education to be never-married mothers.[10]

One useful way to think about these trends is to compare changes in the timing of first births and first marriages. If a woman's first birth precedes her first marriage, she becomes a never-married mother, at least temporarily. The first row of table 2.1 shows the percentage of women born between 1940 and 1944 who had had either their first marriage or their first birth by the time they were twenty-five, thirty, and forty years old. The second row shows these percentages for women born between 1960 and 1964. Among white women we see an 18-point decline in the percentage who had married by age twenty-five and a 22-point decline in the percentage who had borne a child by that age. By the time white women had turned forty, however, the changes were far less dramatic: a 6-point decline in the percentage who had married and an 8-point decline in the percentage who had had a child.

Table 2.2 Change in Age at First Marriage and at First Birth
by Education

Birth Year	Percentage with First Marriage by a Given Age			Percentage with First Birth by a Given Age		
	Age Twenty-Five	Age Thirty	Age Forty	Age Twenty-Five	Age Thirty	Age Forty
High school dropouts						
1940 to 1944	83	89	91	82	88	90
1960 to 1964	66	75	82	78	83	86
Difference	−17	−14	−09	−04	−05	−04
High school graduates						
1940 to 1944	87	93	95	77	88	90
1960 to 1964	70	81	88	64	79	84
Difference	−17	−12	−07	−13	−09	−06
Some college						
1940 to 1944	86	92	95	71	83	87
1960 to 1964	65	79	90	49	70	81
Difference	−21	−13	−05	−22	−13	−06
College graduates						
1940 to 1944	74	87	92	47	71	82
1960 to 1964	50	75	85	20	50	73
Difference	−24	−12	−07	−27	−21	−09

Source: Authors' tabulation of June and March CPS data.
Note: For women born between 1960 and 1964 estimates at age forty are extrapolated by combining percentages married or with children at ages thirty to thirty-five with the fraction of unmarried or childless thirty- to thirty-five-year-olds in the 1955 to 1959 cohorts who had a child within the next ten years.

Black women show far greater declines in marriage than white women. Only about 68 percent of black women in the most recent cohort will have married by age forty, compared to 87 percent of those born two decades earlier. But while more white than black women have married by age forty (89 versus 68 percent), more black than white women have had children (85 versus 80 percent). Note that while white women are more likely to marry than to have children, the opposite is true for black women.

Table 2.2 shows changes by level of education.[11] Marriage patterns for

Figure 2.8   Mothers Who Were Not Married, by Race and Ethnicity

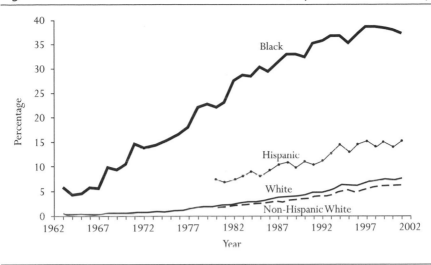

Source: Authors' tabulations from the March Current Population Survey.

the cohort born in the early 1940s were quite similar across all education levels, except that college graduates married a little later. By age thirty education no longer mattered much. In the cohort born twenty years later, women at all education levels married later, but the fraction who had married by age thirty still looked quite similar for women at all education levels.

The trends are very different for childbearing. The fraction of college graduates with a first birth by age twenty-five fell from 47 percent to 20 percent. Even by age thirty the fraction of college graduates who had had a child fell from 71 to 50 percent. The least educated women, in contrast, had hardly postponed childbearing at all.

In sum, highly educated women are postponing both marriage and childbearing, while less-educated women are postponing marriage but not childbearing. The result has been a rapid rise in the fraction of less-educated women who have had children but have not married (see figures 2.8 and 2.9). Figure 2.8 shows this trend by race and (after 1980) Hispanic origin. Figure 2.9 shows the trend by mother's education. Note that the racial differences in figure 2.8 are far larger than the educational differences in figure 2.9. The racial differences in figure 2.8 are also too large to be accounted for by economic factors alone.

Trends in divorce also differ by race and education. Figure 2.10 shows the fraction of ever-married black and white mothers who were separated

Figure 2.9   Mothers Who Were Not Married, by Education

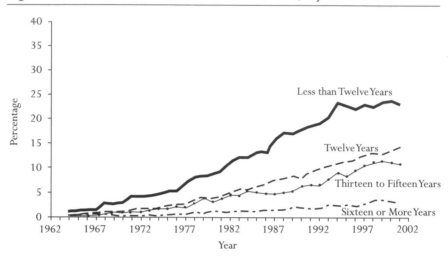

Source: Authors' tabulations from the March Current Population Survey.

Figure 2.10   Ever-Married Mothers Who Were Separated or Divorced, by Race-Ethnicity

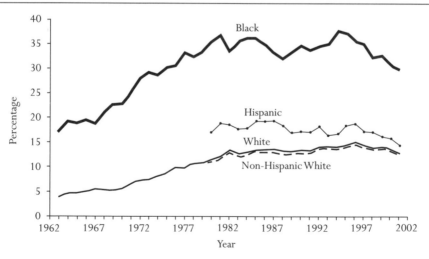

Source: Authors' tabulations from the March Current Population Survey.

Figure 2.11   Ever-Married Mothers Who Were Separated or Divorced, by Education

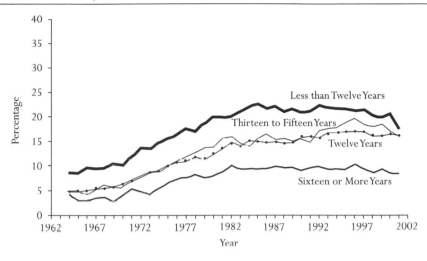

Source: Authors' tabulations from the March Current Population Survey.

or divorced. (These estimates include some mothers who had had a nonmarital birth, subsequently married, and then divorced. The estimates exclude mothers who had divorced and remarried.) In any given year the chances that a previously married mother would be divorced or separated were highest for blacks and lowest for non-Hispanic whites. Divorced mothers became much more common in all groups during the late 1960s and 1970s but the trend levels off in the early 1980s and begins to fall in the late 1990s. It is not entirely clear why divorce leveled off in the 1980s or why nonmarital births continued to rise. The fact that most couples were marrying later (and some were not marrying at all) should have reduced the proportion of "high risk" marriages, but we do not know how much of the decline in divorce is explained by rising reluctance to marry.

Figure 2.11 shows that the percentage of ever-married mothers who were divorced also rose for every education group between the early 1960s and the early 1980s. College-educated women were less likely to be divorced in all years. These patterns hold within both the black and white populations. But once again the racial disparity is much larger than the educational disparity.

These data sharpen the questions we need to answer. First, why did the tendency to postpone childbearing differ by education and race? Why did the considerations that led less-educated women to delay marriage not lead them to delay parenthood as well? Second, why are college-educated women postponing childbearing so much? And third why did divorce rates flatten out when nonmarital childbearing was accelerating?

THE TRADITIONAL ECONOMIC MODEL

Much of the empirical literature on family structure has been based on a broad class of economic models that we will refer to as the "traditional economic model" (TEM), which derives to a great extent from theories developed by Gary Becker (summarized in Becker 1991). The adjective "traditional" reflects the fact that far more elaborate formulations are now found in the economics literature. The adjective "economic" is more ambiguous. Economists played a central role in developing these models, but sociologists have proposed models in which economic variables play similar roles. Still, since this model lies at the core of much current empirical work, some label is needed.

The traditional economic model seeks to explain decisions about marriage, not decisions about fertility, but it assumes that marriage leads to parenthood. It treats marriage as a contract from which both the husband and wife expect to reap economic benefits.[12] Becker emphasizes gains associated with specialization among marrying partners. If one partner has a comparative advantage in either market work (because of higher wages) or home production (because of either a stronger taste for nurturing children or greater skills in such work), it will generally make sense for at least one partner to specialize. Thus most men might specialize in market work and most women in home production. By improving efficiency, specialization creates gains from marriage analogous to gains from trade. This model yields fairly straightforward predictions. If male and female wages converge, the advantages of specialization and the gains from marriage will decline. Likewise, if men and women derive increasingly similar non-monetary benefits from either employment or childrearing, the gains from marriage will also fall.

Yoram Weiss (1997) highlights three other ways in which marriage can generate economic benefits: overcoming credit market imperfections (one partner can invest in the other's schooling, for example); sharing collective goods (such as a home); and sharing risk (if one partner becomes unemployed, the other can enter the labor force or share earnings). These advantages of marriage should be more sensitive to changes in the overall income level than to changes in the relative earnings of men and women. As incomes rise, both men and women will find it easier to live alone rather than sharing their home with someone they do not find congenial. Those with more income also face fewer credit constraints and have less need to share economic risks. These considerations suggest that if all else were equal marriage should be more common among those with lower potential earnings. Since that is not what we observe, other influences must also be at work.

The traditional economic model also predicts that external economic support for single adults, particularly single parents, will make marriage less common. If a parent who wants to specialize in household production can get money from public assistance or from relatives, the advantages of marriage diminish. Rising welfare benefits should therefore reduce marriage rates, while falling benefits should raise marriage rates. What matters for marriage, however, is not the absolute benefit level but the difference between a mother's standard of living when she is unmarried rather than married. Thus if real welfare benefits fall but unskilled men's potential earnings fall even more, marriage rates among unskilled women may fall.

Economic factors figure prominently in the work of sociologists as well as economists. The best known theory is the one proposed by William Julius Wilson and Kathryn M. Neckerman (1986). Unlike most economists, Wilson and Neckerman focus on blacks living in inner cities. But like many economists they emphasize the importance of male earning power, along with the ratio of young black men to young black women. They argue that high levels of unemployment, weak connections to mainstream employers, rising levels of imprisonment, and a low ratio of young black men to women created a shortage of "marriageable" black men in the 1970s and 1980s. They do not say much about the role of improved economic opportunities for black women.

In summary, traditional economic models highlight the potential importance of four factors:

1. *Male earnings.* All else equal, improvements in men's economic opportunities should be associated with higher marriage rates and lower levels of single-parenthood.

2. *Female earnings.* All else equal, improvements in women's economic opportunities should be associated with lower marriage rates and higher levels of single-parenthood.

3. *Sex ratio.* All else equal, when one sex is in short supply, marriage rates for the other sex should fall.

4. *Public assistance.* All else equal, more generous benefits for single-parent families should lead to less marriage and more single-parent families.

Each of these predictions assumes that the other three factors remain constant. Thus, one can only test these hypotheses rigorously by looking at all four factors simultaneously.

Empirical tests of these predictions generally use one of three methods: comparisons of geographic areas, comparisons of individuals observed at a single point in time, or changes over time in the behavior of the same individuals ("hazard models"). Comparisons of geographic areas examine variation in the likelihood that members of a given age, race, and education group have children and are either married, divorced, or never-married. These area averages are typically regressed on the area's economic characteristics. Comparisons of individuals link the odds that an individual has a given marital or family status to that individual's labor market opportunities, the characteristics of potential spouses, and local welfare benefits. Both individual and area models are sometimes estimated by pooling cross-sectional data for a number of years.

Unfortunately, studies that use these methods seldom distinguish changes in timing from changes in the probability that an event will ever occur. Many studies examine changes in the prevalence of marriage among twenty-five- to thirty-four-year-old women, for example. These studies almost all find that marriage rates have fallen over time. But because they look at relatively young women, these studies cannot distinguish those who are postponing marriage from whose who will never marry. This limitation would not be a problem if the factors leading women to delay marriage were the same as those leading women to eschew marriage entirely, but that may not be the case. Goldstein and Kenney (2001) argue, for example, that higher education leads women to delay marriage but increases the probability that they will eventually marry. We are not certain whether this is true, but analyses that focus exclusively on women between the ages of twenty-five and thirty-four cannot address the possibility.

Hazard models use longitudinal data to estimate the odds that an unmarried person will marry at a given point in time. Such models can yield predictions about the timing as well as the overall likelihood of marriage, but they are seldom estimated in a way that allows the effect of variables such as women's labor market opportunities to vary by age. If higher education leads women to marry less when they are in their twenties but more when they are in their thirties, for example, the hazard models in the literature would seldom detect this pattern.[13] Like other models, longitudinal hazard models also have trouble measuring the characteristics of a respondent's potential spouses. This is largely a data problem rather than a modeling problem: until recently surveys of unmarried adults seldom tried to identify respondents' potential spouses.[14]

Findings on Marriage and Divorce

David T. Ellwood and Christopher Jencks (2004) summarize many of the articles on marriage and divorce, as well as discussing their strengths and weaknesses. The four main conclusions are that:

1. All empirical methods suggest that men's economic opportunities exert a strong influence on marriage and divorce. Improved male earnings appear to hasten marriage and may also increase the overall prevalence of marriage.
2. The role of women's economic opportunities is unclear. In cross-sectional studies of areas and individuals, women with more economic opportunities are less likely to be married and in some cases more likely to be divorced. But hazard models that follow the same women over time seldom find this pattern. These divergent findings cast doubt on the hypothesis that improvements in women's economic opportunities discourage marriage. Better economic opportunities may, however, lead women to *postpone* marriage.
3. A lower ratio of men to women reduces marriage.
4. Welfare has ambiguous effects on marriage but may increase divorce.

Several authors have also sought to explain trends over time in marriage. Changing patterns of male work and earnings cannot explain much of the trend.[15]

Findings on Female Headship and Unwed Motherhood

Another part of the literature focuses on female headship and unwed motherhood. Most of this work is preoccupied with the role of welfare. There have been a number of careful reviews of this literature, including Gregory Acs (1995), Hilary Hoynes (1997), and Robert Moffitt (1998). We agree with Moffitt's overall conclusion:

> Based on this review, it is clear that a simple majority of the studies that have been conducted to date show a significant correlation between welfare benefits and marriage and fertility, suggesting the presence of such behavioral effects. However, in addition to this finding not being able to explain the time-series increase in non-marital fertility and decline in marriage, the majority finding itself is weakened by the sensitivity of the result

to the methodology used and to numerous other differences in specifica-
tion. A neutral reading of the evidence still leads to the conclusion that
welfare has incentive effects on marriage and fertility, but the uncertainty
introduced by the disparities in research findings weakens the strength of
that conclusion. (Moffitt 1998, 75)

For our purposes the key point is that regardless of whether welfare
impacts are large or small, the traditional economic model suggests that
if all else had been equal the gradual cuts in welfare benefits since the
1970s would have reduced the number of single parent families.[16]

Why don't economic models perform better? The fact that empirical work
generates such divergent results and does such a poor job of explaining
trends over time poses a challenge for those who think that economic
change has played a major role in family change. In our view, however,
the main problem may be with the way the traditional economic model
has been used, not with the hypothesis that economic change explains
family change.

First, as Valerie Kincade Oppenheimer (1997) points out, the traditional model is meant to explain *whether* people will marry, not *when* they
will marry. If the economic gains associated with marriage decline, fewer
unmarried adults should marry and more married adults should divorce,
lowering the fraction of adults who are married at any given time. The
fraction of adults who are married has indeed fallen, but it has fallen far
more among young adults than among older adults. Because the traditional economic model makes no predictions about how economic change
will affect the age at which people marry, it is not especially helpful in
explaining the delay in marriage.

A second limitation of the traditional economic model is that it pays
little attention to fertility decisions, especially outside marriage (Hotz,
Klerman and Willis, 1997).[17] Since the gains from marriage derive chiefly
from specialization in the care and nurturing of children, the model im-
plicitly assumes that marriage should lead immediately to childbearing.
Yet one of the most important changes over the past generation is that
the timing of marriage and childbearing has become decoupled. These
changes are quite dramatic.[18] Among women who married for the first
time in 1960, 71 percent had their first child during their first three years
of marriage. Among women who first married in 1990, only 37 percent
had their first child during their first three years of marriage. The decoupling of marriage and childbearing occurred not just because more
women are now having children before marriage but also because childless women postpone their first birth longer after marriage. Over 75
percent of childless women who married in 1960 had a child within three

years. Less than 50 percent of childless women who married in 1990 had a child within three years. Since this decoupling of marriage and child-bearing is a large part of what we seek to explain, models that treat marriage and childbearing as inextricably intertwined are unlikely to be helpful.

NONECONOMIC EXPLANATIONS

The traditional economic model largely ignores the interpersonal relation-ships associated with marriage. Instead, it treats a family like a firm that generates profits (in the form of increased well-being) for its owners (the husband and wife). If the family ceases to improve the well-being of either partner, it is dissolved. But a marriage, like a business partnership, requires constant negotiations about how the enterprise will be run and how the profits will be divided. These negotiations raise issues about power and control. The outcome of such negotiations depends partly on societal norms and expectations, as well as the legal environment, all of which change over time. Such changes may well affect the likelihood that couples can achieve a mutually satisfactory outcome.

Sociologists, anthropologists, social psychologists, and even some econ-omists have investigated the interpersonal, social, and legal forces that might influence family formation and dissolution. Here we consider four types of explanations: gender role conflict, limited confidence and per-sonal efficacy, altered attitudes and social norms, and technological and legal change.

Gender Role Conflict

One popular explanation for the rise of single motherhood has been that women are less willing to put up with the way the men they meet treat them. This change is often attributed to the breakdown of consensus about gender roles (Furstenberg 1996, 2001). Both the women's move-ment and the increase in women's employment certainly appear to have changed the way many prospective husbands and wives think about their obligations to one another. If male and female expectations have changed in different ways or at different rates, that could have produced an ex-tended period in which marriages were slow to form and often dissolved because couples had incompatible views about their respective roles. This could also have contributed to the spread of single motherhood. If these changes were unevenly distributed by education or race, that would help explain why single motherhood increased more among black women and among women without college degrees.

Arland Thornton and Linda Young-DeMarco (2001) review changes in the role expectations of men and women. Using data on the attitudes of high school seniors from 1976 to 1998, they report that disagreement with the statement "the husband should make all the important decisions in the family" rose from 72 to 85 percent among women and from 44 to 49 percent among men. Disagreement with the statement "it is usually better for everyone involved if the man is the achiever outside the home and the woman takes care of the home and family" rose from 42 to 71 percent among women and from 17 to 37 percent among men. If these attitudinal changes led to parallel behavioral changes among prospective spouses, that could help explain why men and women have become more reluctant to marry and have had more trouble staying married. But the published data do not tell us whether the gender gap is wider among blacks than whites or among those who do not go on to college than among those who do.

The General Social Survey also asks adults two questions about gender roles. One question asks whether respondents agree with the statement "women should take care of running their homes and leave running the country to men." The second asks whether the respondent approves of "a married woman earning money in business or industry if she has a husband capable of supporting her." We found that more recent birth cohorts were more likely to endorse gender equality. Among those who had completed college, the trend was the same for men and women. Among those who had not completed college, egalitarian responses to the question about women's place being in the home increased significantly more among women than among men. This area deserves more systematic study.

Efficacy and Control

Social psychologists typically posit an interactive relationship between the results of people's behavior, their feelings of confidence, and their perceptions of control. Behavior that is validated by perceived success builds confidence. Behavior that leads to perceived failure can lower self-esteem, reduce sense of control, and sometimes generate dysfunctional behavior. Poor information on subjects such as contraception can also weaken people's sense of control.

Nurturing children can often provide women with avenues for success and validation that the market does not provide. Women who feel they have few opportunities in the labor market may therefore turn to child-rearing sooner in order to gain a greater sense of self-worth and efficacy. Whereas the traditional economic model suggests that better job opportunities for women reduce the benefits of marriage, efficacy models suggest that better job opportunities could reduce women's chances of becoming young mothers and thus increase the proportion who marry before having children. Furthermore, if women with better jobs are better able to maintain a sense of control or power in their marriage, this might conceivably increase their chances of remaining married. However, if men have less power in a relationship, they might be less inclined to marry or more inclined to divorce.

The notion that low efficacy causes early out-of-wedlock births among disadvantaged women comes up repeatedly both in the social sciences literature on teen pregnancy and in programs designed to prevent it.[19] Robert D. Plotnick (1992), for example, finds that a variety of measures of self-esteem, attitudes toward school, educational expectations, and the presence of an employed adult woman in a teenager's household influence teen pregnancy and its resolution. But the National Academy of Sciences' Panel on Adolescent Pregnancy and Childbearing (1987) noted that "several studies of social and psychological factors associated with adolescents' sexual behavior conclude that self-perception (not self-esteem)—that is who one is, can be, and wants to be—is at the heart of teenagers' sexual decision making" (Panel on Adolescent Pregnancy and Childbearing 1987, p. 120). Lack of knowledge about contraception and inability to resist peer influence and pressure from men are also frequent themes in this literature.

Struggles over power and control also seem to play a role in explaining why single mothers decide not to marry. Kathryn Edin (1999) reports that:

> In a non-marital relationship, women often felt they had more control than they would have had if they were married. Even if the couple cohabited, they nearly always lived with her mother or in an apartment with her name on the lease. Thus, mothers had the power to evict fathers if they interfered with childrearing or they tried to take control of the financial decision making. . . .
>
> When we asked single mothers what they liked best about being a single parent, their most frequent response was, "I am in charge," or, "I am in control". . . . (Edin 1999, 22, 24)

Edin emphasizes that single mothers want to marry, but only if men bring something valuable to the table, namely economic resources. Much of Edin's work focuses on the consequences of the fact that unskilled men not only have trouble bringing in much money but are often unwilling to do their share of the housework and childcare, especially when the children in a household are not their own. Her story is consistent with both traditional economic models and gender role conflict, but power struggles played a central role in what Edin's informants told her. Women wanted to maintain control of their household, and the "primary way that mothers thought they could maintain power in a marriage relationship was by working and contributing to the family budget" (Edin 1999, 25).

Orlando Patterson (1998) makes a related argument about why marriage is less common among blacks than other groups. He sees high levels of gender conflict as having been endemic in both African American and Afro-Caribbean culture and traces this to the legacy of slavery, not poverty. Patterson argues that because of slavery there has always been a big difference between the families of blacks and whites in North America. This argument remains controversial, partly because one would expect the cultural legacy of slavery to diminish over time, and the difference between black and white parents' living arrangements did not narrow during the late twentieth century and by some measures widened. Patterson argues that this is because African American men and women are moving on "very different socioeconomic trajectories" with men "falling behind in both absolute and relative terms" (Patterson 1998, 160). Because black men's economic position has deteriorated while black women's position has improved, the economic benefits of marriage are smaller and persistent gender conflict is more likely to drive couples apart. Patterson's story thus combines a traditional economic explanation for recent trends with a cultural explanation for the long-standing difference between blacks and non-blacks in similar economic situations.

Altered Attitudes and Social Norms

Sociologists and anthropologists often see culture as people's collective interpretation of their situation and as their initial a guide to appropriate behavior. Different cultures and subcultures have different definitions of what is rational, reasonable, desirable, and good, and these ideas often influence individuals' responses to particular opportunities and stimuli. Most anthropologists and sociologists also believe that culture is adaptive. In particular, if a given norm of behavior fails to achieve its intended result, it is unlikely to persist indefinitely. New definitions of success and failure may also emerge if old goals are no longer attainable. The adaptive nature of norms and values makes it hard to investigate their causal role unless an exogenous source of change can be identified and changes in a norm or value can be directly observed rather than just inferred.

Norms and values could be linked to changing family patterns in several different ways. The simplest case is when some exogenous shock alters attitudes, which then alter family patterns. The origins of the "sexual revolution" that de-stigmatized premarital sex, for example, are often (if not altogether convincingly) traced to the pill. Once sexual activity outside of marriage became socially acceptable, this change could easily have reduced marriage rates, since one of the strongest incentives to marry was reduced or removed.

Another possibility is that changes in social norms amplify the initial impact of exogenous shocks. If economic conditions reduce the appeal of marriage, for example, marriage rates will fall. But if marriage rates fall, social pressure to marry may also fall, which could lower marriage rates even among couples whose economic situation had not changed. Because social norms change slowly, the full impact of an economic change might not be felt for some years. The uncertain pace of normative change poses a problem for quantitative social scientists, because strong empirical tests usually rely on evidence that changes are closely linked in time. The longer and more uncertain the interval between a cause and its presumed effect, the harder it is to separate that effect from the effect of other changes.

Norms and culture also play a prominent role in discussions of the "culture of poverty" and the "underclass." In Charles Murray (1984), new social policies adopted in the 1960s reward behavior that is dysfunctional within the larger society and ultimately undermine traditional mores. In Wilson (1987), declining economic opportunities for less educated black men plus the out-migration of the black middle class leave an impoverished inner-city ghetto with few mainstream economic opportunities, and an urban underclass is the result.

Parental religion can also be treated as an exogenous cultural influence on children. Evelyn Lehrer (2000) finds that even after controlling for parental SES, education, family structure and the like, children raised in fundamentalist Protestant households are significantly more likely to marry early than mainstream Protestants, who in turn are more likely to marry early than Jews. Mormons are the most likely to marry early. Melvin Zelnik, John F. Kantner, and Kathleen Ford (1981) report that religion also affects the likelihood of premarital intercourse, although it does not seem to affect the likelihood of becoming pregnant before marriage. Presumably young people from more "liberal" denominations are more likely to have sex before they marry but also more likely to practice birth control.

There is considerable controversy about whether surveys of attitudes can provide reliable data about social norms. If survey respondents who say that premarital sex is "wrong" make sexually active unmarried friends aware of their beliefs, one can say that premarital sex violates a social norm. But if those who think that premarital sex is wrong never tell those who are sexually active that they are doing something wrong, one cannot say that premarital sex violates a social norm. Attitude surveys seldom ask about such matters. Nonetheless, attitude surveys probably provide *some* useful evidence regarding normative change. Adult attitudes about sex and family formation changed far more during the 1960s and 1970s than during the 1980s and 1990s. Thornton (1989) reports that in a 1965 NORC survey, 69 percent of women under the age of 30 said that it was always or almost always wrong if a woman "has intimate relations with a man *to whom she is engaged and intends to marry*" (italics ours). Seven years later, in the 1972 General Social Survey (GSS), only 34 percent of women under 30 said it was always or almost always wrong "if a man and a woman have sex relations before marriage." By 1974 the number had fallen to 24 percent, and it has hardly changed since.

More permissive attitudes toward nonmarital sex have been accompanied by greater acceptance of women choosing not to marry. According to Joseph Veroff, Elizabeth Douvan, and Richard A. Kulka (1981), the fraction of respondents who agreed that a woman who remained unmarried was "sick, neurotic, or immoral" fell from 80 percent in 1957 to 25 percent in 1978. Just as with attitudes toward premarital sex, Axinn and Thornton (2000) find virtually no changes in attitudes toward marriage since the mid-1970s. But while few Americans now disapprove of remaining single, both ethnographic and survey data still find widespread interest in marriage, even among inner-city blacks whose marriage rates are quite low (Edin 1999).

Overall, surveys suggest a substantial change in attitudes during the 1960s and early 1970s on everything from divorce to gender roles to premarital sex. But with the exception of attitudes toward cohabitation, surveys show relatively little change in attitudes since the 1970s. Published time series seldom report trends by race or level of education, making it difficult to determine whether attitudinal changes could account for the uneven spread of single-parent families. This issue requires further work.

The Pill and Abortion

George Akerlof, Janet Yellen, and Michael Katz (1996) argue that new contraceptive technologies and legal abortions altered the character of sexual relations between unmarried couples. Until the 1960s engaging in premarital sex usually implied a commitment to marry if the woman became pregnant. "Shot-gun" marriages were the frequent result. Akerlof, Yellen, and Katz argue that the invention of the pill and legalizing abortion made unmarried women more willing to participate in uncommitted, premarital sex by reducing the odds of a pregnancy. Women who sought to hold men to the old rules (no sex without a commitment to marry) therefore found it harder to compete successfully for boyfriends. Even women who were unwilling to get abortions responded to this competitive situation by engaging in more premarital sex. When such women became pregnant, however, they could no longer rely on social pressure to ensure that their boyfriends married them. Nonmarital births therefore rose. Akerlof, Yellen, and Katz (1996, 268) estimate that "about three-fourths of the increase in the white out-of-wedlock first birth ratio, and about three-fifths of the black increase, between 1965–1969 and 1985–1989" can be traced to a decrease in the fraction of premarital pregnancies that led to marriage.

Akerlof, Yellen, and Katz rest their argument primarily on a clever theoretical construction and a loose connection between the timing of changing events. Several other authors have sought to tighten the case by investigating whether the legalization of abortion led to changes in teen birthrates. There is an obvious direct effect: if pregnancy rates remain unchanged, birth rates will almost inevitably fall when abortion is legalized. But when the risk of pregnancy falls, the expected cost of premarital sex falls. When costs (or risks) fall, demand normally rises, often more than proportionately. As a result, cutting prices sometimes raises a firm's total revenue. This logic can also apply to nonmarital sex. If halving the risk that nonmarital sex will lead to a nonmarital birth more than doubles the frequency of nonmarital sex, the total number of nonmarital births will rise, not fall.

Several scholars, notably Phillip B. Levine et al. (1996) and June Sklar and Beth Berkov (1974), have shown that birth rates among both married and unmarried women fell in states when abortion became legal. Conversely, Philip Morgan and Allan Parnell (2002) found that funding restrictions lowered abortions and raised births in North Carolina. But Thomas Kane and Douglas Staiger (1996) found that that modest new restrictions on abortion actually *reduced* teen motherhood. They speculate that small increases in the obstacles to obtaining an abortion may have made some teenagers more careful about avoiding pregnancy without reducing abortions among those who were likely to abort before the new restrictions were imposed.

Claudia Goldin and Lawrence F. Katz (2000) examine the diffusion of the pill among college-educated women and argue that by facilitating sexual activity prior to marriage, easy availability of the pill reduced the cost of delaying marriage and staying in school (Goldin and Katz 2000). Others have investigated the possible effects of more liberal divorce laws on marriage and divorce rates, property settlements, and even suicide and spousal murder.[20] In virtually every case, legal and institutional changes appear to have had an impact, but whether they affected the fraction of children living with their biological parents is unclear.

While the literature on contraception, abortion, and divorce law suggests that changes in these domains have influenced sexual behavior, fertility, and marriage, this literature has not investigated whether technical or legal changes might account for racial and educational variation in the spread of nonmarital births, divorce, and single-parent families. All these technical and legal innovations occurred during the 1960s and 1970s. Invoking such innovations to explain changes in family patterns during the 1980s and early 1990s requires a rather complicated story in which technical and legal changes have delayed effects, perhaps because it takes a long time to alter traditional social norms. While this story is theoretically plausible, the rather skimpy evidence on attitudes that might be expected to affect family structure does not show many big changes after 1980. Changes in family structure after 1980 may, therefore, be largely due to other influences, such as the declining economic fortunes of less educated men.

WHERE MIGHT WE LOOK FOR BETTER ANSWERS?

Our review of existing research has not uncovered any simple explanation for changes in the American family. We found consistent evidence that deteriorating job opportunities for men modestly reduce marriage and increase single parenthood. But both the theoretical and empirical literature is more ambiguous about the effects of improved job opportunities for women. Contraceptive technology, access to abortion, and attitudes all changed during in the 1960s and early 1970s, but there is little direct evidence that these innovations contributed to family change in subsequent decades.

Nonetheless, if we take a broad view of the trends and findings, we believe a fairly plausible hypothesis emerges. Like Megan Sweeney (2002), we think that the relationship between economic opportunity and marriage has changed over the years. Three factors are likely to have altered the preferred timing of marriage and parenthood.

First, *the pill and legalized abortion* weakened the link between marriage and childbearing. Previous forms of contraception, such as condoms, withdrawal, rhythm, and diaphragms, were less reliable, required interruption of sexual activity, or gave males control. The pill and legalized abortion gave sexually active couples, and particularly women, far more control over the timing of births, allowing other factors (including economic incentives) to exert more influence on the timing of marriage and parenthood.[21]

Second, *changing sexual mores* made it more acceptable for unmarried couples to engage in sexual activity and live together. This change also reduced the non-economic incentives to marry, making economic considerations more likely to be decisive.

Third, *gender roles and expectations changed dramatically, particularly with respect to maternal employment.* As late as March 1968, less than a quarter of married mothers with a child under five were working, and the percentage did not vary much by the mother's education. Even among mothers with elementary school children, only about 40 percent worked and even fewer worked full-time. By March 2000, roughly two-thirds of married mothers with children under five were working, and the fraction was even higher among mothers with older children. Despite welfare reform, moreover, rates of employment in 2000 were substantially higher among college-educated mothers than among those with less schooling. Because women now expect to spend more of their life working, they know that their decisions about the timing of fertility have greater financial implications.

Why should these changes lead college-educated women to delay childbearing more than women with less schooling? First, college-educated women have more attractive labor market options, so they may postpone motherhood simply because it would interfere with another satisfying activity. Second, the career costs associated with early childbearing appear to be greater for more skilled women. College-educated women may need to invest more heavily in the early parts of their careers in order to maximize their lifetime earnings (by becoming a partner in a law firm, for example). David Ellwood, Ty Wilde, and Lily Batchelder (2004) find strong evidence that early childbearing reduces the earnings of women with high test scores more than the earnings of women with low test scores. Finally, college-educated women may anticipate using more paid childcare and may therefore wait until they can afford the amount of help they want.

Our hypothesis, then, is that women's economic opportunities now play a more important role in the timing of motherhood than they did a generation ago. College-educated women have probably always had somewhat more economic incentive to delay childbearing than less-educated women had. But this difference has widened over the past generation, both because college-educated mothers now spend more of their life working and because the earnings gap between more- and less-educated women has widened. In addition, growing acceptance of premarital sex and cohabitation, combined with greater control over the timing of births, has made family formation less sensitive to the hormonal influences that traditionally encouraged women to marry early.

Meanwhile, less-educated women who want to have children at a relatively early age see less reason to marry, because their potential spouses have fared so badly in the labor market. As a result, many of these women delay marriage but not childbearing. More-educated women who are in no rush to have children are also in no rush to get married. Hence they delay both marriage and childbearing, even when their boyfriends are doing well economically.

This hypothesis can also help explain the sudden change in many trends during the late 1990s. For the first time in almost thirty years, both marriage and delayed childbearing became more common. Jobs became plentiful. Real wages of less-skilled men rose by about 2 percent per year from 1995 to 2001 (Mishel, Bernstein, and Boushey 2003). The Earned Income Tax Credit and other supports also made work more lucrative for some parents. Welfare reform pushed more women into paid employment. And perhaps welfare reform also signaled a modest shift in attitudes toward single-parenthood.

This explanation is far from perfect. It cannot explain why racial differences have grown so large. It says nothing about divorce or remarriage. We offer this hybrid hypothesis only as a starting point, which is meant to suggest that if social scientists estimate multivariate models and allow the importance of different influences to change over time, we may eventually be able to explain far more than we have to date about why American families changed.

THE POLICY MORASS

Like the weather, everyone complains about family change, but no one seems able to do anything about it. Nor is it obvious that a better understanding of past changes in family structure would change this situation. We understand the weather far better than we used to, after all, but while better understanding has produced better forecasts, it has not produced better weather. For those who want to alter family structure, we can offer only one bit of advice: treat anyone who claims to know how to do this with a high degree of skepticism.

Still, our review does suggest that a few things might help reduce the prevalence of single-parent families. First, improving job opportunities for less-skilled men seems to be an unambiguously positive step. Second, improving job opportunities for less-skilled women has more ambiguous effects. Third, supports for two-parent families, such as refundable tax credits, childcare subsidies, and health insurance subsidies, seem likely to reduce their vulnerability.

This chapter was prepared with support from the Russell Sage Foundation's New Inequality Program. Jencks was also supported by a Hewlett Foundation Fellowship while he was working on these issues at the Center for Advanced Study in the Behavioral Sciences. We also thank Andrew Clarkwest, David Harding, Elisabeth Riviello, Joseph Swingle, Zoua Vang, Beth Welty, and Chris Wimer for excellent research work and thoughtful suggestions, and Steve Martin for sharing his unpublished data on divorce. Andrew Cherlin, Paula England, Frank Furstenberg, Irv Garfinkel, Patrick Heuveline, Eric Wanner, and two anonymous reviewers provided very helpful comments, as did participants in the Russell Sage New Inequality Project, the MacArthur Network on the Family and the Economy, and seminars at Cornell University, Harvard University, Syracuse University, and the University of Wisconsin.

NOTES

1. Calculated from U.S. Census Bureau (2000), table B-3.

2. One potential limitation of McLanahan and Sandefur's (1994) findings is that they generally controlled income in a single year, which is a very imperfect proxy for long-term income or for most forms of consumption. To the extent that family structure is a proxy for unmeasured income differences, their results underestimate the importance of family structure's economic effects and exaggerate the importance of its noneconomic effects.

3. These estimates come from Harding and Jencks (2003). The estimate for the 1960s is from Gallup data for 1969, but Harding and Jencks find little evidence of change between 1962 and 1969. The estimate for the 1980s is from the General Social Survey, which uses a different question, but Harding and Jencks find that the change in wording only accounts for about 5 percentage points of the shift.

4. The Survey of Income and Program Participation is an exception.

5. The estimates in figure 2.1 will overstate the fraction of children living with both of their own parents early in the century if, as seems likely, such children live longer than children raised in other arrangements. We have no data on the magnitude of this bias, but we doubt that it is large enough to alter the basic picture in figure 2.1.

6. Both nonmarital births and divorce among married parents with children have now leveled off, but the proportion of sixteen-year-olds living with both of their own parents is likely to keep falling for at least another decade, because a child born to a lone mother in 1994 will not be sixteen until 2010.

7. The difference between the estimates for the United States in figures 2.1 and 2.2 are probably a byproduct of methodological differences. The estimates in figure 2.2 are analogous to life expectancies in that they are projections based on the rates at which parental unions dissolved during the seven-year interval shown for a given country. Because dissolution rates have been rising, the observed rate among fifteen-year-olds in any given year is likely to be lower than the projected rate using dissolution rates among younger children in the same year. The estimates for the 1990s in figure 2.1 are based on a relatively small sample of GSS respondents, most of whom turned sixteen in the first half of the 1990s.

8. Both birth certificates and Census data on household composition are usually based on self-reports, although some states do not ask whether the mother and father listed on the birth certificate are married. The discrepancies in figure 2.4 are partly explained by the fact that some couples marry after the birth of their child, and some children born out of wedlock are adopted by another married couple.

9. It is tempting to suppose that single motherhood has risen among the less educated because mothers at each educational level have become a less and less select group since 1964. But if one assigns women to the top, middle, or bottom third of the educational distribution for their birth cohort and then tracks trends for each third of the distribution, the results are essentially identical to those shown in figure 2.7 (Ellwood and Jencks 2004).

10. In 2001, for example, 19 percent of white non-Hispanic dropout mothers had never married compared to 54 percent for blacks. Among white mothers who had completed college less than 2 percent had never married, compared to 18 percent of black mothers who had completed college. For Hispanics the figures were 16 percent for dropouts and 4 percent for college graduates.

11. Education may, of course, be partly endogenous. Women who have children early are presumably likely to get less education and are thus more likely to show up in the bottom education third. Ideally

one might like to do such tables based on parental education or some other non-endogenous variable.

12. There are several excellent recent reviews of the theoretical literature. In particular see Yoram Weiss (1997) and Joseph Hotz, Jacob Alex Klerman, and Robert J. Willis (1997).

13. Suppose that improvements in women's economic opportunities lower the odds that a young unmarried woman will marry in the next year, but raise the odds that an older unmarried woman will marry in the next year. Unless one allows both the magnitude and sign of the effect of female opportunity to vary by age, one will not find this pattern.

14. Recent research on cohabiting couples (Smock and Manning 1997) has begun to overcome this limitation, as has the Fragile Families study, which has been quite successful in tracking the fathers of children born out of wedlock (see the working papers available at http://crcw.princeton.edu/fragilefamilies/ffpapers.html).

15. David Ellwood and David Rodda (1990) employ a hazard model with little control for female work. This combines both timing and avoidance effects, thus providing an upper bound for the impact of male earnings. Yet even they conclude, along with Christopher Jencks (1992) and Robert Wood (1995), that male labor market performance can explain only a tiny share of the decline in marriage.

16. As the cost of medical care rose, the value of Medicaid also rose. This change could offset the declining value of cash benefits for families with serious medical problems.

17. As will be discussed later, there have recently been a few attempts to integrate models of fertility and childbearing, such as Willis (1999).

18. All the data on the decoupling of marriage and first births is from David T. Ellwood and Christopher Jencks (2004).

19. For excellent reviews of the recent literature see Kristin A. Moore et al. (1995a) and Moore et al. (1995b).

20. See for example, Leora Friedberg (1998) and Justin Wolfers and Betsey Stevenson (2003).

21. See, among others, Goldin and Katz (2000).

REFERENCES

Acs, Gregory. 1995. "Do Welfare Benefits Promote Out-of-Wedlock Childbearing?" In *Welfare Reform: An Analysis of the Issues,* edited by Isabel V. Sawhill. Washington, D. C.: Urban Institute.

Akerlof, George A., Janet L. Yellen, and Michael L. Katz. 1996. "An Analysis of Out-of-Wedlock Childbearing in the United States." *The Quarterly Journal of Economics.* 111(2, May): 277–317.

Andersson, Gunnar. 2001. "Children's Experience of Family Disruption and Family Formation: Evidence from 16 FFS Countries." Rostock, Germany: Max Planck Institute for Demographic Research.. Available at: www.demogr.mpg.de (accessed May 24, 2004).

Axinn, William G., and Arland Thornton. 2000. "The Transformation in the Meaning of Marriage." In *The Ties That Bind: Perspectives on Marriage and Cohabitation,* edited by Linda J. Waite. New York: Aldine de Gruyter.

Becker, Gary. 1991. *A Treatise on the Family (Enlarged Edition).* Cambridge, Mass.: Harvard University Press.

Blau, Francine D. 1998. "Trends in the Well-Being of American Women, 1970–1995." *Journal of Economic Literature* 36(March): 112–65.

Bumpass, Larry and Hsien-Hen Lu. 2000. "Trends in Cohabitation and Implications for Children's Family Contexts in the United States." *Population Studies* 54(March): 29–41.

Cigno, Alessandro, and John Ermisch. 1989. "A Microeconomic Analysis of the Timing of Births." *European Economic Review* 33(4, April): 737–60.

Edin, Kathryn. 1999. "Why Don't Low-Income Mothers Get Married (or Remarried)?" Mimeo. Philadelphia: University of Pennsylvania.

Ellwood, David T., and Christopher Jencks. 2004. "The Uneven Spread of Single Parent Families: What Do We Know? Where Do We Look for Answers?" In *Social Inequality,* edited by Kathryn Neckerman. New York: Russell Sage Foundation.

Ellwood, David T., and David Rodda. 1990. "The Hazards of Work and Marriage: The Influence of Employment on Marriage." Mimeo. Cambridge, Mass.: Harvard University.

Ellwood, David T., Ty Wilde, and Lily Batchelder. 2004. "The Mommy Track Divides: The Impact of Childbearing on the Wages of Women of Differing Skill Levels." Mimeo. Cambridge, Mass.: Harvard University.

Friedberg, Leora. 1998. "Did Unilateral Divorce Raise Divorce Rates? Evidence From Panel Data." *American Economic Review* 88(8, June): 608–27.

Furstenberg, Frank. 1996. "The Future of Marriage." *American Demographics* 18(6, June): 34–40.

————. 2001. "The Fading Dream: Prospects for Marriage in the Inner City." In *Problem of the Century: Racial Stratification in the United States,* edited by Elijah Anderson and Douglas Massey. New York: Russell Sage Foundation.

General Social Survey. 1972–2000. *National Opinion Research Center's General Social Surveys, 1972–2000.* Storrs, Conn.: The Roper Center for Public Opinion Research. Available at: http://www.ropercenter.uconn.edu/gss.html (accessed May 21, 2004).

Goldin, Claudia, and Lawrence F. Katz. 2000. "The Power of the Pill: Oral Contraceptives and Women's Career and Marriage Decisions." NBER Working Paper No. 7527. Cambridge, Mass.: National Bureau of Economic Research (February).

Goldstein, Joshua, and Catherine Kenney. 2001. "Marriage Delayed or Marriage Foregone? New Cohort Forecasts of First Marriage for U.S. Women." *American Sociological Review* 66(August): 506–19.

Harding, David, and Christopher Jencks. 2003. "Changing Attitudes Toward Premarital Sex: Cohort, Period, and Aging Effects." *Public Opinion Quarterly* 67(2, Summer): 26.

Hotz, V. Joseph, Jacob Alex Klerman, and Robert J. Willis. 1997. "The Economics of Fertility in Developed Countries." In *Handbook of Population and Family Economics,* edited by Mark R. Rosenzweig and Oded Stark. Amsterdam: Elsevier Science.

Hoynes, Hilary. 1997. "Work, Welfare, and Family Structure: What Have We Learned?" In *Fiscal Policy: Lessons From Economic Research,* edited by Alan Auerbach. Cambridge: Cambridge University Press.

Jencks, Christopher. 1992. *Rethinking Social Policy: Race Poverty, and the Underclass.* New York: HarperCollins.

Kane, Thomas J., and Douglas Staiger. 1996. "Teen Motherhood and Abortion Access." *Quarterly Journal of Economics* 111(May): 467–506.

Lehrer, Evelyn. 2000. "Religion as a Determinant of Entry into Cohabitation and Marriage." In *The Ties that Bind: Perspectives on Marriage and Cohabitation,* edited by Linda J. Waite, Christine Bachrach, Michelle Hindin, Elizabeth Thomson, and Arland Thornton. Hawthorne, N.Y.: Aldine De Gruyter.

Levine, Phillip B., Douglas Staiger, Thomas J. Kane, and David J. Zimmerman. 1996. "*Roe v. Wade* and American Fertility." NBER Working Paper No. 5615. Cambridge, Mass.: National Bureau of Economic Research (June).

London, Kathryn. 1989. "Children of Divorce." *Vital and Health Statistics,* Series 21, No. 46. DHHS Pub No. (PHS)89-1924. Washington: U.S. Government Printing Office.

McLanahan, Sara, and Gary Sandefur. 1994. *Growing Up with a Single Parent: What Hurts, What Helps.* Cambridge, Mass.: Harvard University Press.

Mishel, Lawrence, Jared Bernstein, and Heather Boushey. 2003. *The State of Working America 2002/2003.* Ithaca, N.Y.: Cornell University Press.

Moffitt, Robert. 1998. "The Effect of Welfare on Marriage and Fertility." In *Welfare, The Family, and Reproductive Behavior,* edited by Robert Moffitt. Washington, D.C.: National Academy Press.

Moore, Kristin A., B.C. Miller, D.R. Morrison, and D.A. Glei. 1995a. "Adolescent Sex, Contraception and Childbearing: A Review of Recent Research." Washington, D.C.: Child Trends, Inc.

Moore, Kristin A., B.W. Sugland, C.S. Blumenthal, D.A. Glei, and N.O. Snyder. 1995b. "Adolescent Pregnancy Prevention Programs: Interventions and Evaluations." Washington, D.C.: Child Trends, Inc.

Morgan, S. Philip, and Allan Parnell. 2002. "Effect on Pregnancy Outcomes of Changes in the North Carolina State Abortion Fund." *Population Research and Policy Review* 21(4, August): 319–38.

Moynihan, Daniel Patrick. 1986. *Family and Nation.* New York: Harcourt, Brace, Jovanovich.

Murray, Charles. 1984. *Losing Ground.* New York: Basic Books.

Oppenheimer, Valerie Kincade. 1997. "Women's Employment and the Gain to Marriage: The Specialization and Trading Model." *Annual Review of Sociology* 23: 431–53.

Panel on Adolescent Pregnancy and Childbearing. 1987. *Risking the Future: Adolescent Sexuality, Pregnancy, and Childbearing.* Washington, D.C.: National Academy Press.

Patterson, Orlando. 1998. *Rituals of Blood.* Washington, D.C.: Civitas/Counterpoint.

Plotnick, Robert D. 1992. "The Effects of Attitudes on Teenage Premarital Pregnancy and Its Resolution." *American Sociological Review* 57(6, December): 800–11.

Sklar, June, and Beth Berkov. 1974. "Abortion, Illegitimacy, and the American Birth Rate." *Science* 185(4155, September 13): 909–15.

Smock, Pamela J., and Wendy D. Manning. 1997. "Cohabiting Partners' Economic Circumstances and Marriage." *Demography* 34(3, August): 331–41.

Sweeney, Megan M. 2002. "Two Decades of Family Change: The Shifting Economic Foundations of Marriage." *American Sociological Review* 67 (February): 132–47.

Thornton, Arland. 1989. "Changing Attitudes Toward Family Issues in the United States." *Journal of Marriage and the Family* 51(November): 873–93.

Thornton, Arland, and Linda Young-DeMarco. 2001. "Four Decades of Trends in Attitudes Toward Family Issues in the United States: The 1960s Through the 1990s." *Journal of Marriage and the Family* 63(November): 1009–37.

U.S. Census Bureau. 2000. "Poverty in the United States, 1999." *Current Population Reports*, P60–210. Washington: U.S. Government Printing Office.

————. Various years. *Statistical Abstract of the United States*. Washington: U.S. Government Printing Office.

Veroff, Joseph, Elizabeth Douvan, and Richard A. Kulka. 1981. *The Inner American*. New York: Basic Books.

Weiss, Yoram. 1997. "The Formation and Dissolution of Families: Why Marry? Who Marries Whom? and What Happens Upon Divorce?" In *Handbook of Population and Family Economics,* edited by Mark R. Rosenzweig and Oded Stark. Amsterdam: Elsevier Science.

Willis, Robert J. 1999. "A Theory of Out-of-Wedlock Childbearing." *Journal of Political Economy* 107(6, 2): S33–S64.

Wilson, William Julius. 1987. *The Truly Disadvantaged: The Inner City, the Underclass, and Public Policy*. Chicago: University of Chicago Press.

Wilson, William Julius, and Kathryn M. Neckerman. 1986. "Poverty and Family Structure: The Widening Gap Between Evidence and Public Policy Issues." In *Fighting Poverty: What Works and What Doesn't,* edited by Sheldon H. Danziger and Daniel H. Weinberg. Cambridge, Mass.: Harvard University Press.

Wolfers, Justin, and Betsey Stevenson. 2003. "Bargaining with the Shadow of the Law: Divorce Laws and Family Distress." Stanford Law and Economics Olin Working Paper No. 273. Available at http://papers.ssrn.com/abstract/478162 (accessed July 14, 2004).

Wood, Robert G. 1995. "Marriage Rates and Marriageable Men: A Test of the Wilson Hypothesis." *The Journal of Human Resources* 30(1): 163–93.

Zelnik, Melvin, John F. Kantner, and Kathleen Ford. 1981. *Sex and Pregnancy in Adolescence*. Beverly Hills, Calif.: Sage Publications.

CHAPTER THREE

Unmarried Cohabitation and Parenthood: Here to Stay? European Perspectives

Kathleen Kiernan

IN MANY Western European nations and North America few developments in family life have been quite as dramatic as the recent rises in unmarried cohabitation and out-of-wedlock childbirth. Such developments raise questions about the hegemony of legal marriage as the basis of family life and many of the assumptions on which public policies are built. However, the extent to which these changes have taken hold and the policy responses to them have not been uniform across nations. The past shapes our cultures, institutions, laws, and welfare regimes, which in turn can constrain behaviors and responses to changed circumstances. A comparative approach assists us in identifying commonalities in changing family behavior across nations, highlighting those developments that require more global rather than particular explanations. On the other hand, identifying exceptions and outliers provides insights into what might constrain or facilitate new developments.

COHABITATION AND UNMARRIED PARENTHOOD IN THE PAST

Although cohabitation is often regarded as a recent development, it includes a range of living arrangements, some novel, others more traditional. Prior to the 1970s such unions were statistically largely invisible, and may well have been socially invisible outside of the local community or milieu. In some European countries there were subgroups of the population more prone to cohabitation than others: the poor, those whose marriages had broken up but were unable to obtain a divorce, certain groups of rural dwellers, and groups ideologically opposed to marriage.

Although there are few statistical data on how common cohabitation historically was there is evidence from parish register data for Britain that stable, nonmarital procreative unions in earlier periods, going back several centuries, often acquired the status of legal marriage (Laslett, Oosterveen, and Smith 1980). Moreover, cohabitation after a marriage breaks down and cohabitation between marriages are unlikely to be recent developments: common sense alone would suggest that when divorce was more difficult people might well choose to cohabit. Charles Booth noted in his studies of the laboring population in London that those most likely to be cohabiting were older formerly married persons. He noted that "more license is granted by public opinion to the evasion of laws of marriage by those who have found it a failure, than is allowed to those whose relations to each other have not yet assumed a permanent form" (Gillis 1985, 232). Similarly, in other European countries there are a number of historical sources from around the beginning of the twentieth century suggesting that the phenomenon was sufficiently visible to attract some comment. In Sweden, according to Trost (1978), there were two types of cohabitation: one known as "marriage of conscience," practiced by a group of intellectuals as a protest against only church marriages being permitted at the time, which protests led to the introduction of civil marriage in 1909, and another known as "Stockholm marriages," found among poor people who could not afford to marry. These unions were probably akin to those observed in poorer sections of British, French, and German urban society (on Britain, see R. Roberts 1973; on France, see Villeneuve-Gokalp 1991; on Germany, see Abrams 1993).

A New Form of Cohabitation

It is likely that cohabitation following marital breakdown persisted throughout the twentieth century, and postmarital cohabitation was the most prevalent form in the 1950s and 1960s. For example, in Britain among women marrying in the latter half of the 1960s only 6 percent of never-married women reported having lived with their husband prior to marriage, compared with 25 percent of those who were remarrying (General Household Survey 1989). Moreover, with the growth in divorce across European nations, "postmarital" cohabitation has become even more prevalent, either in preference to, or as a prelude to, remarriage.

Whether the poor continued to enter into informal unions is unknown, although in France there is some evidence that they did (see Villeneuve-Gokalp 1991). However, given the growing popularity of marriage, and in particular the youthful marriage of the 1950s and 1960s, it is likely that informal unions among single people were rare in these decades. A so-called golden age of marriage prevailed in Western Europe from the 1950s to the early 1970s (Festy 1980), when marriage was youthful and almost universal. This pattern receded during the 1970s. Marriage rates declined and the average age at marriage increased. It is a new type of cohabitation, which is strongly implicated in the decline in marriage, a form of cohabitation that escalated during the 1980s and 1990s, and saw young people living together as a prelude to, or as an alternative to, marriage.

The Rise of Cohabitation: Evidence from Fertility and Family Surveys

Until recently, detailed data on cohabitation were scarce and in large part came from ad hoc surveys. This presented problems for comparative analyses because sample sizes, coverage, and definitions tended to vary. During the 1990s, however, more information from standardized questionnaires became available from a series of Fertility and Family Surveys carried out primarily in the first half of the 1990s under the auspices of the UN Economic Commission for Europe (ECE) (United Nations 1992). Similar data had been collected in the 1992 wave of the British Household Panel Survey and the 1995 U.S. National Survey of Family Growth. These included partnership histories that incorporated dates of marriages and other coresidential heterosexual intimate relationships, permitting more in-depth examination than vital registration data or cross-sectional current status surveys. Here we present data from some of our earlier analyses on a number of European countries and the United States (Kiernan 2001a; Kiernan 2004) .

To illustrate the rise in cohabitation and how it varies from country to country, figure 3.1 shows the proportion of women who began their first coresidential partnership with cohabitation, the complement being the proportion who did so with marriage, for two age cohorts of women. It is clear from these data that the younger women, those aged twenty-five to twenty-nine, were much more likely to have cohabited than the older women. Overall, however, the increase in cohabitation is marked for both groups in most countries. In France, for example, 45 percent of the older women and 79 percent of the younger women cohabited, a pattern repeated across many of the nations. The main exceptions are Sweden and the southern European countries. In Sweden cohabiting was

Figure 3.1   First Unions Beginning with Cohabitation

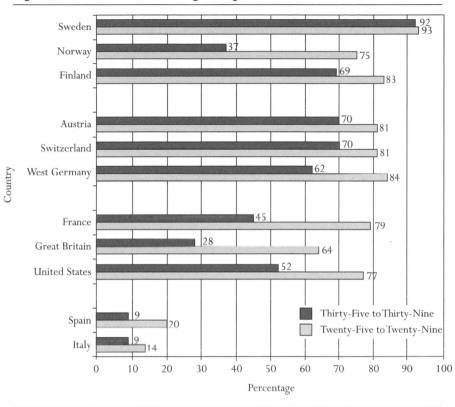

Source: Author's analysis of Fertility and Family Surveys.

already well established among older women. In Italy and Spain there are indications of a rise in cohabitation, but for the majority of women marriage still heralds the start of first partnership.

It appears, then, that by the early 1990s cohabitation had eclipsed marriage as the marker for entry into first union in many Western countries. Was there any evidence that it was becoming a durable alternative to marriage? To examine this issue we asked how long first partnerships that begin with cohabitation last. There is, however, no straightforward answer: estimates on the duration of cohabiting unions need to take into account exit through marriage, exit through dissolution, and—for those unions that continue—censoring at the time of the interview. Life table analysis was used to estimate the extent to which cohabitations had converted into marriages or dissolved by a specified time from the start of the union. We found that there was some variation across nations in the propensity to marry. Sweden had the lowest conversion rate: only one in three of the cohabitations had become marriages within five years of the start of the partnership. In most other countries more than one in two had done so (Kiernan 2001a; Kiernan 2004). With respect to how quickly cohabiting unions dissolve we found that in most of our countries about one in three had done so within five years. We also found that the propensity for cohabiting unions to either convert or to dissolve is somewhat higher in the United States than in Europe (Kiernan 2004).

Our analyses of the most recent available comparable data show marked variation across Western nations in partnership formation. In the first half of the 1990s, marriage was still the preeminent entry in the southern European countries, but in most western and northern European countries and in the United States cohabitation had eclipsed it. Across all nations included in the study, only a minority of cohabiting unions were intact after five years, the rest having either converted into marriages or dissolved. Sweden was the only country where there was evidence of longer-term cohabitation. But there may well be changes under way. Our analyses related primarily to the behavior of cohorts forming partnerships in the early 1990s, since which time there have been further increases in the level and duration of cohabitation in several nations (Haskey 2001; Noack 2001).

LEVELS OF COHABITATION

As a more up-to-date guide to the levels of cohabitation and the popularity of marriage across European nations we have used data from a series of Eurobarometer Surveys carried out in 2000 and 2001 in the fifteen member states of the European Union (European Commission 1998–2001). Cohabitation is on a rising trend line so it is important to have recent information. Eurobarometer data fulfill this need and provide standardized information for a wide range of nations. However, they have their drawbacks. They are primarily opinion surveys carried out under the auspices of the administration of the European Union and thus unlikely to be as accurate as those obtained in dedicated family and fertility surveys. Moreover, they contain only very basic current status information on marital status and provide only limited insights into the nature of cohabitation; on the other hand they do provide us with an up-to-date guide as to the relative position of different European countries in these developments in family life.

For this analysis we have combined five surveys carried out in late 2000 and the first half of 2001, which provides us with a sample size of around 90,000 people aged sixteen and over. We report on data for four-teen countries plus eastern and western Germany. These two parts of unified Germany, which now constitute the largest country in Europe, had substantially different postwar histories and as we will see in the realms of family behavior they also tend to differ.

Another issue for our analysis is that the marital status categories have been constructed in a nonconventional way and also differ from how they were collected in the mid-1990s, so we cannot make direct comparisons. The respondents were asked to choose from a card the letter that corre-sponded best to their current situation, according to specific categories: married, remarried, unmarried living with a partner, unmarried having never lived with a partner, unmarried having lived with a partner but now alone, divorced, separated, widowed, other (spontaneous answers).

Table 3.1 shows the combined proportions of men and women aged 25 to 34 in the fifteen European Community countries who were ever married (includes remarried, separated, divorced, and widowed); those who were never partnered; and the two groups of unmarried cohabitants, those who were currently cohabiting and those who were unmarried hav-ing previously cohabited. The tiny proportion (0.7 percent) who re-sponded "other" have been excluded from the table. This categorization of less than ideal data provides us with some insights into the saliency of marriage and cohabitation in the partnership behavior of recent genera-tions of young Europeans. The age range of twenty-five to thirty-four was chosen because by this time most people are likely to have left home, finished their full-time education, and be settling down into partnerships and contemplating or having children.

It is clear from table 3.1 that there is a good deal of diversity across European states in the incidence of cohabitation among the unmarried. Three broad groupings can be discerned. Cohabitation is strikingly com-mon in the Nordic countries of Denmark, Sweden, and Finland, and in France. At the other extreme are the southern European countries with relatively low levels of cohabitation, 10 percent or less in the case of Greece, Italy, and Portugal. There is a middle group including the Bene-lux (the Netherlands, Belgium, and Luxembourg), Great Britain and Ire-land, West and East Germany, and Austria with intermediate levels of cohabitation. Evidence from U.S. surveys suggests that the United States would fall into this group (Raley 2000). The evidence from earlier sur-veys in 1996 (Kiernan 2000) suggest that Ireland has only recently moved from the southern European set to the western European.

It is also clear from these data that there is a good deal of variation in the proportions of young people who have ever married. Marriage is popular in Greece and Portugal but not as much so in Italy and Spain, which have low proportions of ever-married and the highest proportions

Table 3.1   Marital Status, Men and Women Aged Twenty-Five to Thirty-Four in 2000 to 2001

Country	Ever Married, Percentage	Never Partnered, Percentage	Unmarried Currently Cohabiting, Percentage	Unmarried Previously Cohabited, Percentage	Number in Sample
Sweden	28%	13%	39%	20%	891
Denmark	37	14	32	17	957
France	39	15	31	15	1,094
Finland	43	17	30	11	860
Austria	52	13	22	13	1,013
The Netherlands	47	23	22	8	954
East Germany	46	17	21	15	718
Great Britain	57	16	18	16	992
Luxembourg	65	11	17	9	512
West Germany	50	19	15	6	905
Ireland	45	32	15	7	913
Belgium	59	20	15	6	964
Spain	44	41	11	4	984
Greece	56	29	10	5	929
Italy	34	55	8	4	964
Portugal	61	32	5	2	753
Total	47	23	19	10	14,730

Source: Author's tabulations from Eurobarometer 54.1 November–December 2000, 55.0 March–April 2001, 55.1 April–May 2001, 55.10VR April–May 2001, and 55.2 May–June 2001.

of never-partnered. In the Nordic countries and in France, among the unmarried, cohabiting or having cohabited is as popular as marriage at these ages. Marriage tends to be more popular in countries with intermediate levels of cohabitation, with relatively high proportions in Great Britain, Belgium, and Luxembourg.

Another perspective is evident in figure 3.2, where we show the proportions of first marriages and unmarried current cohabitations among our set of men and women aged twenty-five to thirty-four. In most western and northern European countries more than 50 percent of unions are cohabitions, with highs in the Nordic countries of over 70 percent, and lows in the southern European countries of around 40 percent or less.

Educational Level and the Incidence of Cohabitation

When cohabitation came to prominence in the 1980s, European researchers tried to determine where in the social structure it first took hold. In Norway, the results were inconclusive (Blom 1994; Ramsoy 1994). Some analyses suggested that it began among university students, others that it began among the poor (a legacy of the past). Similarly, in France there is evidence (Villeneuve-Gokalp 1991) that it developed first among upper class children and university students and then spread down, but initially was more common among lower social groups, particularly the unemployed. In Sweden, the rise in cohabitation was initially observed among the working classes (Hoem 1992). But Bernhardt and Hoem (1985) also observed that in the case of working-class women cohabitation was a setting for having children, whereas among the daughters of salaried workers, it was a relatively long lasting childless phase. This alerts us to the possibility that there may be different impetuses behind childless and fertile cohabiting unions. In Britain, cohabitation as a marker for first unions was embraced so rapidly across the social spectrum that it is difficult from the extant data to clearly identify the initiators (Kiernan 1989). The same may be the case for other countries.

Here we examine for a wide range of European nations whether there is any variation in the incidence of cohabitation according to educational level. Respondents to the Eurobarometer 2000–1 surveys were asked how old they were when they finished full-time schooling. We use this as a proxy for educational level. For our analysis of cohabitation among young adults aged twenty-five to thirty-four we coded the data into three categories: finished at age seventeen and under; at ages eighteen to nineteen; and at age twenty or older or still a full-time student. For our analysis, twenty-five- to thirty-four-year-old full-time students were included in the twenty and older category. Across our sixteen countries 33

Figure 3.2 Cohabiting and Married Men and Women, Aged Twenty-Five to Thirty-Four in
2000 to 2001

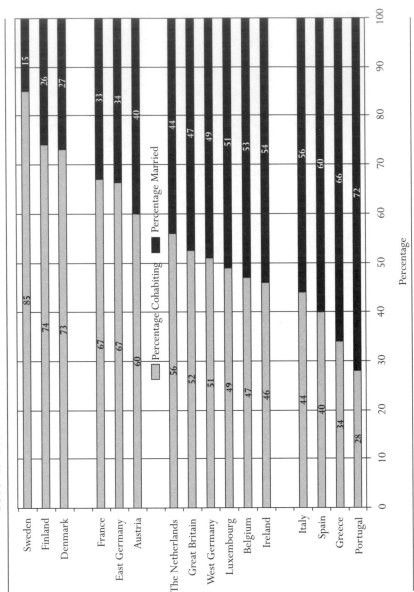

Source: Author's analysis of Eurobarometer Surveys, 2000 to 2001.

Table 3.2   Percentage of Men and Women Aged Twenty-Five to Thirty-Four Cohabiting, by Age Left Full-Time Education

Country	Left at Age Seventeen and Under	Age Eighteen to Nineteen Years	Age Twenty and Older	Number in Sample
Sweden	38%	38%	38%	346
Denmark	29	31	32	307
France	28	27	34	339[a]
Finland	23	29	30	255
The Netherlands	19	18	24	210
Austria	17	23	25	221[a]
East Germany	20	18	26	154
Great Britain	17	17	23	139
Luxembourg	12	17	20	88
West Germany	12	15	20	139[a]
Ireland	15	11	18	141
Belgium	10	13	15	143
Spain	10	11	11	149
Italy	8	7	8	73
Greece	7	7	15	91[a]
Portugal	4	4	8	39
Total	14	17	24	2,872

Source: Author's tabulations from Eurobarometer 54.1 November December 2000, 55.0 March–April 2001, 55.1 April–May 2001 55.1OVR April–May 2001 and 55.2 May–June 2001.
[a]Significant differences at 5 percent or less.

percent of the twenty-five- to thirty-four-year-olds finished education at under age eighteen, 25 percent left at ages eighteen to nineteen and 42 percent left at age twenty and older. But, there was a good deal of variation across nations. Denmark, at 81 percent, had the highest proportions reporting having left education at age twenty or later and Great Britain, at 18 percent, had the lowest. Across the European Union as a whole there are indications that the oldest leavers, who are in the main graduates, are more likely to be cohabiting: 24 percent compared with 17 percent of the eighteen- to nineteen-year-old leavers and 15 percent of the seventeen-year-old leavers (see table 3.2). But within-nation analyses showed that only in East and West Germany, Greece, France, and Austria were there significant differences (5 percent or less) in the propensity to cohabit across educational levels. There is, then, no coherent and consistent pattern with respect to educational level; cohabitation has seemingly been embraced across the social spectrum.

Figure 3.3   Out-of-Wedlock Births

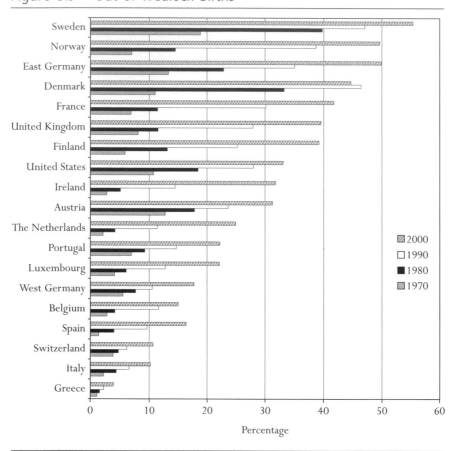

Source: Author's tabulation of Council of Europe data.

Unmarried Parenthood

Until the closing decades of the twentieth century marriage was the conventional setting for having children in most European nations, but as we see in figure 3.3 this situation has changed of late.

It is very clear that across all nations from 1970 onward the incidence of childbearing outside of marriage has risen (see figure 3.3), but there continues to be a good deal of variation in the level, and the pace of change has also varied (Council of Europe 2001). In 1970, only five of the nineteen countries shown here had out-of-wedlock birth ratios of more than 10 percent: Sweden, the frontrunner at 19 percent, and then

East Germany, Austria, Denmark, and the United States in the 11 to 13 percent range. The relatively high rates in Austria and East Germany are long-standing. In Austria there is a well-established tradition of marriage following first birth in one large region. (Prinz 1995) and in East Germany public policies relating to housing allocation created a tendency for couples to marry after the birth of their first child (Hohn 1991). Only in Sweden and Denmark was there strong evidence that the level of out-of-wedlock childbearing observed in 1970 was directly associated with the rise of cohabitation (Hoem and Hoem 1988).

In 2000, Greece was the only country with an out-of-wedlock birth ratio of less than 10 percent; over half of the countries were above 30 percent. Norway and Finland moved up with Sweden and Denmark. Generally speaking, countries with low ratios in 1970—Greece, Spain, Italy, Switzerland, and Belgium—still had them in 2000. Ireland, a noteworthy exception, has seen a spectacular increase since 1980, from 5 percent to 14 percent in 1990 and to 32 percent in 2000. Austria and the United States saw decreases. The United States also has not exhibited as marked a rise in out-of-wedlock childbirth as Europe since the 1990s. There was only a 5-percentage-point difference between the U.S. ratios of 1990 and 2000 versus a 12-point difference in many other countries. Lawrence Wu, Larry Bumpass, and Kelly Musick (2001) show that the U.S. rate flattening occurred after 1995, a period that coincides with welfare reforms, declines in teenage pregnancy, and increases in teenage contraceptive use. There are also signs that the level of out-of-wedlock childbearing may have peaked in Denmark (little change between 1990 and 2000) and the pace of change in Sweden seems to have slowed. France and the United Kingdom have had remarkably similar trends, and the pace of change has not slackened over the last decade in either country.

The data in figure 3.3 refer to all births. It is likely that there are more first births outside marriage than amongst later births. Moreover, over time the proportion of later births in out-of-wedlock childbearing has probably increased. These tendencies may vary across nations. Unfortunately we cannot disentangle them because many countries do not collect parity information for out of wedlock births in their vital registration systems.

Cohabitation is undoubtedly the engine driving the rise in out-of-wedlock childbearing in Europe, particularly since the beginning of the 1980s. While there is a good deal of diversity across Europe, the correlation is usually direct. However, there are exceptions. Britain and Ireland have higher levels of childbearing outside marriage than one would expect from cohabitation estimates alone, and the Netherlands and the former West Germany have lower, suggesting that norms about marriage being the conventional setting for having children may be stronger in some countries than others.

Figure 3.4   Child Under Fifteen in Household According to Marital Status, Men and Women Aged Twenty-Five to Thirty-Four, 1998 to 2000

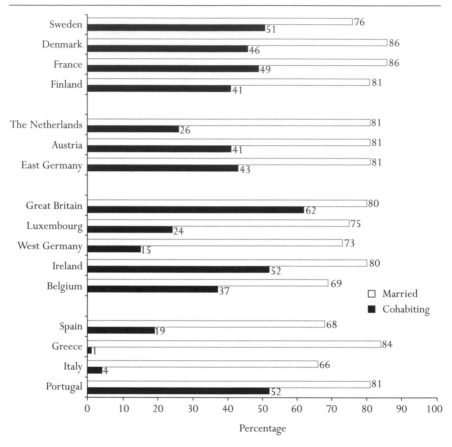

Source: Author's analysis of Eurobarometer Surveys, 1998 to 2000.

Cohabitation and Children

Eurobarometer surveys for 1998 to 2000, though not 2001, also collected information on whether there was a child under age fifteen living in the household for both cohabiting and married couples aged twenty-five to thirty-four (see figure 3.4). Unfortunately these data do not reveal if the families are biological, but it is probably reasonable to assume that the majority are.

Across all nations married couples are more likely than cohabiting to have a resident child, in most 70 percent or more, ranging from 66 percent in Italy to 86 percent in France and Denmark. However, there is much more variation in cohabiting couples with a resident child. Excluding the southern European countries, the proportions range from 15 percent in West Germany to 62 percent in Britain. In most northern and western European countries 40 percent or more of the cohabiting couples have a child, the notable exceptions being the Benelux countries and West Germany, again indicating that norms about marriage as the appropriate context to have children are stronger in some nations than others.

Education Level Among Cohabiting Couples with Children

We also examined whether education was related to the proportions of cohabiting couples with resident children (figure 3.5). The relatively crude data—those aged twenty-five and older with a child under age fifteen in the household, who had finished school either at or younger than seventeen or at or older than twenty—indicate that in the Nordic countries and Germany there is not much difference. Elsewhere in Europe the ratio is inverse: less educated cohabiting couples are more likely to have children in the household than more educated. It would appear that the less advantaged are more likely to have children within such unions but that childfree cohabitation tends to be popular across the social spectrum. This echoes the Swedish findings of Bernhardt and Hoem (1985) and detailed analyses of British cohabitation (Kiernan and Estaugh 1993; Kiernan 2002).

Over the last few decades, then, many European countries have witnessed a weakening between marriage and parenthood. However, it should be emphasized that this is not a decoupling of partnership and parenthood. The evidence suggests that most of the rise in out-of-wedlock births is attributable to cohabiting couples. Our analyses of Eurobarometer data provide limited but up-to-date descriptive information on these issues. More informed insights come from our analyses of the partnership and fertility histories collected in the UN ECE Fertility and Family Surveys (Kiernan 2001b; Kiernan 2004).

Partnership Context of First Birth

The union and fertility histories collected in these surveys have allowed us to examine the partnership context of first birth in more detail. We look at the proportions of women in the various countries who made the transition to motherhood in one of four settings: before they had any

Figure 3.5   Cohabitants Aged Twenty-Five and Older with
Child Under Fifteen, According to Age Cohabitant Left
Full-Time Education

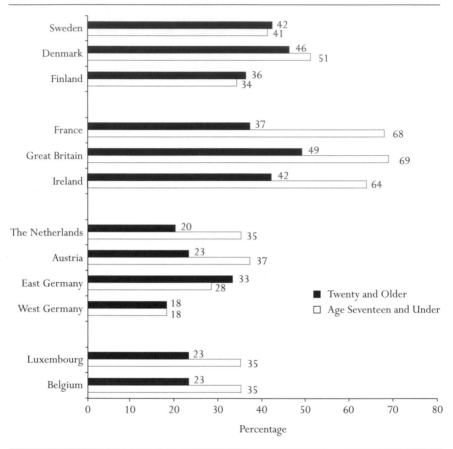

coresidential partnership; within their first partnership which was a cohabitation; within first marriage; and after their first partnership, whether
cohabitation or marriage (table 3.3).

A number of findings stand out. In almost all these countries most
women become mothers in their first partnership. However, there are
signs of change in Sweden, where first parenthood occurring in later
partnerships increases from 12 to 19 percent over the two age cohorts.
Having a child prior to a partnership is a minor practice in many coun-

tries, regardless of the rate of out-of-wedlock childbirth. For example, the overall proportion of women who had a child prior to any union was 7 percent in Sweden and 6 percent in France. The figure is somewhat higher in Norway and notably higher in Austria, but Austria has a long history of marriage following a first birth. A simple comparison of the two age cohorts aged twenty-five to twenty-nine and thirty-five to thirty-nine shows that in most countries the proportions of births occurring before a first partnership have hardly changed in recent years. Intriguingly, the figure has risen in Great Britain and the United States. In Spain and Italy, and to a lesser extent Switzerland, first marriage continues to be the preeminent context for first births. While the picture is less clear-cut in the other countries, across most there is a discernible movement away from having a child within marriage to having one within a cohabiting union.

Parental Separation and Context of First Birth

Undoubtedly, children born to a single mother are more likely to be poor than those born to a couple, but does it matter whether a child is born to a cohabiting union or married couple? From a child's perspective, on a day-to-day basis, there may be little to distinguish between them. However, there is a good deal of evidence that cohabiting unions are more fragile than marital. We have posed the question whether children born into cohabiting unions, compared with those born to married parents, were more or less likely to see their parents separate, and whether their parents marrying after their birth made any difference to family stability. We used life-table analysis to estimate the survival probabilities of partnerships where the clock started with the birth of the child rather than the beginning of the union. We studied the proportions of unions surviving five years after the birth of the first child for all marital unions and, for the two subsets of cohabiting unions, those that had converted into marriages by the time of the survey and those that had not (see figure 3.6).

In all countries children born within marriage were less likely to see their parents separate than those born in a cohabiting union (not shown). Cohabiting unions not converted into marriages were the most fragile, with at least one in five having dissolved by the time the child was five years old. Fewer than one in ten born within marriage or cohabiting unions that subsequently converted to marriages saw their parents' marriage break up by their fifth birthday in Sweden, Norway, Austria, and Germany. In France and Switzerland and the United States, however, and most noticeably in Great Britain, children born within marriage were more likely to see their parents remain together until their fifth birthday.

Table 3.3 Percentage of Women by Partnership Status at First Birth, By Age of Woman

Country and Age of Woman	Before Partnership	First Cohabitation	First Marriage	After First Partnership	First Birth by Survey
Norway					
Twenty-five to twenty-nine	12%	28%	53%	8%	68%
Thirty-five to thirty-nine	13	7	75	4	91
Twenty to forty-five	12	18	65	5	62
Sweden[a]					
Twenty-five to twenty-nine	6	53	23	19	66
Thirty-five to thirty-nine	6	53	30	12	92
Twenty to forty-five	7	51	29	13	74
Austria					
Twenty-five to twenty-nine	21	29	47	3	70
Thirty-five to thirty-nine	20	20	53	7	91
Twenty to forty-five	20	22	53	5	73
Switzerland					
Twenty-five to twenty-nine	4	8	78	10	45
Thirty-five to thirty-nine	5	8	76	11	83
Twenty to forty-five	5	7	77	11	66
West Germany					
Twenty-five to twenty-nine	11	17	64	8	38
Thirty-five to thirty-nine	11	8	73	8	75
Twenty to thirty-nine	10	13	70	7	45
France					
Twenty-five to twenty-nine	9	22	62	7	56
Thirty-five to thirty-nine	5	11	80	4	91
Twenty to forty-five	6	14	74	6	71

Great Britain

Twenty-five to twenty-nine	15	17	59	8	54
Thirty-five to thirty-nine	4	4	82	9	80
Twenty to forty-five	9	9	75	8	65

United States

Twenty-five to twenty-nine	20	15	54	11	70
Thirty-five to thirty-nine	14	8	66	12	86
Twenty to forty-five	17	11	60	12	80

Italy

Twenty-five to twenty-nine	4	5	90	1	36
Thirty-five to thirty-nine	5	3	90	1	83
Twenty to forty-five	5	3	90	1	61

Spain

Twenty-five to twenty-nine	8	6	85	—	47
Thirty-five to thirty-nine	4	3	92	1	92
Twenty to forty-five	5	3	90	1	65

Source: Author's analysis.
[a] Sweden 1954 and 1964 cohorts: Thirty-five to thirty-nine and twenty-five to twenty-nine equivalent. Norway 1950 and 1960 cohorts: thirty-five to thirty-nine and twenty-five to twenty-nine equivalent.

Figure 3.6   Unions Surviving Five Years After Birth of First Child

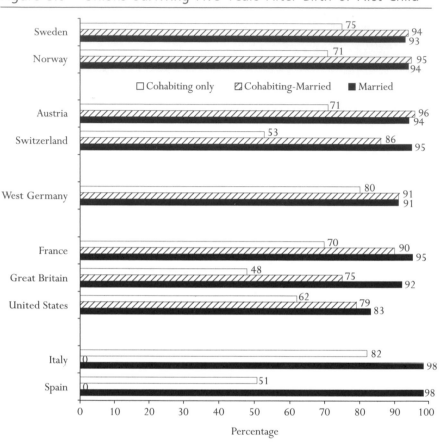

Source: Author's analysis of Fertility and Family Surveys.

In Italy and Spain the numbers of dissolutions of converted unions were too small for reliable estimates to be made.

Our analyses of the UN ECE Fertility and Family Surveys have shown that in most western European countries, excepting Great Britain, there is little evidence that more women are having babies on their own. The United States is also an exception to this. The data from the FFS for the first half of the 1990s showed that a recent generation of first-born Europeans were born to parents in a union and typically the first union. However, it is also important to stress that there is still a good deal of variation within Europe in levels of out-of-wedlock childbearing (see figure

Table 3.4   Percentage Considering a Cohabiting Couple with Children a Family, by Age and Sex

Age Group	Men	Women	Total	Sample Number
Fifteen to twenty-four years	61%	67%	64%	(2666)
Twenty-five to thirty-four years	66	68	67	(3130)
Thirty-five to forty-four years	63	65	64	(2998)
Forty-five to fifty-four years	59	62	61	(2552)
Fifty-five to sixty-four years	51	56	54	(2255)
Sixty-five and older	44	44	44	(2622)
Total	58	60	59	(16223)

Source: Author's tabulations from Eurobarometer 51.0 November–December 1998.

3.3), though substantial increases in those levels during the 1990s may have altered the picture.

ARE COHABITING COUPLES WITH CHILDREN CONSIDERED FAMILIES?

Some insights in the extent to which cohabiting couples are perceived as families comes from a Eurobarometer survey carried out in the winter of 1998 that included family issues as a special topic. Overall 59 percent considered those with children a family, but only 27 percent considered those without children one; for married couples the responses were 95 and 48 percent respectively. Children, then, appear to be the deciding factor. Overall there was little gender difference in responses, with 58 percent of men and 60 percent of women considering a cohabiting couple with children a family (see table 3.4). Older people, particularly those over fifty-five, were somewhat less likely to consider a cohabiting couple with children as a family.

Cohabiting couples were more likely than their married counterparts to consider cohabiting couples with children to be families: 79 to 56 percent. Our analyses by individual country (not shown here) showed that these observations held within nations and that some of the most noteworthy variation was found across them. The proportions considering an unmarried couple with children a family are tabulated for all respondents and for the age group twenty-five to thirty-four (see table 3.5). This age group was selected because it is one in which couples are most likely to begin having children and one that provides a handle on the attitudes of younger generations. The sixteen European countries in the

Table 3.5   Percentage Considering a Cohabiting Couple with Children a Family, by Nation

Country	Age Group Twenty-Five to Thirty-Four Years	All Ages	Sample Numbers
Sweden	91%	88%	(1000)
Finland	91	80	(1026)
Denmark	88	80	(1010)
France	76	68	(1002)
Austria	70	64	(1085)
Great Britain	70	57	(1039)
East Germany	69	64	(1012)
West Germany	66	56	(1041)
Spain	65	57	(1000)
Ireland	63	52	(1000)
Luxembourg	62	57	(598)
Belgium	58	56	(1058)
Portugal	54	50	(1001)
The Netherlands	51	49	(1017)
Italy	51	44	(1004)
Greece	41	31	(1009)
Total	67	59	(16224)

Source: Author's tabulations from Eurobarometer 51.0 November–December 1998.

survey have been ordered according to the responses of the twenty-five-to thirty-four-year-olds. Our comments relate primarily to this group.

It is clear that respondents in countries with the highest incidences of cohabiting unions—Sweden, Denmark, and Finland—are the most likely to regard cohabiting couples with children as families, 90 percent. In most of the other countries 60 percent or more did so. Although the responses were broadly in accord with the level of cohabitation in a given nation there were some interesting anomalies. Spain, for example, is more permissive than one might expect and the Netherlands more traditional. The Dutch attitudes may associate more with low levels of out-of-wedlock childbearing than with the level of cohabitation.

A PARTNERSHIP TRANSITION?

There is no question that social control over the way that men and women become couples in the majority of European countries has loosened, albeit to different degrees. Several scholars have suggested that societies may be undergoing a transition (see Prinz 1995 for a review). Most draw on the experience of Sweden, which has gone furthest in these developments, and from which a number of stages can be identified (Hoem and Hoem 1988). In the first, cohabitation emerges as a deviant or avant garde phenomenon practiced by a small group. In the second, cohabitation, predominantly a childless phase, functions as either a pre-lude to or a probationary period where the strength of the relationship may be tested before committing to marriage. In the third, cohabitation becomes socially acceptable as an alternative to marriage and parenting is no longer restricted to marriage. In the fourth and final stage, cohabita-tion and marriage become indistinguishable. These stages may vary in duration, but once a society has reached a new stage, regression is un-likely and all previous types of cohabitation can coexist.

We have attempted to categorize countries based on where they are in this transition. Greece, Italy, and Spain are in the first stage, with marriage still the preeminent marker for first union; the Netherlands, Switzerland, and western Germany are in the second, with cohabitation relatively popular but marriage remains the context within which children are born; Austria, Great Britain, and Ireland are in the third; and Sweden and Denmark have made it to the fourth, with France and eastern Ger-many hovering around this stage. The United States, I believe, is now between the second and third stages.

These stages refer to the societal level but there are also parallels for the individual or couple. Cohabitation at a given time may well have different meanings for those involved (Manting 1996), for example, it may be viewed as an alternative to being single, or as a precursor to marriage, or as a substitute for marriage. Moreover, how a couple per-ceives the cohabitation may change over time and their perceptions may also vary. Dissecting cohabitation this way highlights the diversity and complexity of the phenomenon and suggests that it, more than marriage, is a process rather than an event. Its inconstancy poses challenges for analysis, understanding, and appropriate policy responses.

POLICY BACKGROUND AND RESPONSES

European countries have responded to the developments in cohabitation and unmarried parenthood in different ways. With respect to children, the issue has been discussed and codified in recent years in most countries and is much less controversial than cohabitation. Justifications for changes in the laws and regulations relating to cohabitation include needing to adapt to changing family behavior, protecting weaker family members, and avoiding differences in rights and benefits between married couples and cohabiting couples. Incentives to promote marriage have generally played a minor role in recent debates, though care has been taken not to undermine the institution (Noack 2001; Martin and Thery 2001). Underlying the debates is the need to respect the individual's right to decide his or her kind of relationship. This is not say, however, that moral and religious authorities have not vocalized their concerns (Martin and Thery 2001). Interestingly, cohabitants have neither played a major part in the public debates nor formed pressure groups. The most likely explanation for this is their heterogeneity: with relationships ranging from recent lovers to marriage-like long-term relationships, the opinions of cohabitants on regulation are likely to be very diverse. In many nations the demand for the recognition of unmarried couples has come from the gay communities (Schrama 1999; Martin and Thery 2001; International Lesbian and Gay Association website).

COHABITATION

To date in different European countries there have been a variety of policy responses to the emergence of cohabitation. At the beginning of 1998 the Netherlands, a country with intermediate levels of cohabitation and low rates of out-of-wedlock childbearing, instituted formal registration of partnerships for both heterosexual and homosexual couples, which made legally registered cohabitation functionally equivalent to marriage. In the early 1990s Denmark had instituted the legal registration of homosexual partnerships, but the Netherlands was the first in Europe to formalize heterosexual cohabitation. However, registered partnerships in the Netherlands were instituted primarily to meet the needs of gay couples, who did not have the option of marriage (Schrama 1999). In September 2000 a new bill was passed, which took effect in 2001, that allowed gay couples to convert their current registered same-sex partnerships to full-fledged marriages. It may therefore be that the registration of heterosexual cohabitation may be short-lived (International Lesbian and Gay Association website).

The French, perhaps, have come up with the most innovative approach with their Civil Solidarity Pacts (PACS), instituted in late 1999. Under PACS unmarried heterosexual and homosexual couples, rather than simply registering their relationship and thereby opting into a preordained set of rights and responsibilities, as in the Netherlands, are required to register a contract that sets out their rights and responsibilities. The contract between the couple then in effect institutionalizes the cohabitation. The longer the pacte stands, the more public benefits it attracts. PACS were originally conceived as meeting the demands of gay organiaations for a form of legally recognized marriage ceremony. To avoid homophobic attacks from the right wing, however, the government broadened the idea to include heterosexuals (Martin and Thery 2001). There has been uptake by heterosexual couples, suggesting that there is a desire for a real alternative to marriage. If couples choose to cohabit to avoid the traditional marriage contract and the assumption of more traditional roles that seem to go with it, they may not necessarily object to a pacte, which does not carry the same ideological baggage as marriage. Pactes have no history and no particular gender-division of roles associated with them, which is reinforced by the fact that this new form of contract is open to both homosexual and heterosexual couples.

Sweden, Finland, and Denmark have taken a more pragmatic approach. Over time family law has come to be applied to married and cohabiting couples in the same way (Bradley 1996). Norway, where cohabitation emerged later than in the other Nordic countries, established a commission to examine the issue. Reporting in late 1999, it accepted the need for a law regulating heterosexual cohabitation where this was "marriage like," that is, where there were children or where the relationship had lasted for two years or more (Noack 2001). In Germany, the protection of the family enshrined in the constitution applies only to marriage and not to "marriage-like partnerships" (Ditch, Barnes, and Bradshaw 1996; Ostner 2001), which implies a principled commitment not to equate married and cohabiting relationships, though the law could be changed.

Children Born Outside Marriage

Over the course of the twentieth century there have been shifts towards improving the legal status of out-of-wedlock children, but the speed and extent of changes have been quite variable across nations. For example, as early as 1917 Sweden banned the use of the term illegitimate in all official documents but it was not for another seventy years that similar legislation was enacted in England and Wales. Progress has tended to be slower in terms of, for example, children's rights to inherit from their father. Norway was the forerunner in tackling this issue by granting rights of inheritance in 1916 (Eekelaar and Katz 1980) but Sweden did not follow until 1969. In all European Union nations married couples have automatic parental rights and responsibilities as soon as the child is born, as do unmarried mothers, whether cohabiting or married. The position of cohabiting fathers is less clear-cut. In all countries once paternity has been established, unmarried fathers have a financial duty to maintain their children but no automatic rights, although in most countries they can establish parental responsibility by making some form of formal declaration (European Observatory on National Family Policies 1996). Generally speaking, across European nations the public policy debate has moved from a focus on the obligations and responsibilities arising from marriage to those of parenthood (Millar and Warman 1996).

The debate that first emerged in Sweden in the early 1970s (Eekelaar and Katz 1980) continues to vex policy makers: how can policies best accommodate two opposing points of view? One argues that the legal distinction between marriage and cohabitation should be maintained because removing it would undermine marriage. The other is reluctant to accord cohabitation full recognition on the grounds that it forces on cohabiting couples a legal framework, which by cohabiting they may be trying to avoid. A focus on children tempers this debate and may explain why unmarried parenthood rather than unmarried partnerships has been the preferred focus of public policy.

DISCUSSION

Across all the European countries included in this study, the signs all point in the direction of cohabitation and unmarried parenthood being here to stay. But they also point to legal institutions and regulatory authorities continuing to formalize such relationships.

Although cohabitation and unmarried parenthood are intimately related, identical forces may not necessarily lie behind them. The rise of cohabitation has typically been viewed as a positive development: a response to increased participation in education among the young, greater female autonomy in the workplace and in the home, and the contraceptive revolution, along with higher expectations of relationships and marriage. It may symbolize, particularly for women, the avoidance of the notion of dependency typically implicit in the marriage contract. On the other hand, for some it may be a response to insecurity. For example, rising divorce rates may well have increased the perceived risks of investing in marriage and cohabitation may have been a logical response.

There are clues that unmarried parenthood may be more closely associated with impoverishment than empowerment. British, Swedish, and U.S. research has shown that women who become mothers in a cohabiting union are more likely to have partners who are either unemployed or in partly skilled or unskilled occupations, which may account for why cohabiting couples with children are among the poorest two-parent families (Kiernan 2002, Bjornberg 2001, McLanahan et al. 2001). Similarly, French research shows that before the 1980s unmarried parents differed significantly from married but now are more similar, though unmarried parents still tend to be disproportionately from lower socioeconomic groups (Munoz-Perez and Prioux 1999). Why do the less advantaged choose to cohabit rather than marry, if it is a choice? One might point to a range of reasons. Pregnancy is one. With the dramatic growth in having children outside of marriage and the decline in the stigma attached to having a child outside marriage, cohabitation for some may be preferable to single motherhood or marriage. Studies of British cohabiting families suggest that some mothers prefer cohabitation to single motherhood or to marrying a man whom they were uncertain they could rely on for support (Smart and Stevens 2000). These findings resonate with Wilson's thesis (1987) of the shrinking pool of "marriageable"—that is, economically stable—men and the influence that joblessness has had on family structure. He argues that the decline in marriage among U.S. blacks is associated with the declining economic status of black men. This may have a corollary in European countries in the declining status of men who have uncertain job prospects. Cohabitation, for some, may be a rational choice in the face of uncertainty, insecurity, unemployment, and socio-economic disadvantage, just as it was in times past. In effect, a poor person's marriage.

Why are people excluding themselves from formal marriage and does it matter? The anxiety expressed in the literature, notably U.S. and British (Waite and Gallagher 2000; Morgan 2000), stems largely from the fact that cohabitation is a more fragile union than marriage. However, this difference may be largely due to the stronger and more committed partnerships being selected into marriage. There were clues to this being the case in our analysis of childbearing in cohabiting unions. We showed that in a number of countries if parents subsequently married the risk of breakdown was similar to those parents who had their first child within marriage. Moreover, if the general trend and future course of cohabitation is for parents who live together to eschew marriage, then cohabitations, other things being equal, should become more durable.

I conclude with a quote from a U.S. senator giving evidence to a hearing in 1968 on the Population Crisis and the issue of fertility control. Senator Ernest Gruening noted that "the taboo of the day before yesterday becomes the controversial of yesterday and the accepted of today, and the wanted of tomorrow" (U.S. Congress 1970, xxi). This is a plausible description of the pathways of cohabitation and out-of-wedlock childbearing over the last four decades. The taboo and controversial hurdles are past and from where we stand today both have become reasonably acceptable forms of behavior in many European nations, and there are signs that they are becoming normative forms of behavior in the Nordic countries. Whether they become normative in other European countries and the United States awaits the future. But, as yet there is no reason not to hold to Westermarck's thesis propounded in his book on the *Future of Marriage in Western Civilisation* published in 1936, that the family founded upon some form of marriage, based on deep rooted sentiments both conjugal and parental, will last as long as these sentiments last.

The Economic and Social Research Council United Kingdom provided the funding for this project. The ESRC Data Archive supplied the Eurobarometer data. The Fertility and Family Survey data were supplied by the Population Activities Unit at the UN Economic Commission for Europe at Geneva. Thanks are also due to the Advisory Group of the FFS program of comparative research for permission granted to use the FFS data in this study.

REFERENCES

Abrams, Lynn. 1993. "Concubinage, Cohabitation and the Law: Class and Gender Relations in Nineteenth-Century Germany." *Gender and History* (5): 81–100.

Bernhardt, Eva M., and Britta Hoem. 1985. "Cohabitation and Social Background: Trends Observed For Swedish Women Born Between 1936 and 1960." *European Journal of Population* (1): 375–95.

Bjornberg, Ulla. 2001. "Cohabitation and Marriage in Sweden. Does Family Form Matter? *International Journal of Law, Policy and the Family* 15(3): 350–62.

Blom, Svein. 1994. Marriage and Cohabitation in A Changing Society: Experience of Norwegian Men and Women Born in 1945 and 1960. *European Journal of Population* (10): 143–73.

Bradley, David. 1996. *Family Law and Political Culture: Scandinavian Laws in Comparative Perspective.* London: Sweet and Maxwell.

Council of Europe. 2001. *Recent Demographic Developments in Europe.* Strasbourg: Council of Europe Publishing.

Ditch, John, Helen Barnes, and Jonathan Bradshaw. 1996. *A Synthesis of National Family Policies 1995.* Brussels: Commission of the European Communities.

Eekelaar, John M., and Sanford M. Katz, eds. 1980. *Marriage and Cohabitation in Contemporary Societies.* Toronto: Butterworth.

European Commission. 1998–2001. Eurobarometer (ESRC Data Archive). Essex: European Commission.

European Observatory on National Family Policies. 1996. *A Synthesis of National Family Policies, 1995.* Brussels: European Commission.

Festy, Patrick. 1980. "On The New Context of Marriage in Western Europe." *Population and Development Review* (6): 311–15.

General Household Survey Report. 1989. Office of Population, Censuses and Surveys (OPCS) and Her Majesty's Stationery Office (HMSO). London.

Gillis, John R. 1985. *For Better or Worse: British Marriages 1600 to the Present.* Oxford: Oxford University Press.

Haskey, John. 2001. "Cohabitational in Great Britain: Past, Present, and Future Trends and Attitudes." *Population Trends* (103): 4–25.

Hoem, Britta. 1992. "Recent Changes in Family Formation in Sweden." *Stockholm Research Report in Demography.* No. 71. Stockholm: Stockholm University, Demography Unit.

Hoem, Jan M., and Britta Hoem. 1988. "The Swedish Family: Aspects of Contemporary Developments." *Journal of Family Issues* (9): 397–424.

Hohn, Charlotte. 1991. "Germany." In *European Population, vol. 1: Country Analysis,* edited by Jean-Louis Rallu and Alain Blum. Paris: John Libbey.

International Lesbian and Gay Association. Available at: http://www.ilga-europe.org (accessed May 20, 2004).

Kiernan, Kathleen E. 1989. "The Family: Fission or Fusion." In *The Changing Population of Britain,* edited by Heather Joshi. Oxford: Basil Blackwell.

———. 2000. "European Perspectives on Union Formation." In *Ties That Bind: Perspectives On Marriage and Cohabitation,* edited by Linda J. Waite, Christine Bachrach, Michelle Hindin, Elizabeth Thomson, and Arland Thornton. New York: Aldine de Gruyter.

———. 2001a. "The Rise of Cohabitation and Childbearing Outside of Marriage in Western Europe." *International Journal of Law, Policy and the Family* 15(1): 1–21.

———. 2001b. "Non-Marital Childbearing: A European Perspective." In *Out of Wedlock: Causes and Consequences of Nonmarital Fertility,* edited by Lawrence L. Wu and Barbara Wolfe. New York: Russell Sage Foundation.

———. 2002. "Demography and Disadvantage: Chicken and Egg?" In *Understanding Social Exclusion,* edited by John Hills, Julian Legrand, and David Piachaud. Oxford: Oxford University Press.

———. 2004. "Cohabitation and Divorce Across Nations and Generations." In *Human Development Across Lives and Generations: The Potential for Change,* edited by P. Lindsay Chase-Lansdale, Kathleen E. Kiernan, and Ruth J. Friedman. Cambridge: Cambridge University Press.

Kiernan, Kathleen E., and Valerie Estaugh. 1993. *Cohabitation Extra-Marital Childbearing and Social Policy.* London: Joseph Rowntree Foundation/Family Policy Studies Centre.

Laslett, Peter, Karla Oosterveen, and Richard M. Smith. 1980. *Bastardy and Its Comparative History*. London: Edward Arnold.

Manting, Dorien. 1996. "The Changing Meaning of Cohabitation." *European Sociological Review* 12: 53–65.

Martin, Claude, and Irene Thery. 2001. "The PACS and Marriage and Cohabitation in France." *International Journal of Law, Policy and the Family* 15(1): 135–58.

McLanahan, Sara, Irwin Garfinkel, Nancy E. Reichman, and Julien O. Teitler. 2001. "Unwed Parents or Fragile Families? Implications for Welfare and Child Support Policy." In *Out of Wedlock: Causes and Consequences of Nonmarital Fertility*, edited by Lawrence L. Wu and Barbara Wolfe. New York: Russell Sage Foundation.

Millar, Jane, and Andrea Warman. 1996. *Family Obligations in Europe*. London: Family Policy Studies Centre.

Morgan, Patricia. 2000. *Marriage-Lite: The Rise of Cohabitation and Its Consequences*. London: Institute for Civil Society.

Munoz-Perez, Francisco, and France Prioux. 1999. "Les Enfants Nés Hors Mariage Et Leurs Parents. Reconnaissances Et Légitimations Depuis 1965." *Population* 54 (3): 481–508.

Noack, Turid. 2001. "Cohabitation in Norway: An Accepted and Gradually More Regulated Way of Living." *International Journal of Law, Policy and the Family* 15(1): 102–17.

Ostner, Ilona. 2001. "Cohabitation in Germany: Rules, Reality and Public Discourses." *International Journal of Law, Policy and the Family* 15(1): 88–101.

Prinz, Christopher. 1995. *Cohabiting, Married Single*. Aldershot: Avebury.

Raley, R. Kelly. 2000. "Recent Trends and Differentials in Marriage and Cohabitation: The United States." In *The Ties that Bind: Perspectives On Marriage and Cohabitation*, edited by Linda J. Waite, Christine Bachrach, Michelle Hindin, Elizabeth Thomson, and Arland Thornton. New York: Aldine de Gruyter.

Ramsoy, Natalie R. 1994. Non-Marital Cohabitation and Change in Norms: The Case of Norway. *Acta Sociologica* 37: 23–37.

Roberts, Robert. 1973. *The Classic Slum: Salford Life in the First Quarter of the Century*. London: Pelican.

Schrama, Wendy M. 1999. "Registered Partnerships in The Netherlands." *International Journal of Law, Policy and the Family* 13 (3): 315–27.

Smart, Carol, and Pippa Stevens. 2000. *Cohabitation Breakdown*. London: Family Policy Studies Centre.

Trost, Jan. 1978. "A Renewed Social Institution: Non-Marital Cohabitation." *Acta Sociologica* 21: 303–15.

United Nations. 1992. *Questionnaire and Codebook Fertility and Family Surveys in Countries of the ECE Region*. New York: United Nations.

U.S. Congress. 1970. *Population Crisis Hearings, 1965–1968.* Washington, D.C.: Socio-Dynamics Publications.

Villeneuve-Gokalp, Catherine. 1991. "From Marriage to Informal Union: Recent Changes in the Behaviour of French Couples." *Population (An English Selection)* 3: 81–111.

Waite, Linda, and Maggie Gallagher. 2000. *The Case for Marriage.* New York: Doubleday.

Westermarck, Edward A. 1936. *The Future of Marriage in Western Civilisation.* London: Macmillan.

Wilson, William J. 1987. *The Truly Disadvantaged.* Chicago: University of Chicago Press.

Wu, Lawrence L., Larry L. Bumpass, and Kelly Musick. 2001. "Historical and Life Course Trajectories of Nonmarital Childbearing." In *Out of Wedlock: Causes and Consequences of Nonmarital Fertility*, edited by Lawrence L. Wu and Barbara Wolfe. New York: Russell Sage Foundation.

CHAPTER FOUR

Single-Parent Poverty, Inequality, and the Welfare State

Lee Rainwater and Timothy M. Smeeding

OUT-OF-WEDLOCK childbirth and divorce combine, then, to produce a wide array of family types and child living arrangements. Family change also brings economic changes. While the causes and consequences of father absence are not yet fully understood (see chapter 5), the economic consequences are much easier to trace.

Our intent is to examine how income support policies help or hinder single-parent families. Children in single-mother families are widely understood to be economically vulnerable. In all countries in recent years policy has focused special attention on this problem. Single mothers are seen as caught between their responsibilities as mothers and heads of families on the one hand, and their need and desire to earn money on the other (McLanahan and Sandefur 1994; Ellwood 1988). In some countries public policy is specifically designed to provide economic assistance in such cases, France for example, while in others support systems are more fragmented and challenging (Rainwater and Smeeding 2003).

DATA AND PERSPECTIVE

Our focus is the economic well-being of children in single-mother families. For perspective we compare the situation of American children with their counterparts in other wealthy countries. Most of these are in Western Europe: Belgium, Denmark, Finland, France, Germany, Italy, the Netherlands, Norway, Spain, Sweden, Switzerland, and the United King dom. Two others are Australia and Canada. The surveys on which our analysis is based are in the database of the Luxembourg Income Study (LIS), a data bank available to social scientists throughout the world containing more than 100 income surveys (see appendix 1). The results reported here are from surveys in the 1990s.

We deal only with money income and near cash benefits such as food stamps and housing allowances. We omit other in-kind benefits, though we know they contribute significantly to the well-being of children and parents, particularly children's health and education, because while they moderate the effects of poverty they do not reverse it (see Smeeding 2002a).

Our definition of a single-mother family is that in which a woman is the head of a household with minor children and no spouse or partner. If the mother is cohabiting with another adult the arrangement is considered a two-parent family. Some European surveys make no distinction between married and "living-together-as-married" (see chapter 3).

Among our fifteen countries we find a wide variation in the number of children who live in single-mother families. At the high end are the United States and the United Kingdom, with some 21 percent of children in such families. Next is Sweden at 19 percent; then Denmark, Norway, and Canada in the 14 to 15 percent range; then Germany, Finland, and Australia at 11 percent; then Belgium, France, and Switzerland at 9 percent; and the Netherlands at 7 percent. At the low end of the scale are Spain and Italy with about 5 percent (authors' tabulations of LIS data, see also Andersson 2002).

In some of these families there are also other adults present, mostly older children, whom one would expect would be likely to contribute to families' income. We find that in Spain and Italy more than 50 percent of the single-mother families have another nonpartner adult in the household. In the United States approximately 30 percent do. In the other countries, however, more than 75 percent of children in single-mother families live with only one adult.[1]

COMPARATIVE LIVING STANDARDS AND GOVERNMENT SUPPORT FOR POOR CHILDREN

We present several measures of the economic status of single-parent children in cross-national perspective. Poverty and income distribution estimates are mixed with aggregate Organization for Economic Cooperation and Development (OECD) figures and our own LIS estimates to paint a

Table 4.1   Single-Mother Child Poverty Rates

	Poverty Rate
United States	51.4%
Germany	47.6
Australia	46.2
Canada	43.2
United Kingdom	38.8
Italy	33.6
France	28.2
The Netherlands	25.5
Spain	24.2
Switzerland	14.3
Norway	13.9
Belgium	13.3
Denmark	11.4
Finland	8.0
Sweden	6.4

Source: Authors' calculations from the Luxembourg Income Study.
Note: Poverty rates are the percentage of households with a lone female parent and children under eighteen who have incomes less than half of the national median income after adjusting for family size using an equivalence scale.

portrait of how economically disadvantaged American children compare to their counterparts in a number of rich OECD nations.

Poverty in Single-Mother Families

First we consider the proportion of children in single-mother families who are poor.[2] Over half of America's, 51 percent, are in families with incomes below the median size-adjusted income in the country (table 4.1). Next are Germany at 48 percent, Australia at 46 percent, Canada at 43 percent, and the United Kingdom at 39 percent. The median are France, the Netherlands, and Spain, at or near 25 percent. The lower rates range down from Switzerland and Norway at 14 percent, Belgium at 13 percent, Denmark at 11 percent, Finland at 8 percent, to Sweden at 6 percent.

One might think that the single-mother employment rate would affect the poverty rate. It is, however, only slightly correlated with the child poverty rate across the fifteen countries surveyed. For example, the five with the highest poverty rates have employment rates ranging from 37 percent to 81 percent. The Netherlands, with the median poverty rate of 25 percent, has the lowest employment rate, 28 percent, of all. We will consider this apparent anomaly in more detail later.

Simulation: Why Do Poverty Rates Differ So Greatly?

In general, demographic differences among countries seem not to explain much about the wide range in single-mother child poverty rates (see table 4.1). In a recent simulation experiment, a range of demographic characteristics of single-mother families in each country was imposed on the mean and median income of households with children in the United States-LIS survey and vice versa (Rainwater and Smeeding 2003). One can then distinguish between effects of variations in demography and income packaging in producing or reducing poverty and inequality.[3] The factors simulated include number of earners, numbers of adults, elders and children, and age of family head. The results show that for more than half of the countries, simulating U.S. demography with each country's own income package (earnings, benefits) produces only small differences between the simulated and actual single-mother poverty rates (Rainwater and Smeeding 2003). But in the rest of the countries the simulated rate is as high or higher than the actual (see table 4.1). It is therefore the very great income differences between the northern European countries and the United States that produce the differences in the poverty rates, not any real differences in the demographic structure of single-mother households.

Patterns of Social Spending

Redistributive social expenditures vary greatly across nations. In the developed countries, total social expenditures—including government spending on the elderly, on health care, and education as a percent of 1998 GDP ranged from 15 percent in the United States to 26 percent in the United Kingdom to over 30 percent in Sweden (OECD 2003).[4] The available evidence indicates that total social expenditures as a fraction of total government spending in OECD nations range from 0.67 in Australia to 0.90 in Denmark and Sweden (Smeeding 2002a). That is, 67 to 90 percent of all government spending in rich OECD nations is in the form of redistributive cash or in-kind benefits.[5] Thus the topic of "social expenditure" is about most of what governments actually do. The relevant grouping for single parents includes benefits for the nonelderly, primarily cash and near cash (food stamps, housing allowances) support for families with children.

We can trace the trend in nonelderly cash and near cash benefits for OECD countries back over the past twenty years using 2002 OECD data (see figure 4.1). Seventeen OECD nations—all of the major nations except for the Central and Eastern Europeans—have been grouped into seven clusters: Nordic Scandinavia (Finland, Norway, Sweden); Northern Europe (Belgium, Denmark, Netherlands); Central and Southern Europe (Austria, France, Germany, Italy, Luxembourg, Spain); Anglo Saxony (Australia, United Kingdom, and Canada); the United States and Mexico.[6]

The Nordic Scandinavians and northern Europeans follow similar patterns—high levels of spending showing responsiveness to the recession of the early 1990s, especially in Sweden and Finland, and a tapering afterward. The central and southern Europeans and the Anglo-Saxon nations show remarkably similar spending patterns, again rising in the early 1990s but overall at a level distinctly below the other two groups. The United States is significantly below all these others and by the late 1990s is spending at a level closer, in terms of a fraction of GDP per capita, to Mexico than to the other richer OECD nations.

These figures illustrate the wide differences in both levels and trends in social spending, using figures that abstract from financing of health care and education, and from retirement for the elderly. They also correspond very closely to the measures of money and near-money income inequality used by LIS and in the analytic literature in this area.

Well-Being in a Broader Context

A poverty rate serves as an index of the distribution of income in the lower ranges. We get a much better understanding of how countries compare if we expand our concern to more levels of income. Figure 4.2 shows the proportion of children in single-mother families who are extremely poor (below 30 percent of median adjusted income), poor (30 percent to less than 50 percent) and near poor (50 percent to below 70 percent of median adjusted income) on a relative basis.

We see that well over 50 percent of the poor American children in single-mother families are in fact extremely poor; their families exist on less than 30 percent of the median income.[7] Only 2 percent or fewer of such children in Belgium, Denmark, Finland, and Sweden are so poor. France follows closely at 4 percent and Norway at 5 percent. Taking the extremes we find that an American child in a single-mother family is more than twenty times more likely to be extremely poor than a comparable Swedish child, about nine times more likely to be simply poor than the Swedish child, and about as likely to be near poor. The Swedish child's odds of escaping poverty altogether are nine times better than the American's.

Figure 4.1   Nonelderly Social Expenditures in Six Sets of
              Seventeen Nations

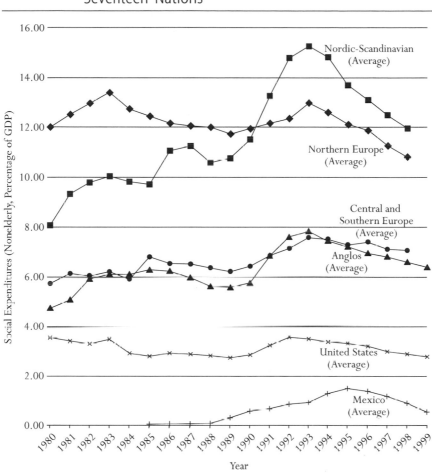

Source: Authors' compilation.
Notes: Total nonelderly social expenditures (as percentage of GDP), including all cash
plus near cash spending (for example, food stamps) and public housing but excluding
health care and education spending (OECD 2003). Anglos include Australia, United
Kingdom, and Canada; Scandinavia includes Finland, Norway, and Sweden; Northern
Europe includes Belgium, Denmark, and the Netherlands; Central and Southern Europe
includes Austria, France, Germany, Italy, Luxembourg, and Spain.

Figure 4.2   Children of Single Mothers with Low Income

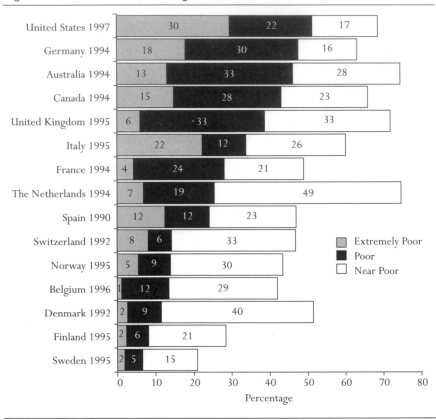

Source: Authors' calculations from the Luxembourg Income Study.
Note: Extremely poor is below 30 percent of adjusted median income; poor is at 30 percent to less than 50 percent of median; and near poor is 50 percent to 70 percent of median.

There are three countries with more poor or near poor children (over 70 percent) but with far fewer extremely poor children than in the United States—Australia, the United Kingdom, and the Netherlands. These are also the countries with the lowest proportion of single-mother families with earnings, and therefore their income packaging relies heavily on social transfers (see figure 4.1). The British and Dutch programs protect very well against extreme poverty. Australia has about twice as many extremely poor children as the United Kingdom and the Netherlands, and the Netherlands has far fewer simply poor children. But that seems to be the limit of Dutch antipoverty programs: half of Dutch children in these families are near poor. The lesson to be learned is that strong safety nets can reduce abject poverty among single parents, but even in most of the generous nations of Europe, single parents are disproportionately poor.

American child poverty rates are so high that even children in two-parent families often fare worse than single-mother children in other countries. The poverty rate of children in two-parent families in the United States is 11 percent. In two countries the poverty rate of children in single-mother families is in fact lower—in Finland, 8 percent, and in Sweden, 7 percent (adding extremely poor and poor in figure 4.2). We therefore need to ask what it is about the income packaging in these countries that allows single-mother families to escape poverty so much more frequently than even two-parent families in the United States.[8] But, first we need to understand that American children's comparative living standards, in a rich country context, are poor by any standard.

"Real" Standards of Living

Consider the relative and real U.S. dollar incomes of children on different points in the distribution of overall adjusted income. We rank the single-mother children in each country according to the family income relative to the median income in that country (relative incomes) and then to the U.S. family income once all incomes have been changed to U.S. dollars (real incomes) (see table 4.2). We can ask, for example, what the income of a child at the twenty-fifth percentile in country X is compared to that of the American child at the U.S. twenty-fifth percentile. We can also convert this relative income amount to 1997 U.S. real income by using purchasing power parities and ask what is the child's real income relative to the twenty-fifth percentile child in the United States in U.S. dollars.[9]

Well over 90 percent of single mothers' children in four countries— Switzerland, Spain, Finland, and Sweden—have higher relative incomes than their counterparts in the United States. This is true of over 80 percent of the children in the other countries except for Germany at 72 percent, the United Kingdom at 64 percent, the Netherlands at 63 percent, and Australia at 58 percent (see table 4.2).

An observer would conclude that the majority of single-mother children in all of these countries are better off by the standards of their societies than comparable children in the United States. This is not because single-mother children are well off in these other countries, but because their American counterparts have very low relative incomes.

To counter the claim that American living standards are so much higher, that U.S. children in single-parent families are still better off in an absolute income sense, even if not in a relative one, we convert all

Table 4.2   Children of Single Mothers with Higher Incomes than U.S. Children

	Relative Income[a]	Real Income[b]
Switzerland	100	100
Spain	99	3
Finland	97	60
Sweden	90	66
Belgium	88	66
France	88	58
Norway	83	76
Canada	82	77
Denmark	80	59
Germany	72	30
United Kingdom	64	28
The Netherlands	63	38
Australia	58	33

Source: Authors' calculations from the Luxembourg Income Study; Rainwater and Smeeding (1998, 2003).
[a]Relative incomes refer to the incomes of children relative to the national median income. Thus, at all points of the Swiss relative income distribution (10th, 20th, 90th) Swiss children in single-parent families have incomes that are higher than the incomes available to U.S. children at the same percentile of the U.S. income distribution. In Australia, only 58 percent of children are as well off as U.S. children compared to the median overall incomes in each nation.
[b]Real income comparisons first convert all incomes into 1997 U.S. dollars using OECD purchasing power parities and then make the same comparisons relative to the U.S. overall median real income. Thus, in Switzerland (a rich and child-friendly country), U.S. children are worse off and Swiss children are better off in the same real terms, relative to the U.S. median child. In a poorer country such as Spain or the United Kingdom, a much smaller proportion of children are better off in the same real dollar terms.

incomes into equivalent purchasing power in U.S. dollars (table 4.2, second column). Even in real income American children of single mothers fare worse than the majority of their counterparts in eight of these countries. The proportion that is better off in real terms ranges upward from close to 60 percent in Finland, France, and Denmark to 66 percent in Belgium and Sweden to 75 percent in Canada and Norway and to all children in Switzerland. A substantial minority, from 28 to 38 percent, are better off in the Netherlands, Australia, Germany, and the United Kingdom. In Spain almost none are.

Stated differently, comapring the real incomes of the half of American children in single-mother families who are poor (the lowest 51 percent of these children from table 4.1) to those of their opposite numbers in other countries, American incomes are higher in five cases and lower in eight. And in four other countries half to two-thirds of the poor children enjoy higher real incomes than American children. Only compared to Spain is the great majority of poor American single-mother children better off in real terms. In short, the poverty gap of the children of American single mothers is so great that even in countries with much lower "average" real incomes, their single-mother children fare better in real comparable U.S. dollar terms.

The Role of Government and Market Income

In most of these countries a solid majority of children in single-mother families would be poor if their families had only income from the market, almost entirely earned income. This proportion of poor ranges from just under 50 percent in Denmark and Finland to over 80 percent in the Netherlands and the United Kingdom (figure 4.3-horizontal axis). Switzerland, Spain, Belgium, and Sweden are in the 55 to 60 percent range if one considers market income alone. Canada, Germany, Italy, France, Norway, and the United States cluster in the 62 to 66 percent range. Then there is a rather large gap to Australia, the Netherlands, and the United Kingdom, where the rate is around 80 percent.

There are very large differences in the proportion of those who are moved out of poverty by transfer—that is, unearned—income. In the Nordic countries, Belgium, and Switzerland it is 75 percent or more, in Sweden over 90 percent, in the Netherlands almost 70 percent. In Spain, France, and the United Kingdom a little over 50 percent, slightly less than that in Italy and some 40 percent in Australia. In Canada it is 30 percent, and in the United States and Germany only 25 percent.

It is clear that most single-mother families cannot depend on market income alone to rescue them from poverty or near poverty. Social transfers are an integral part of single-mother income in every nation. Figure 4.4 highlights the role of market and transfer income in a different way. Here we plot the average market (earnings and much smaller amounts of asset income) income and average transfer income received in single-mother families in the lowest child income quintile. All American children are poor in the bottom quintile. The figure charts the average income from market sources and the average income from transfer sources as a percent of median adjusted income. The poverty rate is given in parentheses after the country abbreviation. The further to the right of the diagonal line, the higher is average total disposable income; the further to the left, the lower that income.

The five countries with the lowest poverty rates vary quite a bit in the mix of income types. Denmark has a high average of market income and

Figure 4.3   Child Poverty Rates in Single-Mother Families

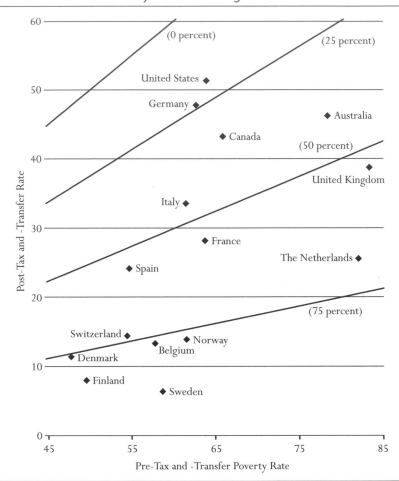

Source: Authors' calculations from the Luxembourg Income Study.
Note: The diagonal lines from top to bottom denote 0, 25, 50, and 75 percent poverty reduction by transfers.

a relatively low one of transfers. Sweden and Finland have lower market income and higher transfer income, followed by Norway. Belgium relies most heavily on transfer income.

There is the same variation in the mix of income types among the counties with middling and high child poverty rates. Switzerland and Spain show a higher reliance on market income than France and, in par-

Figure 4.4   Income of Single-Mother Children in Bottom
Child Quintile

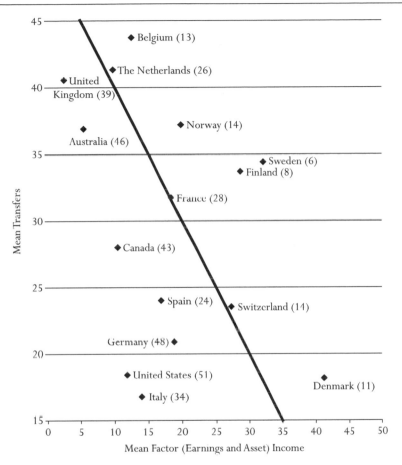

Source: Authors' calculations from the Luxembourg Income Study.
Note: The diagonal line represents a total disposable income of 50 percent of median income. Figures in parentheses are poverty rates.

ticular, the Netherlands, which relies on transfers to a much greater extent. Yet the four countries have somewhat similar poverty rates. Finally, among the countries with very high poverty rates the United States and Germany rely most heavily on market income while the United Kingdom and Australia rely on transfers. Thus, countries may differ a great deal in the content of the income package and yet produce similar poverty rates. Overall, however, the correlation between market income and poverty rate is much stronger than with transfer income. If the poverty gap is small because of higher real earnings by the poor then it does not take a large social transfer to move them out of poverty.

Low-Income Single Mothers' Participation in the Labor Force

Almost all the market income for low-income single-mother families comes from earnings. In most cases, as we have seen, there is only one adult in the household and therefore only one set of earnings. The variations in market income are thus for the most part in the earnings of the single mother who heads the household. We consider here the labor force participation of single mothers whose children are in the lower third of the equivalent income distribution.[10]

The fact that in the four Nordic countries around 75 percent of single mothers have earnings is very much a product of the growth of the social service sectors (figure 4.4, horizontal line). This growth, which has occurred over the past half century, is in turn the major factor in the increase in women's labor force participation overall. In Denmark and Sweden approximately two-thirds of the single mothers with earnings in this low-income group have jobs in the government or social service sector. In Finland the proportion is smaller but nevertheless, at about half, fairly high. We do not have industry data for Norway. The jobs tend to the less skilled, such as caregivers in day care centers, in schools, for the elderly, and in medical settings. They do, however, have a certain amount of security, with full fringe benefits and standard wages.

Belgium has a somewhat similar pattern in terms of government versus private sector jobs though the overall proportion of these mothers with earnings, 40 percent, is quite a bit lower than in the Nordic countries. But we do find that the majority of those with earnings have jobs in the government sector. In France the majority are also in the government sector, but the proportion of low-income single mothers with earnings, about 65 percent, is lower than in the Nordic countries.

A very different pattern is found in the United States, the Netherlands, and the United Kingdom. Despite the fact that 65 percent of these single mothers in the United States have earnings, fewer than 20 percent of them work in the government sector. Instead they take the low wages and marginal security of the least desirable jobs in the private sector. In the Netherlands and the United Kingdom, the proportion with government jobs is quite small because the proportion with any job is small, less than 30 percent.

When the mother has earnings we find a similar variation across countries in how much she earns relative to the median. But there is only a weak association between the likelihood of a single mother having earnings and the average amount earned by those who do. The working mothers with the highest earnings relative to median adjusted disposable income are in Denmark, Finland, Sweden, Switzerland, Germany, and Belgium—averaging from 40 percent to a high of 60 percent in Denmark. Those earning the least, 30 percent or less, are in Australia, the United Kingdom, and the United States.

In sum, if we think of the poverty rate for children in single mother families as a function of their mothers' earnings and social transfers we find that across these fifteen countries market income (principally earnings) seems to play a larger role than transfers, though both are important. The correlation of the single-mother child poverty rate with low-income single mothers' mean market income is -0.70. Its correlation with mean transfers is much lower (-0.25).

Summary

This section suggests that the U.S. policy stance and income support for single parents differs considerably from that in other nations. Child poverty in America is a product of both low wages and low levels of social support for both working and nonworking parents (Smeeding 2002a; 2002b). In fact, low-income American parents, singles and couples, work longer hours for lower pay than their counterparts elsewhere (Osberg 2002). Thus, we also need to pay some attention to how American support systems differ from others, beyond the aggregate statistics shown in figure 4.1.

THE ROLE OF TRANSFERS FOR CHILDREN IN THE LOWER THIRD OF THE DISTRIBUTION

In this section we examine the role of the public sector through family oriented transfer programs for single-mother families. We report the average amount received by children in the lower third of the adjusted disposable income, and the percentage of children in low-income single-mother families who receive these benefits. There are other types of transfer programs (pensions and unemployment and labor market programs, for example) that can be important but we omit them to concentrate on the benefits that most help low-income children.[11]

Child allowances are nearly universal in these countries, save France where there are none for the first child. Parental insurance, which allows parents to take "sick leave" with pay when their children need them, is also universal. In Spain, Italy, and Switzerland, child allowances are paid as part of earnings and there is no separate accounting of them. From aggregate data we know that child allowance spending is not as great as in most other European countries. Only in the United States is there no child allowance program and no guaranteed parental leave with pay. And American refundable tax credits are paid only to children whose parents' income is high enough for income tax, thus excluding the bottom third of children and the poorest 23 percent of all single-parent families without benefits (Lee and Greenstein 2003).

The average amount of child allowances and parental insurance payments received by children in low-income single-mother families ranges from Finland at 14 percent, to Belgium and Norway at 12 percent, to France and Australia at 11 percent, to Denmark at 10 percent. In France, for the 75 percent who receive them, the benefits amount to 15 percent. Canada, the Netherlands, the United Kingdom, and Sweden average 8 or 9 percent and Germany only 5 percent.

Child allowances are clearly important to the single-mother families in that they top up income from other sources, but they are not the major source of transfers in any country, especially for those families with no or very little market income.

Another important source of income for some single-mother families is transfers from absent parents or other relatives. In some countries when the absent father does not make his child support payment the government makes it, the so-called advance maintenance payment. In Sweden and Norway, some 89 and 82 percent of children receive child support either from the absent parent or government. Their benefits average 10 and 8 percent of median income respectively. The combination of child allowance, parental insurance, and child support averages almost half of the poverty line.

In Belgium some 50 percent of children receive support that amounts to 10 percent of median income and in Australia just over 30 percent, also averaging 10 percent of the median. In the United States 25 percent receive child support, amounting on average to 8 percent of the median, and in the Netherlands and the United Kingdom, about 15 percent, the former averaging 21 percent of median income, and the latter 12 percent.

In Spain help from relatives for the 28 percent of children who receive such income averages 26 percent of median income. The pattern is similar in Germany, 40 percent of children receiving benefits averaging 15 percent of the median.

Finland, Switzerland, and France are distinctive for having fairly substantial benefits from both child support and other private transfers. In Switzerland 41 percent of eligible children receive child support and 45 percent receive other private transfers. The average benefits amount to 23 percent of the median in the first case and 15 percent in the second. It is primarily these transfers that account for the fact that 75 percent of the Swiss children of single mothers are moved from poverty by transfers. We find a similar pattern in Finland, but the benefits are quite small. The heavy lifting by transfers in Finland comes from the more standard child allowances and labor market programs.

We find child support fairly important in France, where 25 percent of the children receive child support payments that average 12 percent of the median income. Other private transfers are less frequent; only 9 percent of children receive them, and when they do, benefits average only 9 percent of the median.

Income-tested social protection programs are an important source of income for single-mother families in almost every country. Cash social assistance may be general or linked to specific kinds of eligibility, such as being unemployed or a new single mother. So-called near cash programs are a standard part of the welfare state in most countries—the principal ones are food stamps in the United States, housing allowances in many countries, and a range of smaller programs that provide income in connection with education.

We find that in seven countries 75 percent or more of low-income single-mother children are in families that receive benefits from cash or in-kind income-tested programs—Denmark, Australia, France, the Netherlands, Finland, the United Kingdom, and the United States. In Sweden 67 percent are recipients. In Canada, Norway, and Germany slightly more than 50 percent receive benefits, in Belgium 38 percent, in Switzerland 30 percent, and in Spain fewer than 10 percent.

Average benefits to recipient families, however, vary a great deal. The average amount in the Netherlands is the highest at 46 percent, next highest in the United Kingdom at 35 percent, then Australia and Canada at 23 percent, Finland and Germany at about 18 percent, and in the other countries from 10 to 14 percent.

In most countries cash social assistance programs, as opposed to in-kind programs, are the most important components of the income-tested programs targeted on low-income families. Only in Finland, France, and Sweden does the largest share of this kind of income come from in-kind programs. In fact, in eight of the countries three-quarters or more of this income comes in cash. Cash income is mostly social assistance—a general program that dispenses cash to those whose income is below some subsistence standard. But in a few countries there are more specifically targeted programs. In Australia 75 percent of single mothers qualify for an unmarried mother's allowance with quite generous benefits amounting to almost 25 percent of the median. In Finland, Germany, and the Netherlands unemployment assistance for those who do not qualify for the unemployment insurance program is an important part of cash assistance.

While almost all of these countries have in-kind programs that benefit low-income single-mother families the size of benefits is considerable in only five. The leader is the United Kingdom, where housing benefits go to 75 percent of the children in low-income single-mother families, and average 15 percent of the median. Finland and France come next with about the same proportion of housing allowance recipients and an average benefit of around 10 percent of the median. Sweden has fewer housing allowance beneficiaries, 62 percent, who average 9 percent of the median. The United States has even more food stamp beneficiaries, 85 percent, but the average benefit is lower at 6 percent of the median. In Germany, the Netherlands, and Norway housing benefit recipients are in the 40 percent range but their benefits are only around 5 or 6 percent of the median, as is the case for the 30 percent in Belgium whose average benefit amounts to 4 percent of the median. In the other countries there are either no or very few recipients of in-kind programs.

SUMMARY

We can conclude that the varying social policies of nations make an enormous difference in the well-being of children of single mothers. Countries with low single-mother poverty rates compared to the United States have them because of a combination of labor market and social protection policies. The complex of family-oriented labor market programs in most nations encourages earnings by single mothers—not just as such, but more generally facilitating the participation of women and all mothers in particular in the labor force—by supporting family leave and subsidizing child care. The highly varied social transfer programs—particularly the combination of child allowance, guaranteed child support insurance, and assistance to the unemployed—and housing allowances for low-income families top up earnings in such a way that countries that have strong labor market presence of single mothers and high levels of social transfers to working single mothers have low child poverty rates. But, for the most part the benefits single mothers receive do not depend on their status as single mothers but on their having children (child allowance) or that the breadwinner is unemployed or that the family has a low income.

In most of these nations the same benefits would go to a two-parent family in the same circumstances.

There are a variety of transfer programs and no single way to provide support for families with children that is universally accepted across all nations. Instead, social values, institutions, and history combine to produce a unique "income package" for low-income children and their families in each country. The differences across countries are therefore tied to the benefit adequacy of the set of programs each nation has chosen for its children (Smeeding 2002a).

We conclude that American values, institutions, and political priorities toward children in low-income families differ significantly from other countries, and in clear ways that can be documented by both aggregated statistics and microdata. Given that we choose not to provide much in the way of a social support package for mothers, and faced with the stark contrast in income support policy outlined here, we turn to the policies we as a nation have formulated for low-income families with children.

We would like to thank Christopher Jencks for comments on earlier version of this paper and the Ford and Russell Sage Foundations for their support of the Luxemburg Income Study (LIS).

NOTES

1. Single-father families are too few to examine separately, as are children living in other arrangements, for example, with neither birth parent. This group is impossible to separate from children living with both biological parents using LIS data, as are blended families where only one parent is the biological parent.

2. Here we define poor as having an income of less than half the median, after an equivalence scale adjustment for differences in family sizes. For a data detailed explanation see Burtless, Rainwater, and Smeeding (2001). Data years are the most recently available to LIS and span the period from 1992 to 1998.

3. Here we report results comparing single-mother families in our fifteen countries. We ask to what extent the differing poverty rates of single-mother families can be explained by differing demographic characteristics among the single-mother families in these countries. The methodology we use is to take the income packages in a country X and the demographic breakdown in a country Y and to mix the two by imposing one set of characteristics on the other nation.

Thus the effects of United States demography and United States comparative income packages are separated out in a way that allows one to change one set of factors in any other country by "reweighing" according to the other country's demography, or by imposing one country's income package on another nation. For more, see Rainwater and Smeeding (1998; 2003).

4.   The variation in nonelderly total social expenditures is even more pronounced. There, the Northern European (Belgium, Denmark, Netherlands) and Scandinavian (Finland, Norway, Sweden) countries spend markedly more (as a percentage of GDP) on social expenditures than do the Anglo (Australia, Canada, United Kingdom, United States) countries (OECD 2003).

5.   We estimate this ratio by adding OECD Social Expenditures and OECD Final Government Outlays and dividing this total into OECD Social Expenditures. For more on this method, see Smeeding (2002a; 2002b) and OECD (2003). Both we and the OECD do not include tax expenditures as public benefits in these calculations.

6.   No comparable time series exists that includes both health care and education spending. But United States figures show that spending in elementary and secondary education has actually fallen as percent of GDP from 1970 to 2000. Health care spending on the nonelderly is high in the United States, but only because of employer subsidies. Disproportionately large numbers of working adults, for example single mothers, are not enrolled in employer plans.

7.   In fact, Duncan et al. (1998) shows that being born into such families has a serious negative impact on child well-being. See also Sigle-Rushton and McLanahan (chapter 5).

8.   The relative comparisons look at the incomes available to children in single-parent families relative to overall adjusted incomes within each nation. The real income comparisons differ because here we convert all incomes to U.S. 1997 dollars using OECD Purchasing Power Parities (PPP). This gives us the real value of the incomes of each child in 1997 U.S. dollars relative to the U.S. median overall income in 1997. For more on this technique, see Rainwater and Smeeding (2003); and Smeeding (2002a).

9.   These figures are taken from Rainwater and Smeeding (2003).

10.   These statistics and programs should give the reader a notion of the breadth of different policy options for single parents before moving to the "United States only" discussion.

11.   For more detail see Rainwater and Smeeding (2003).

REFERENCES

Andersson, Gunnar. 2002. "Children's Experience of Family Disruption and Family Formation: Evidence from 16 FFS Countries." *Demographic Research* 7(7): 343–63. http://www.demographic-research.org.

Burtless, Gary, Lee Rainwater, and Timothy M. Smeeding. 2001. "United States Poverty in a Cross-National Context." In *Understanding Poverty*, edited by Sheldon H. Danziger, and Richard Haveman, 162–89. New York: Russell Sage Foundation; Cambridge, Mass.: Harvard University Press.

Duncan, Greg J., Wei-Jun Yeung, Jeanne Brooks-Gunn, and Judith Smith. 1998. "How Much Does Childhood Poverty Affect the Life Chances of Children?" *American Sociological Review* 63(3): 406–23.

Ellwood, David. 1988. *Poor Support*. New York: Basic Books.

Lee Andrew, and Robert Greenstein. 2003. "How the New Tax Law Alters the Child Tax Credit and How Low-Income Families Are Affected." Washington, D.C.: Center on Budget and Policy Priorities (May).

McLanahan, Sara, and Gary Sandefur. 1994. *Growing Up with a Single Parent*. Cambridge, Mass.: Harvard University Press.

Organization for Economic Cooperation and Development (OECD). 2003. *Social Expenditures 2002 Database*. Paris: OECD.

Osberg, Lars. 2002. "Time, Money and Inequality in International Perspective." Presented at "Income Distribution and Welfare International Workshop," organized for the Bocconi University Centennial, Milan, Italy (May 30–June 1).

Rainwater, Lee, and Timothy Smeeding. 1998. "Demography and Income Packaging: What Explains the Income Distribution?" In *Empirische Forschung und wirtschaftspolitische Beratung (Empirical Research and Economic Policy Discussion): Commemorative Volume for Hans-Jurgen Krupp*, vol. 38, edited by Heinz P. Galler and Gert G. Wagner, 99–118. Frankfurt and New York: CAMPUS-Publisher.

———. 2003. *Poor Kids in a Rich Country*. New York: Russell Sage Foundation.

Smeeding, Timothy M. 2002a. "Real Standards of Living and Public Support for Children: A Cross-National Comparison." Presented at "Income Distribution and Welfare International Workshop" organized for the Bocconi University Centennial, Milan, Italy (May 30–June 1).

———. 2002b. "No Child Left Behind?" *Indicators* 1(3): 6–30.

CHAPTER FIVE

Father Absence and Child Well-Being: A Critical Review

Wendy Sigle-Rushton and Sara McLanahan

PATTERNS OF family formation have changed dramatically in the United States over the last several decades. Cohabitation has replaced marriage as the preferred first union of young adults; premarital sex and out-of-wedlock childbearing have become increasingly commonplace and acceptable; and divorce rates have recently plateaued at very high levels. One of three children in the United States today is born outside marriage, and the proportion is twice as high among African Americans (Ventura and Bachrach 2000). Recent estimates suggest that 54 percent of American children will spend some time living apart from one of their parents, usually their father, by the time they are fifteen (Heuveline and Timberlake 2001; Andersson 2002).

Although similar changes have occurred in most other developed countries, the United States has the highest proportion of children born outside of a union, either marriage or cohabitation, and the highest rates of divorce and union dissolution. Thus, relative to its own history and to other industrialized nations, the United States has a larger share of children living apart from their fathers.

These changes might generate less concern if they did not appear to have deleterious consequences for both the families and society. Single-mother families in the United States have high rates of poverty and rely disproportionately on public assistance. Children in these families may

Figure 5.1   Children Aged Zero to Seventeen with a Single
             Mother or Father

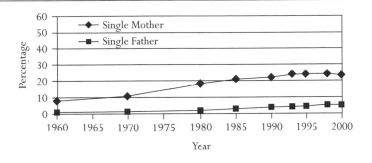

Source: Authors' compilation.

thus be deprived of important economic resources. Furthermore, a large body of research demonstrates that, while the average differences are not large, children who grow up with only one biological parent are disadvantaged, relative to others across a wide range of outcomes (Amato and Keith, 1991a, 1991b; Amato 1993; McLanahan 2002). If changes in family formation undermine the life chances of future generations, the costs to society could be extremely high.

We review what is known about the life chances of children raised in single-mother families and the extent to which they are disadvantaged relative to their peers. Because we are concerned about life chances, most of the outcomes we consider are measured in adolescence and early adulthood. While there is good evidence that father absence has negative consequences for young children, our main concern is whether these disadvantages persist into adulthood.

THE PREVALENCE OF SINGLE-PARENT FAMILIES: 1960 TO 2000

Single parent families increased dramatically in the United States during the second half of the twentieth century. In 1960, about 9 percent of children under 18 were living with a single parent; by 2000, the figure was nearly 27 percent. The largest growth in single parenthood occurred between 1970 and 1985 when the proportion almost doubled from 12 percent to 23 percent (figure 5.1). After the mid-1980s, the growth of single-mother families leveled off at about 25 percent while the growth of single-father families continued but from a very small base. Single-

Figure 5.2   Children Aged Zero to Seventeen with
              One Parent, By Race

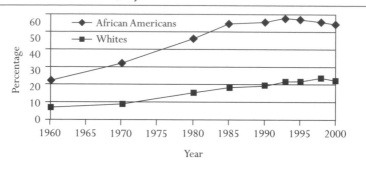

Source: Authors' compilation.

father families are still relatively rare and have not contributed much to
the growth or prevalence of one-parent families.

When we examine blacks and whites separately, we find that the levels
and growth patterns of differ substantially (see figure 5.2). In 1960, 22
percent of black but only 7 percent of white children were living with
just one parent. By 2000, the levels for both were much higher, 53
percent for African American children and 22 percent for white, yet the
racial gap had narrowed only moderately. In 1960, African American
children were about 3 times as likely as white children to live in a one-
parent family; today they are about 2.5 times as likely to do so. In fact,
in 2000, the proportion of white children living with only one parent
was about equal to the proportion of black children who were in 1960.
For white children, the biggest increase in single parenthood occurred
during the 1970s, a full 75 percent. For black children, big increases
occurred during both the 1960s and 1970s, 45 percent in each decade.
After 1985, the increase leveled off for both.

Children may be in a single-parent family for any number of reasons.
While death was once a major path into single parenthood, it is much
less common today (Hernandez 1993). In 1998, only 3 percent of white
children in single-mother households were living with a widowed mother,
and only 5 percent of African American children were.[1]

Since the 1960s, divorce has been the major path into single parenthood for the average child in the United States, accounting for about
two-thirds of the increase in single mother families between 1960 and
1980 (Hernandez 1993).[2] Divorce is a particularly important path for
white children, accounting for about 70 percent of the growth in single-

mother families between 1960 and 1980 (Hernandez 1993). Divorce is a less important, but nonetheless substantial, factor for African American families, accounting for about 38 percent of the overall growth between 1960 and 1980.

Out-of-wedlock childbearing is the second most important component of the growth in single-mother families and the most important among African Americans. The proportion of black children who live in families headed by a never-married mother increased from 7 percent in 1960 to 36 percent in 1980 and to 63 percent in 1998. The increase was much less dramatic for white children, from about 2 percent in 1960 to 8 percent in 1980 to 28 percent in 1998 (Hernandez 1993).

Since 1985, out-of-wedlock childbearing has become increasingly important. By 2000, about 41 percent of all U.S. children in single-mother families were living with a never-married mother. Part of this increase is due to a rise in children born to cohabiting couples who never married so many of these children are actually living with two parents (Bumpass and Lu 2000). In the early 1980s about 21 percent of out-of-wedlock births to blacks and about 33 percent of out-of-wedlock births to whites were to cohabiting couples (Bumpass and Lu 2000). By the early 1990s, the percentage for blacks remained stable at 22 percent, but the percentage for whites increased dramatically to 50 percent. Cohabiting unions are less stable than marital unions, however, and many dissolve before the child reaches adulthood (Andersson 2002; Heuveline and Timberlake 2001).

Unfortunately, these "snapshots" of living arrangements do not provide us with very complete information on the family experiences of children. Some children who are living with married parents when these snapshots are taken will experience a divorce before they reach adulthood. And some who now live with two parents (a mother and stepfather) have experienced single motherhood in the past. Moreover, if divorced mothers form new partnerships at a faster rate than widowed or never-married mothers, the relative importance of the different routes to single-motherhood, as seen from the snapshots, may be somewhat biased. Researchers thus prefer to use life history data to obtain a more complete picture of children's exposure to single parenthood (Andersson 2002; Heuveline and Timberlake 2001). The more sophisticated estimates for the United States indicate that about 78 percent of children born to cohabiting parents and about 35 percent of those born to married parents will spend some time in a single-parent family before the age of fifteen (Andersson 2002). Taken together, these estimates imply that between 50 and 54 percent of all children will spend part of childhood in a single-parent family (Andersson 2002; Heuveline and Timberlake 2001).[3] In the United States, the average child can expect to spend about 10.1 years with two biological parents, 3.3 years with at most one parent, and another 1.5 years with a parent and stepparent during the first fifteen years of life (Andersson 2002).

INTERGENERATIONAL EFFECTS

As noted, changes in family formation would provoke less concern if children were not involved or if it appeared that the changes were innocuous. Unfortunately, the empirical evidence suggests otherwise. On average, children who live with a single-mother fare poorly across a wide range of adolescent and adult outcomes, including educational achievement, economic security, and physical and psychological well-being. Some researchers have suggested that these longer-term consequences may result from pathways established early in adolescence. For example, children raised apart from their biological fathers may drop out of school, leave home, and/or have a child earlier than children raised in two-parent families, which may create disadvantages later in life.

In what follows, we summarize the various outcomes that have been shown to be associated with father absence. We begin by examining academic success and educational attainment. Next, we present differences in psychological adjustment, antisocial behavior and early life transitions. These outcomes, along with educational achievement, may account for persistent differences in adult physical and psychological well-being, relationship quality, and economic well-being, which we consider last. Except where noted, we focus on simple correlations between family structure and child outcomes. Although zero-order effects are typically larger than those controlling for other factors, the variation in control variables across studies makes it difficult to compare outcomes based on more complicated models. Moreover, simple correlations can easily be interpreted as the probability that a random person, drawn from a given family structure, will experience the outcome of interest.[4] When we turn, further on, to the question of whether the effects are causal, we will take into account the ways in which authors have attempted to control for factors that may be affecting both family structure and child outcomes.

Academic Success and Educational Attainment

In light of the importance of educational qualifications to employment and earnings in post-industrial economies, the negative relationship between family structure and children's academic success is a major concern. Studies demonstrate quite conclusively that children who live in single-mother families score lower on measures of academic achievement than those in two-parent families (Morrison and Cherlin 1995; Entwisle and Alexander 1995, 1996; Lang and Zagorsky 2001). Controlling for age, gender, and grade level, secondary school students living in single-parent families score about one-third of a standard deviation lower on mathematics and science tests than children living in two-parent families (Pong, Dronkers, and Hampden-Thompson 2002). Although children in stepparent families score somewhat higher than those in other one-parent families, their scores are still over one-fourth of a standard deviation lower than those of children with two biological parents. Similar gaps are found when grades rather than test scores are used to measure academic success. Children who live with two biological parents receive the highest grades, as reported by the parent, and children who live with their mother and an unmarried partner receive the lowest grades (Thompson, Hanson, and McLanahan 1994). Finally, children who live with both bio logical parents score highest on academic self-concept, a scale that measures a student's self-assessment of academic performance and potential (Smith 1990).[5] In sum, children who live apart from their biological fathers perform less well in school, have lower grades, and report lower academic confidence than those who live with both biological parents. Even if short-lived, these disadvantages may have long-term consequences if they interrupt important educational transitions.

On average, children living with both biological parents remain in school longer and attain higher educational qualifications than children in one parent families. In particular, children with absent fathers are more likely to drop out of school than children who live with their fathers (Astone and McLanahan 1991; Painter and Levine 1999, 2000; Lang and Zagorsky 2001; Manski et al. 1992; McLanahan and Sandefur 1994; Bethke and Sandefur 1998). For example, one team of researchers found that in a sample of children who completed the eighth grade, high school graduation rates were 90 percent for those in two-parent families, 75 for those in divorced-mother families, and 69 for those in never-married-mother families (DeLeire and Kalil 2002). Compared to those living with both biological parents, children in almost every other family structure, including children in stepfamilies, were less likely to graduate from high school. The pattern is similar for college attendance. About 71 percent of children who lived with two biological parents went on to college, while only 50 percent of those living with only their mothers made this transition. Researchers who have counted the years children spend in different types of families report similar results (Bjorklund, Ginther, and Sundstrom 2002). Controlling for age and gender, each additional year spent with a single mother reduces a child's education by half a year, on average. Time spent in stepparent families has a similar effect. Altogether, a child who spends one-third of her childhood with both biological parents, one-third of her childhood with a single mother, and the final one-third of her childhood in a stepfamily will complete, on average, half a year less of education than one who spends her entire childhood with both parents.

Given the differences in both the level and the sources of single parenthood by race, it is unfortunate that few studies examine child outcomes by family structure and race or ethnicity. In most cases researchers look at the relationship between family structure and outcomes, using race and ethnicity as a separate control, but not interacting family structure with race. Only a few studies have looked at white and African American children separately. In the case of educational outcomes, a recent study using data from the Panel Study of Income Dynamics, showed that among white children, father absence was associated with a 4.4 percent and a 9.6 percent reduction in the probability of high school graduation for males and females respectively. For African American children, the differences were more stark: nearly 15 percent for both males and females (Boggess 1998). An earlier study, using data from the National Longitudinal Surveys, considered years of completed education and found that when they disaggregated by race and sex, whites of both sexes and black males living with single mothers had completed 0.5 to 0.7 fewer years of education than their sample averages. Among black women, those who had lived in single mothers had completed 0.2 fewer years of education than their sample average (Krein and Beller 1988).

Childhood Behavioral and Psychological Problems

Father absence may generate feelings of abandonment and stress. We should therefore not be surprised to learn that father absence is associated with a higher incidence of behavioral and psychological problems. Most research on family structure and children's psychological well-being examines the impact of divorce. Children who experience it are more likely to suffer from behavioral problems, such as shyness and aggression, than others (Jekielek 1998; Cherlin et al. 1991; Thomson, Hanson, and McLanahan 1994; Morrison and Cherlin 1995; Flewelling and Bauman 1990; Matsueda and Heimer 1987; Carlson 1999). In a study of first-grade students in Baltimore, 15 to 20 percent of all students were categorized as needing improvement in conduct, compared with 30 percent of children in single-parent families (Entwisle and Alexander 1996). Covering a wider age range, Elizabeth Thomson, Thomas Hanson, and Sara McLanahan (1994) report that only 11 percent of children who lived with both biological parents had dropped out of school, been suspended or expelled, or had their parents called about a behavior problem. In contrast, 19 percent of children in stepparent families, 21 percent in cohabiting couple families (where the male was not the child's father), 23 percent in divorced mother families, and 26 percent in never-married-mother families reported such problems. In the same study, children living with both parents scored lowest on shyness and aggression and highest on sociability and initiative.

Several researchers report that father absence has more of a negative effect on boys' than on girls' psychological well-being. However, this finding may be due to an emphasis on aggressive behavior in many of the studies. When we look at anxiety and depression (or withdrawal), boys and girls appear to have similar responses to divorce (Jekielek 1998). Children in families that have separated recently appear to have the most problems.

Substance Abuse and Contact with the Police

Given the association between single-parent families and aggressive behavior, we should not be surprised to learn that children who live apart from their biological fathers are more likely to use illegal substances and to have early contact with the police (Comanor and Phillips 1998; Matsueda and Heimer 1987; Carlson 1999; for Britain, see Hobcraft 1995; Harper and McLanahan 1999). Indeed, delinquency is sometimes used as an indicator of aggressive behavior (see, for example, Simons et al. 1999). The number of years spent with a biological father is negatively associated with drug use and police contact (Antecol, Bellard, and Helland 2002). Although the probability of having a conviction before age 15 is low for all children, those who spend time in a single-mother household are about 70 percent more likely to have a conviction and 28 percent more likely to have smoked marijuana. Children who live apart from their biological fathers are also 19 percent more likely to smoke cigarettes regularly than other children. The only negative behavior that shows no significant correlation with single parenthood is drinking alcohol. While these findings are intriguing, they have some problems; children born into cohabiting unions were recorded as living apart from their fathers unless their parents married within three years of the birth.

Along with the other problems discussed above, substance use and delinquency can both have long-term consequences that affect educational achievement and future employability. Even if behavioral problems are short-lived, if they occur at times of crucial transitions, such as finishing high school or becoming sexually active, they may create disorder in the life course that carries lasting penalties (Hogan 1980).

Life Transitions

Numerous studies have found a strong association between time in a single-parent family and early life transitions. Children who spend part of their childhood in a single-mother family are more likely to have sex at an early age (DeLeire and Kalil 2002; Flewelling and Bauman 1990). Indeed the risk of an early sexual debut is more than twice as high among children who are raised by one parent rather than two (Antecol, Bellard, and Helland 2002). Daughters from single-mother families also form partnerships and begin childbearing, marital and nonmarital, at a younger age (Wu 1996; Wu and Martinson 1993; Painter and Levine 1999). Whereas young women from two-parent families have a 6-percent chance of having a child outside marriage by age twenty, young women from single-mother, divorced and never-married, families have an 11- and 14-percent chance respectively. Interestingly, girls in stepfamilies have a 16-percent chance of having a child—the highest of all (Painter and Levine 2000). Once again, children from stepparent families appear to be especially disadvantaged when it comes to leaving home early (Goldscheider and Goldscheider 1998; see Cherlin, Chase-Lansdale, and McRae 1995 for Britain). Because early home leaving and early childbearing may interfere with education, these transitions are of particular concern. Similarly, early sexual experience is a concern if it leads to early childbearing or home leaving. Finally, early partnerships tend to be less stable and more likely to dissolve than relationships formed later in life.

Adult Physical Health and Psychological Well-Being

Relative to other outcomes, only a few studies have looked at the association between father absence and adult physical health. And these studies tend to focus on children that experienced parental divorce.[6] According to these studies, women who grew up with a divorced mother have poorer physical health than adults who grew up in intact families (Glenn and Kramer 1985). Similarly, adults whose parents divorced, and men who experienced a parental death report lower satisfaction with their health.[7] Finally, there is some evidence that parental divorce is related to higher rates of mortality among sons (Tucker et al. 1997).

In addition to poorer physical health, psychological and behavior problems also persist into adulthood. Adults who come from single-mother families report less self-esteem and higher use of mental health services than adults who come from two-parent families (Amato 1988; Glenn and Kramer 1985; Amato and Keith 1991b; Cherlin, Chase-Lansdale, and McRae 1998). One team of researchers found that both men and women who lived with both parents reported higher scores on different measures of mental health (Acock and Kiccolt 1989).

Partnership Satisfaction and Union Dissolution

Like many other outcomes, partnership satisfaction and relationship stability in adulthood are correlated with parental divorce. One study found that parents' marital quality in 1980 was correlated with children's subsequent marital quality in 1992, suggesting that children whose parents divorced may be more likely to have unhappy marriages themselves (Amato and Booth 1997). In addition, children who experienced divorce or separation were more likely to describe their own marriage as unstable (Webster, Orbuch, and House 1995). Although there is some evidence that the association may have declined in recent years (Wolfinger 1999), there is some evidence that children who have experienced divorce are more likely to divorce themselves (Kulka and Weingarten 1979; Glenn and Shelton 1983; McLanahan and Bumpass 1988).

Analyzing data that followed individuals over a twelve-year period, Amato (1996) found that only 11 percent of individuals who were in marriages where neither spouse had experienced a parental divorce had divorced. If only one spouse had experienced a parental divorce, the probability was between 14 and 16 percent, and if both spouses had, it was 28 percent. Amato also presents evidence that much of the increased risk of divorce is mediated through problematic interpersonal behavior.

Economic Well-Being in Adulthood

Finally, researchers have documented a strong link between growing up in a single-mother family and adult earnings and income (Lang and Zagorksy 2001; Powell and Parcel 1997). Using occupational status as a measure of economic success, Powell and Parcel (1997) found that women who were living with both biological parents at the age of sixteen had significantly higher status as adults than their counterparts who were living in other family types. The correlation between their own occupational status and that of the family of origin was weaker among those who had lived apart from their fathers (Biblarz and Raftery 1999). Finally, those adults who grew up in mother-only families were more likely to experience spells of unemployment and to rely on public assistance (McLanahan and Sandefur 1994).

Comparing children who grew up with both biological parents to those who experienced some other family structure, Lang and Zagorsky (2001) found that adults who were raised apart from one of their parents earned, on average, $5,015 less per year in the labor market than those who lived continuously with both throughout childhood. They also found a gap in assets by childhood family structure of more than $37,000. Finally, 7 percent who grew up with two parents were living below the poverty line compared to 14 percent who lived with a single parent. In sum, compared with those raised by single parents, children raised by both biological parents earn more in the labor market, are less likely to be poor, have more assets, and are in a better position to insure themselves against economic uncertainties.

EXPLAINING THE ASSOCIATIONS

Many explanations have been offered for why children in one-parent families do less well than those in two-parent families. In this section we describe some of these arguments and discuss the relevant empirical evidence. Some theoretical predictions overlap, so empirical evidence may support more than one perspective simultaneously. In some cases, data limitations make it difficult to test a particular hypothesis. Moreover, as there is no systematic typology of family structures or family experiences, comparing effects across studies can be difficult.

Selection into Father Absence

A common (and difficult to test) explanation for the association between father absence and child outcomes is selection. According to this view, the negative outcomes that we observe among children who grow up without their biological fathers are due to differences between the kinds of parents who divorce or never marry and the kinds of parents who marry once and stay married.

Divorce and separation, for example, are more common among individuals from lower socioeconomic groups, and their children are on average less successful in adulthood. Similarly, high parental conflict is associated with both union dissolution and poor outcomes in children. Finally, people who have problems with substance abuse, violence, mental illness, or other forms of antisocial behavior are more likely to be poor parents and poor partners. In short, children whose parents break up are likely to be disadvantaged across a range of observed and unobserved characteristics that are related to both father absence and negative outcomes.

Results from the few studies that have looked at differences between the children of cohabiting and married parents could be used to support the selection hypothesis. Research has shown that adults living in cohabiting unions have lower quality relationships and are less committed to remaining in their unions (Nock 1995). Domestic violence is also more common in cohabiting than in marital relationships. Children whose biological parents are cohabiting are more likely to have behavioral problems and reduced engagement in school (Brown 2001; see also Osborne, McLanahan, and Brooks-Gunn 2003 for behavioral problems in young children). Similarly, adolescents who live in cohabiting stepfamilies are less engaged in school and more likely to have been expelled than those who live in married stepfamilies or single-mother families (Nelson, Clark, and Acs 2001). This suggests that differences in the characteristics of families by family structure, even among those families with fathers present, can have a negative impact on a child's well-being.

No study can take account of all the potentially predisposing factors and it is therefore difficult to rule out the selection hypothesis. Indeed, even if researchers could control for all the characteristics we believe might be important, one could still argue that some other characteristic, unobserved by the researcher, was responsible for both father absence and negative child outcomes. Indeed, without running an experiment in which children are randomly assigned to different kinds of families, it is impossible to say conclusively how children in single-mother families would have fared, had they lived with two biological parents.

In spite of this limitation, several second-best solutions have been developed to try and deal with the problem of selection. One method, now common in studies of the effects of family disruption, uses longitudinal data and explicitly attempts to control for observed pre-disruption characteristics of families (Amato, Loomis, and Booth 1995; Jekielek 1998; Cherlin et al. 1991; Cherlin, Kiernan, and Chase-Lansdale 1995; Chase-Lansdale, Cherlin, and Kiernan 1995; Fronstin, Greenberg, and Robbins 2001; Kiernan 1997; Morrison and Cherlin 1995; Ni Bhrolchain et al. 2000). In some instances, a measure of the child's well-being prior to divorce is included in the model, and in others, measures of parental conflict and other characteristics of the family environment (low income, poor parenting) are included.

In general, when pre-divorce circumstances are taken into account, the associations between family disruption and child outcomes become smaller, sometimes statistically insignificant (Amato and Keith 1991a). Also, there is evidence that in high conflict families, children whose parents divorce experience better adult outcomes than those whose parents remain together, although when married and divorced low-conflict families are compared, children whose parents divorce fare worse (Amato, Loomis, and Booth 1995; Hetherington and Stanley-Hagan 1999).

Nevertheless, even after taking account of pre-disruption differences in family characteristics and child well-being, some studies continue to find a negative association between family disruption and successful child development. In some instances, effects that seem to go away at one stage reappear later. For example, a widely cited study using the British

National Child Development Study (Cherlin et al. 1991) reported that the negative effects of family disruption on age-eleven behavior (and for males, academic test scores) became statistically insignificant after controlling for pre-disruption differences. More recent analyses of these same data, however, find that negative effects reappear in young adulthood, even after controlling for pre-disruption differences (Fronstin, Greenberg, and Robbins 2001; Cherlin, Chase-Lansdale, and McRae 1998). In short, controlling for observed differences in children and family well-being prior to union dissolution accounts for some, but not all, of the differences between children from intact and non-intact families.

Another approach to dealing with the selection problem is to compare children who share parents (or a parent) but experience different family structures. For example, if parents separate when one child is ten and the other five, the older sibling will have experienced eight years without a father (eighteen minus ten), and the younger thirteen (eighteen minus five) (Ermisch and Francesconi 2001; Yeung, Duncan, and Hill 1995; Hao and Xie 2002). This approach assumes that the longer a child lives without a father, the greater the negative effect. If this assumption is true and if these children are similar in terms of graduating from high school or some other outcome of interest, researchers may conclude that the associated between divorce and child outcomes is due to something about the family rather than to divorce per se. Other researchers have used a similar strategy to examine the effects of living in a stepparent family (Sandefur and Wells 1997; Gennetian 2001; Hofferth and Anderson 2000; Ginther and Pollak 2000; Case, Lin, and McLanahan 1999, 2001). In these studies, one child has usually experienced a divorce and the second child (half-sibling) has lived with both biological parents. In general, the findings from the sibling studies are quite mixed. In some cases, the differences between children in the various types of family structure become smaller and insignificant when siblings are compared, and in others become or remain significant. It is important to keep in mind that estimating the sibling models changes the nature of the data enormously. Blended families are a select group and what happens in them may not generalize to the whole population. Moreover, sibling models assume that parents treat their children exactly the same and that children respond similarly to divorce, both of which are highly unlikely. It is possible that in some families, parents wait to divorce until the oldest child leaves home, or is older, precisely because they believe the child would be harmed by the divorce. If two children in such a family have similar outcomes, this does not necessarily mean that divorce, or an earlier divorce, would not have harmed the older child.

A third strategy for determining the effect of divorce on children is to compare children who grew up in states where obtaining a divorce was relatively easy to those who grew up in states where it was more difficult. Gruber (2000) and Johnson and Mazingo (2000) have both examined the association between years of exposure to unilateral or "no fault" divorce laws in childhood and a range of adult outcomes including marital status, fertility, educational attainment, and earnings. Gruber (2000) finds that living in a state with unilateral laws is associated with less education, more dropping out of high school, more early marriage, and more divorce. In some instances the effects differ for women and men, but in all cases at least one experiences a negative outcome. Although unilateral divorce is significantly associated with poorer outcomes in children, this strategy is unlikely to identify the causal effect of divorce. Both argue that the changes in divorce law may have altered the bargaining power of husbands and wives in ways that disadvantage their children (Johnson and Mazingo 2000). If this were true, the negative outcomes associated with changes in divorce laws might not be due to increases in divorce but rather to changes affecting parental obligations toward children more generally. Consequently, state level variation in divorce laws does not provide an acceptable instrumental variable for child outcomes and should overestimate the relationship between family structure and child outcomes.

A final approach to dealing with the selection problem is to examine children who have lost a parent through death. Because death is more likely than divorce to be a random event, it can be thought of as a quasi-"natural experiment." If this assumption holds, the effect of parental death is likely to be a reasonable estimate of the effect of father absence under random assignment. In extensive reviews of the literature, Amato and colleagues (1991a, 1991b, 1993) report that adolescents in bereaved families score significantly lower on academic achievement tests and males are less likely to finish high school. Children exposed to a parent's death also have more behavioral problems and lower psychological adjustment than children in two-parent families. The fact that parental death typically has a smaller (less negative) effect on children than parental divorce is consistent with the argument that at least some of the divorce effect is due to selection. However, the fact that death reduces children's well-being suggests that selection is not the whole story.

In sum, selection appears to account for some but not all of the difference in child outcomes. Families who divorce are different from those who do not and studies that do not take account for pre-disruption differences are bound to overstate the negative effect of divorce. Moreover, although longitudinal data allow researchers to take account of observed differences prior to divorce, such data do not allow us to adjust for other differences not observed by the researcher or readily available in large-scale datasets. Attempts to control for unobserved differences, either by exploiting new measures or employing new statistical techniques, frequently reduce the association between father absence and poor child outcomes. However, all of these methods have their own limitations and, in general, do not account for all the differences in children, families, and subsequent outcomes. The fact that parental death is negatively associated with children's outcomes is probably the strongest evidence we have to date that father absence reduces children's well-being, but this conclusion is tempered by the fact that children with resident cohabiting fathers are often as disadvantaged as children in single-mother families.

The Parental Loss Perspective

Apart from selection, there are good theoretical reasons for believing that children raised apart from their fathers might do less well than those raised by two parents. One of the oldest explanations posits that the loss of a parent, for any reason, is detrimental to successful child development. The presence of the same sex parent teaches young children appropriate gendered behavior so that father absence, particularly at young ages, is especially problematic for boys (Demo and Acock 1988). In addition, interactions between two parents teach children essential interpersonal skills such as communication, cooperation, and conflict resolution. Children who are not exposed to this kind of role modeling may not develop the interpersonal skills they need to function properly as adults, which may make them less successful in school, at work, or in their personal relationships. Put simply, the socialization deficit perspective maintains that children are deprived of important parental resources when they do not have two residential parents. Fathers and mothers play different but important roles in socialization and development, the loss of which cannot be compensated by greater (or better quality) time with the custodial parent.

As children reach adolescence, the loss of a father may result in a different kind of deficit. Social control theory underscores the important link between adult supervision and child behavior (Hill, Yeung, and Duncan 2001). The more adults to monitor the children, the greater the social control, and the lower the frequency of problem behaviors. Father absence creates a shortfall in social control unless other adults take over the monitoring and supervisory roles. According to social control theorists, not all adults are equal, however. Stepparents and grandparents may have less authority than a biological parent, their supervisory roles may be poorly defined (Cherlin 1978), and they may therefore not make up for a parental loss in its entirety. Moreover, in homes where biological parents and grandparents live together, a lack of agreement over parenting issues may undermine effective social control.

Both the socialization and the social control perspectives maintain that the absence of a parent and the timing of the absence are critical factors underlying the negative association between father absence and child well-being. If these perspectives were true, we would expect all children from single-mother families to be disadvantaged relative to all those from two-parent families. In other words, two similar children, both of whom lost a parent at the same age for different reasons, should have similar risks of poor outcomes. Of course, nonresident fathers can play a role in their children's socialization and development even when they live in separate households. Thus, everything else constant, we might expect to see better outcomes among children maintaining a relationship with their nonresident fathers. Children whose fathers died should have poorer outcomes than otherwise similar children with nonresident but involved fathers.

Other adults may substitute for the lost resources of the nonresident father, and therefore we would expect children with alternative role models and sources of support, be it a stepparent, male relative or family friend, to have better outcomes than those without substitutes. Finally, because important socialization occurs when children are very young, children born outside of a union may be the most disadvantaged. All else being equal, older children who experience parental loss should be less disadvantaged than those who experience it in early childhood. Conversely, for social control, we would expect to see noticeable disadvantages at older ages when control and supervision are arguably more important (Amato 1987).

EVIDENCE OF PARENTAL LOSS

As noted, parents' divorce, death, and nonmarriage are all associated with negative outcomes for children. Nonetheless, the effects of parental death are usually smaller than those of divorce or separation, which is inconsistent with a parental loss perspective. That divorce has a more negative effect may be due to children whose fathers leave voluntarily being more likely to feel abandoned than those whose fathers die (Rogers and Pryor 1998).

If socialization deficits are important and a parent's death occurs later than divorce, on average, not taking account of the timing of the loss may explain why children of widowed parents do better than children of divorced. Once they controlled for the number of years spent living apart from the fathers, Lang and Zagorsky (2001), found that death and divorce had similar effects on cognitive ability, educational attainment, and earnings.[8] The only significant difference they identified was for son's marriage. Men were significantly less likely to be married if they lost a father through death. Consistent with a socialization perspective, most outcomes appear to be independent of the reason for separation.

Sheila Krein and Andrea Beller (1988) found that father absence during the preschool years had the largest negative effects on education, for blacks and whites of both sexes. Comparing siblings, John Ermisch and Marco Francesconi (2001) found that disruptions before age five were more strongly associated with negative outcomes later in life, such as low academic achievement, economic activity, and smoking, than later disruptions. Using a similar modeling strategy and a different data set, Jean Yeung, Greg Duncan, and Martha Hill (1995) failed to find support for the early absence hypothesis, however.

Evidence consistent with a deficit in social control is also mixed. Despite his conclusions that simpler measures of family structure may be better, Roger Wojtkiewicz (1993) finds that time spent in a single-mother family between the ages of eleven and fifteen was more strongly associated with high school graduation than time at younger ages. When Robert Haveman and Barbara Wolfe (1994) measure differences in completed schooling by the timing of a parental divorce, they find no significant effects. In sum, the information we have does not allow us to conclude that children who experience father absence from birth are either worse off or no different from those who experience it during middle childhood or adolescence.

Historically, the evidence on whether contact with a nonresident parent mediates the disadvantages of father absence has also been mixed (Amato and Keith 1991a; McLanahan and Booth, 1989). Most studies find that, aside from child support, contact with the nonresident father has no benefits for children (Furstenberg, Morgan, and Allison 1987). There are two possible reasons for this. First, most studies have not controlled for the quality of the parents' relationship. If the parents are openly hostile or expose the child to conflict, the benefits of contact with a nonresident father could be negated. Second, measures of contact are often crude, counting only the number of visits between the nonresident parent and child. In a recent meta-analysis, Paul Amato and Joan Gilbreth (1999) found that when measures of father contact included feelings of closeness and authoritative parenting practices, the effects of contact were larger and more often significant.

There is some evidence that the presence of other relatives in the household has a positive effect on child outcomes, mediating the negative effect of father absence. Thomas DeLeire and Ariel Kalil (2002), for example, found that adolescent children who lived with a never-married mother in a multigenerational household had better educational outcomes, were less likely to smoke and less likely to have engaged in sexual activity before graduating from high school than children who lived with a single mother and no other adult. This finding is far from universal, however. Other research indicates that conflict between grandmothers and single mothers over who is in charge may undermine parenting and ultimately child outcomes (Chase-Lansdale, Brooks-Gunn, and Zamsky 1994). Similarly, McLanahan and Sandefur (1994) and Hill, Yeung, and Duncan (2001) find that children do worse when a grandmother is living in the household. Establishing an effect of other adults is difficult, however, because the presence of other adults is likely to be endogenous. Sigle-Rushton and McLanahan (2002) have shown that unmarried mothers who live in multigenerational households when the child is born have less human capital and more problems with drugs and alcohol than those who live independently or cohabit with the baby's father. This kind of negative selection may bias the relationship between child outcomes and the kinds of support other adults provide. Similarly, mothers with children who are experiencing problems may be more likely to seek assistance from family members, which would weaken any mediating effect (McLanahan and Sandefur 1994).

Contrary to what the socialization deficit or a social control perspective would predict, children living in stepparent families often fare just as badly as children living in single-mother families (Amato and Keith 1991a; Sandefur, McLanahan, and Wojtkiewicz 1992; Thompson, Hanson, and McLanahan 1994; Painter and Levine 1999; DeLeire and Kalil 2002; McLanahan and Sandefur 1994). The findings for stepparent families are especially surprising, given that these families have much higher incomes and more time than single-mother families. However, there are many reasons for expecting stepparents to feel less committed to a child, including the biological tie (Daly and Wilson 1998), psychological attachment, and the lack of clear norms about stepparents' rights and responsibilities (Cherlin 1978).

Finally, verifying whether children brought up by never-married mothers or by mothers who divorced very early on fare worse than those whose parents divorced or separated later on is not straightforward. First, until recently few studies examined the outcomes of children born to never-married parents. Most combined children of never-married mothers with those of divorced parents. Second, even when never-married-mother families are identified, researchers rarely know whether the mother ever lived with the child's biological father and for how long. Given the rise in cohabitation and out-of-wedlock childbearing to cohabiting parents, marital status alone is no longer an adequate measure of family structure (Bumpass and Raley 1995). Finally, many women who have children outside marriage eventually marry. In studies that only distinguish between two-parent and one-parent families, the history of living in a mother-only family and the effects of not having a father present at different developmental stages, whether due to initial absence or loss, have not been consistently identified.

These points regarding data limitations are especially salient given findings that suggest children living in a cohabiting stepfamily often fare worse on school engagement and behavior than those living in married stepfamilies. At present, it is difficult to measure the ways in which children living in cohabiting families are different because it is still a relatively rare family structure (Nelson, Clark, and Acs 2001). African American and Hispanic children are more likely than white to live as adolescents with cohabiting biological parents, but the percentages are still very small. Moreover, many cohabiting parents eventually marry, so without good longitudinal data, children born to cohabiting parents who later married are difficult to distinguish from those born to married parents. Nonetheless, because cohabiting unions with children are increasingly common, and because evidence suggests this structure affects children differently, measuring and seeking to understand these differences over time should be a priority. In sum, there is only moderate support in the literature for the parental loss perspective. Regardless of the cause, the loss of a parent is associated with poorer outcomes for children, and there is some evidence, albeit mixed, that the presence of other adults may offset those effects. A few issues remain, however. The fact that stepfathers do not reduce the negative effects of father absence dramatically weakens support for this perspective. Similarly, that the timing of father absence has not been adequately measured in many studies further reduces our ability to evaluate these perspectives effectively. Careful comparisons between children born into mother-only families, and those that enter them at an early age, with children who experience disruption and death at later ages would provide some useful evidence for or against the socialization and the social control perspectives.

Pathways or Life Course Perspective

Rather than focusing on the direct consequences of losing a parent, the pathways or life course model focuses on other changes that typically go along with such a loss. Research points to three important disadvantages that accompany father absence—economic insecurity, inadequate mothering, and reduced social capital. Pathways models suggest that these state effects can go a long way towards explaining the observed differences between two-parent and one-parent families.

Single-mother households are far more likely to have inadequate economic resources than two-parent families, and there is some evidence that the poverty they experience is more extreme than others (Bane and Ellwood 1983). Page and Stevens (2004) estimate that children in families that divorce experience a 70-percent drop in household income right after the divorce. Six years after a divorce (assuming no remarriage) the income of these children is still 40- to 45-percent lower than that of intact families. These researchers also estimate that, compared to women who marry after having an out-of-wedlock birth and stay married, those who remain single for six years after giving birth face income gaps of around 57 percent.[9] Economic hardship can lower food consumption, affecting children's nutrition and health (Page and Stevens 2004). Fewer economic resources also mean that single mothers will be less able to invest in educational resources for their children such as enrichment activities, books, and computers (Amato and Keith 1991a). In addition, children in single-mother families are more likely to live in deprived areas with lower quality schools and these "neighborhood effects" may have negative consequences for children (McLanahan and Booth 1989; McLanahan and Sandefur 1994).

Besides the lower income, individuals living in single-mother households are more likely to experience greater economic insecurity because female workers frequently have lower status, lower income, and less secure jobs. In addition, families with only one parent are limited in their ability to self-insure against unemployment or illness. Whereas a second adult can go to work to help the family in an emergency, a single parent has no such recourse unless an older child goes to work, which could affect school attendance and academic success.

Families undergoing parental separation also experience a good deal of stress, which may undermine the mother's ability to parent. When parents are hostile to one another, children often react with feelings of fear, insecurity, sadness, and stress (Maccoby and Martin 1983). Children being drawn into the conflict can be especially problematic for parent-child relationships and child well-being. Overt interparental hostility and conflict mean poor role modeling for children and a sanction on inappropriate ways to resolve conflict. Furthermore, family transitions are often accompanied by other stressful events, such as moving to a new house, changing schools, and remarriage. The stress of family disruption may make children less resilient in coping with these additional changes. Moreover, if the stress occurs at crucial periods in the life course, such as graduating high school or becoming sexually active, the results could be quite serious in the long term.

Sociologists emphasize the loss of social capital that accompanies divorce. According to Coleman (1988), social capital arises from relationships of cooperation and trust between adults and can be used to promote the development of children's human capital. In a well-functioning two-parent family, parents cooperate and share information with each other about the child. These relationships, in turn, help them do a better job of supervising their child and of imparting the values and skills they believe important. Strong ties between parents and other adults in the community, including teachers and extended family members, are also useful in increasing children's human capital.

Divorce reduces children's access to parents' social capital by undermining the relationship between the parents and between the parents and children. Children born to lone mothers and children who experience a divorce are likely to spend less time with their nonresident parent than if they lived in the same household, and in some cases, no time at all. Perhaps not surprisingly, then, many studies have shown that children in single mother and stepfamilies are less close to their fathers (Furstenberg et al. 1983; Furstenberg and Nord 1985; Seltzer 1991) than children in original two-parent families. Because single mothers frequently work longer hours than married mothers, they may have less time and energy to devote to childrearing. The parenting deficit could be further exacerbated if high levels of stress—accompanying the separation process or because of economic hardship—interfere with the custodial parents ability to provide emotional support and moderate, consistent control. Some research suggests that single mothers have weaker parental authority structures and make fewer demands on their children (Amato 1987; Astone and McLanahan 1991; Hetherington, Cox, and Cox 1982; Nock 1988; Thomson, McLanahan, and Curtin 1992). Less parental support and inadequate supervision may give rise to lower psychological well-being, increased academic problems, and delinquent behavior.

Although stepparents and other social fathers are likely to increase household income, they do not appear to substitute perfectly for the biological father. Research has demonstrated that paternal support is highest for children who live with both biological parents and lowest for those living in stepfamilies (Thomson, Hanson, and McLanahan 1994). In addition, stepparent families are generally characterized by less warmth and support. Stepfathers and social fathers may compete for the mother's time and energy, further compromising her ability to parent effectively. According to the pathways perspective, controlling for the psychological adjustment and parenting behaviors, for income and for the quality of parental relationship and parenting should reduce the negative outcomes associated with father absence.

Because divorce creates an acute state of adversity, the timing of a parental separation relative to the measurement or timing of outcomes should be important. Even if we assume that the stresses accompanying transitions are short term, if shocks to income, parental stress, parenting, and social capital occur at significant times and impair academic success, the result could be lower occupational attainment and more economic insecurity. These problems could then cause or exacerbate marital and psychological problems later on in adulthood.

Evidence for Pathways Perspectives   A substantial body of research has demonstrated that, once income differences are taken into account, differences between children in single-mother and two-parent families are far less pronounced (Amato and Keith 1991a). Previous investigations have concluded that income differentials account for between 30 and 50 percent of the difference in the high school graduation among children living in one- and two-parent families (McLanahan 1985; McLanahan and Bumpass 1988; McLanahan and Sandefur 1994). The effects of family structure on child outcomes frequently attenuate after income differences are controlled, but in some cases remain significant. Gary Painter and David Levine (1999) present some evidence that measurement error reduces the effectiveness of income as a mediating variable in single-mother families, however. Using an improved measure of income, these researchers still find that children living in stepparent families are disadvantaged. The fact that children in stepparent families often fare worse than those in two-parent biological families suggests that, while income is important, it is not the entire story.

There are problems, however, with testing the economic deprivation hypothesis. Most researchers hold income constant but not time and parenting. Mothers with higher incomes are likely to devote fewer hours to child care, especially given that the women generally earn less than men. A general income effect may therefore underestimate the extent to which income transfers, child support, or higher wages improve children's well-being. These other sources of income do not require the same time inputs and may have larger and more positive effects on child outcomes than mother's earnings.

Because income is an endogenous variable and affected by parents' human capital and by the amount of time they devote to work, some researchers have sought to compare the effects of family structure internationally. North American and European countries differ, often dramatically, in the level of support they provide to single-mother families. An international comparison can shed light on the extent to which income deprivation is responsible for the negative effects of single motherhood on child outcomes. We would expect the effects of single parenthood to be much less negative in countries that provide greater levels of support to single-mother families.

Using data from the Third International Math and Science Study (TIMSS), one team of researchers found that the negative effect of living in a single-parent family varies substantially by country, with children in the United States, Britain, and New Zealand showing the largest achievement gap (Hampden-Thompson and Pong 2002; Pong, Dronkers, and Hampden-Thompson 2002). These countries also provide the least support to single-mother families. The study thus provides some evidence that income effects may be important. Using a modest range of controls, TIMSS researchers found no significant achievement gap for mathematics between one- and two-parent families in Austria and Iceland, and none for science in Austria, Ireland, Iceland, and the Netherlands. Family allowances and longer periods of parental leave are also associated with a lower achievement gap by family structure. These findings are weakened to some extent by the fact that children in the social democratic countries of Iceland, Netherlands, and Norway did not have lower achievement gaps than those in the Mediterranean countries of Cyprus, Greece, and Portugal, where welfare is less generous and child poverty rates in one-parent families are higher. Child poverty rates in single-mother families in Mediterranean countries are far more similar to social democratic and continental countries than they are to liberal countries, however. Similarly, Björklund, Ginther, and Sundstrom (2002) found no difference in the effect of family structure on educational attainment for Sweden and the United States, countries with very different welfare systems.

The empirical evidence also documents differences in the parenting practices of single-mother and two-parent families. There is consistent evidence that levels of stress and the psychological adjustment of the custodial parent are associated with child outcomes. Children of depressed mothers have higher average scores on externalizing and internalizing behavior inventories (Downey and Coyne 1990; Covey and Tam 1990). Insofar as mothers suffer short-term depression and anxiety following a divorce, one might expect that mothers' psychological adjustment would be an important mediating factor (Heatherington, Cox, and Cox 1982), but only a few studies have found evidence of this.

Controlling for differences in parenting does little to offset the effects of father absence. For example, Nan Marie Astone and Sara McLanahan (1991) found that controlling for parental input did little to narrow the difference in the risk of dropping out of high school between children in intact and divorced families. Similarly, Thomson, Hanson, and McLanahan (1994) found that parenting practices accounted for practically none of the disadvantage associated with living in a single-mother family but between 13 to 35 percent of that of a stepfather or mother-partner family. Finally, Rachel Dunifon and Lori Kowaleski-Jones (2002) found that maternal warmth and control are significantly associated with reductions in delinquency for African American but not for white children. The size and significance of the effects of years spent living with a single mother or cohabiting parent are little changed by the introduction of these variables, however. This suggests that while parenting is important, especially for

African American adolescents, it does not mediate the effects of family structure, at least as they are measured here.

Consistent with acute stress, most longitudinal studies find that the negative behavioral and psychological effects of family disruption are short term and decline over time. Also consistent with acute stress is the finding that family transitions during adolescence—either because of a marital breakdown or remarriage—are both detrimental to academic success (see Sandefur, McLanahan, and Wojtkiewicz 1992). Although quite a few cross-sectional studies do not support this hypothesis, the inconsistency is likely due to the fact that both age and time effects are operating, which means that the relationship is likely to be curvilinear in cross-sectional data (Amato and Keith 1991a). Consistent with a social capital perspective, James Peterson and Nicholas Zill (1986) found that the quality of the parent-child relationships reduced the effects of divorce on children's depression and behavioral problems. An indirect method of assessing whether stigma accounts for some of the association of father absence with outcomes is to examine change in the effects of father absence over time. If stigma is a problem we would expect the effects of father absence to have declined over time. An early review of the literature reported that divorce effect sizes had decreased (Amato and Keith 1991a), and recent evidence suggests that the positive relationship between parental divorce and own divorce have both weakened over time (Wolfinger 1999). But other recent studies find no changes over time in the associations of father absence with educational achievement and occupational status. Indeed, recent studies suggest that the effects of family structure on education have remained fairly constant in both the United States and the United Kingdom from the 1960s to the 1990s (Ely et al. 1999; Biblarz and Raftery 1999).

In sum, evidence suggests that the effects of father absence, especially the greater income insecurity and economic hardship, mediate the effects of family structure on child outcomes. There is also moderate, but slightly conflicting, evidence that the effects of divorce, at least on behavioral and psychological problems, decrease with time. The evidence on the declining effects of stress must be weighed against the fact that father absence is associated with many outcomes measured in young adulthood. For this reason a better understanding of the importance of education to other longer-term outcomes is essential. Finally, there is evidence that parenting practices change after divorce, although controlling for these changes does not seem to mediate the association between father absence and educational achievement.

SUMMARY

What, then, do we know about the effect of father absence on children? As others have concluded, no one theory seems to prevail. There is some

evidence that the loss of a father has important developmental consequences for children, the effects of which might be mediated by parental-
like inputs from other adults, but not stepparents. Theorists can invoke
evolutionary explanations for this apparent inconsistency, but this explanation requires further elaboration and verification (Biblarz and Raftery
1999; Case, Lin, and McLanahan 1999). That children of widowed parents fare worse than children in two-parent families lends some support
to the parental loss perspective. It also provides evidence that selection
alone is not enough of an explanation because death is more likely to be
an exogenous event than divorce or separation. Differences between children in married and cohabiting families remind us that selection remains
an important concern and parental loss is not sufficient on its own.

Because an important component of the parental loss perspective is the
deficit in socialization or social control that children suffer, researchers
should pay attention to the timing of events, comparing children who
lost a parent through divorce, widowhood, and nonmarriage in early and
middle childhood as well as adolescence. These comparisons would provide more useful tests than mere dichotomies of one- versus two-parent
families.

Parental conflict before, during, and subsequent to a divorce or separation often accounts for a substantial portion of the relationship between
father absence and children's behavior, psychological adjustment, and academic performance. These findings provide evidence for both pathways
models and for selection models. Further evidence for a selection model
comes from findings that children in high conflict families that remain
intact often fare worse than those in high conflict families that have divorced (Jekielek 1998). Controlling for pre-divorce conflict often weakens and sometimes eliminates the negative association between single parenthood and child outcomes. However, by treating family disruption as
an event rather than a process, researchers may have conflated the precursor with the process, making it difficult to distinguish between selection
and pathways perspectives. Finally, to understand the importance of parental conflict, researchers need to further our understanding of the relationships between parents who share a child born outside of a union. If
parents who share a child born outside of a union have low conflict relationships or do not have any contact at all, it will be difficult to attribute
parental conflict to all the negative outcomes associated with single parenthood. Comparing the outcomes of children born outside of a union to
those born within high- and low-conflict unions may provide additional
relevant information.

Compared to two-parent families, economic resources are relatively
scarce in mother-only families. For those children whose parents divorce,
economic resources are severely reduced creating a financial shock, if not

poverty. Many children born outside of a union are born into poverty. There is a good deal of evidence that this accounts for much of the association of father absence with child outcomes. But there is also evidence that income is not the only explanation. In many cases the association between father absence and outcomes shrinks but retains significance. Although researchers need to explore the extent to which measurement error is responsible for the failure of income to account for more, it is clear that other factors, including the timing of important stressors, are likely to be important as well (Painter and Levine 1999). If income were the only explanation, children in stepfamilies should have better outcomes than they do. In addition, we would expect children living in single-mother families in Scandinavian countries to suffer the least disadvantage. Although the "achievement gap" for children in single-mother families is smaller for children in these countries than for children in the United States, Scandinavian countries have a larger achievement gap than children in Mediterranean countries, where the welfare state is far less developed and poverty rates among children in single-mother families are higher, but still much lower than in the United States.

There is good evidence that parenting practices differ across family types, and that parenting practices are associated with child outcomes. It is somewhat surprising then, that measures of parenting practices do not often mediate the association of family structure and child outcomes. On the other hand, the quality of parent-child relationships (social capital) does seem to matter. But relative to income and conflict, the amount by which controlling for relationship quality reduces the adverse effect of living in a single-mother family is rather modest.

In sum, there is limited support for some factors, and there are many more questions that need to be answered. With existing evidence, the role these various factors play in the development and well-being of children is difficult to determine. Often researchers have not introduced the kinds of measures that would allow us to resolve some of our questions. One of the most important limitations has been the reliance (often a result of data limitations) on cross-sectional measures of family structure, and often only a one- versus two-parent dichotomy. Those children who, in cross sectional data, are observed to be living in a single-parent family have had a wide diversity of family experiences. Important differences between children living in two biological parent families and children living in stepfamilies makes the use of a two-parent versus one-parent dichotomy even more questionable. If we are going to develop a better picture of what changing family realities mean, we are going to have to develop richer and more developmentally sensitive measures of family life. In some sense, because rather crude measures of family structure performed so well and because so much of the work has been atheoretical, there has been little incentive to develop more detailed and meaningful measures of children's lives. With better data and larger samples, more detailed measures are now being used, but it is worth noting that one of the realities of working with survey data is that researchers must often choose between using detailed measures of family structure and using more innovative methods like sibling models that reduce samples substantially, making detailed family measures impractical (Hill, Yeung, and Duncan 2001).

We also need better measures of parental relationships both before and after the relationship dissolves and of parenting practices and parent-child relationships. We have now several good explanations for why children might be disadvantaged when they do not live with their biological fathers—low income and poor relationships between parents and parents and children. To move forward, we need to take advantage of new and richer data and devote more time to evaluating and testing the various hypotheses.

Policy Implications

We now ask how our current knowledge can inform parents, policy makers, and other adults who are concerned with improving the well-being of children.

First, several policy makers have suggested that we should make divorce more difficult as a way of reducing father absence and improving child outcomes. Whether this policy would be good for children is difficult to assess with existing evidence because it is not clear how much harder divorce should be made or what the net impact on families would be. Clearly, a world with no divorce would not be in children's best interest because we know that in some families children are better off after their parents separate. Although some children may be better off if their parents remained together, it is difficult to know who these children are and what set of policies would encourage healthy marriages while allowing unhealthy ones to dissolve. On the one hand, extending the time required to obtain a divorce and providing parents with mediation services might be good for children because it might reduce the number of divorces while increasing cooperation and financial support among parents who do divorce. On the other, restricting divorce could prolong periods of conflict and make it more difficult for some parents to remove themselves, and their children, from unhealthy or violent relationships. These situations might make some children worse off. Moreover, making divorce more difficult might discourage more people from getting married or becoming parents in the first place. It is hard to see how either of these situations, particularly the second, would be in the best interests of children or low birth rate societies.

Although existing research does not provide conclusive support for policies that would discourage divorce, there are, nonetheless, many findings that are relevant to policy makers. First, and perhaps most important, parents need to be informed about the risks associated with father absence. We cannot say with certainty how much of the effect of father absence is due to selection and how much is due to other factors triggered by divorce and separation, but we can be fairly confident that at least some of the effects are due to the reduction in children's access to parental time and money, and to declines in the quality of family relationships (social capital) that go along with divorce. Once they know more about the potential risks to children, some parents who are considering a divorce may decide to stay together. Others may decide to divorce, but do so in a way that minimizes their child's exposure to the conditions described. If parents understand the potential costs to children of economic insecurity, parental conflict, and the loss of fathers' time, nonresident fathers may be more willing to pay child support and parents may make a greater effort to cooperate in raising their child even if they are not living together.

In addition, by identifying some of the pathways that mediate the negative effects of divorce and separation, the literature on single parenthood provides policy makers and program administrators with good information about multiple entry points for intervening to improve the life chances of children. Income loss and economic insecurity appear to account for at least half of the negative consequences associated with union dissolution, and possibly more. The government has made great strides toward strengthening child support enforcement during the past two decades and these efforts should be continued. Some nonresident fathers, however, are not able to provide much support, in which case the United States should follow the lead of its European neighbors who are much more generous in helping low-income families. We now have good experimental evidence suggesting that improving the material conditions of low-income families improves child outcomes (Huston et al. 2001; Ludwig, Ladd, and Duncan 2001; Ludwig, Duncan, and Hirschfield 2001; Katz, Kling, and Leibman 2001). In designing income support programs, it is extremely important that benefits be made available to two-parent families as well as single mothers. Otherwise, we may increase the prevalence of single-mother families at the same time we are improving their circumstances. Making benefits available to two-parent families requires not only removing restrictions that limit eligibility to one-parent families, but also revising income tests so that more two-parent families are eligible for help. If designed correctly, income supports for all low-income families might actually increase marriage and family stability while improving the well-being of children in single-mother families. Recent evaluations of the Minnesota Family Assistance Program—a welfare reform initiative that increased the income of two-parent families—recorded a substantial drop in divorce rates among the welfare population (Knox, Miller, and Gennetian 2000; see also Harknett and Gennetian 2001).

Policy makers could also do much more to increase the social capital of children in single-mother households. We now have evidence from several experimental evaluations that mediation programs can reduce parental conflict and increase father involvement among divorcing parents (Emery et al. 2001; Wolchik et al. 2002). We also know that children as well as parents benefit from programs designed to improve parents' relationship skills (Cowan, Powell, and Cowan 1998; Stanley, Blumberg, and Markman 1999). While these programs have not been administered to low-income couples, several pilot programs are being tested. As was true for programs designed to increase income, programs aimed at building parents' relationship skills should be available, not only to parents that are ending their relationship, but also to parents who are still married or hoping to marry. The Bush administration's marriage promotion program, which promises to offer new unmarried parents training in relationship skills, will tell us much more about whether these programs work for low-income parents and whether children's interests are served by such programs (see Garfinkel and McLanahan forthcoming).

In sum, nonexperimental social scientific research has not and probably cannot tell us exactly how well children would fare if their parents had married or stayed together. Nor can it provide strong ex ante support for policies that make divorce more difficult. However, it can provide a good deal of information on the ways in which policies can be designed to address some of the problems and disadvantages that go along with father absence or parental divorce. Moreover, well designed research can assess the extent to which policies aimed at making children better off— such as income support and relationship skills training—work to stabilize marriage as well. This, we believe, is a valuable contribution.

The research was made possible through grants #R01HD36916 and #R01HD19375 from NICHD, and grant #P30HD32030 from NIH. Both authors received support from the MacArthur Network on "The Family and The Economy" and The Center for Research on Child Well-being at Princeton University. Sara McLanahan worked on this paper while she was a fellow at the Center for Advanced Study in the Behavioral Sciences with support from the William and Flora Hewlett Foundation. Wendy Sigle-Rushton was provided support from the Economic and Social Research Council of the United Kingdom while she worked on this project.

NOTES

1. Many children living in one-parent families are living with women who are separated or whose spouse is absent so separation could have preceded widowhood. Moreover, a widowed woman may have had an out-of-wedlock birth, so that the real pathway into a mother-only home was out-of-wedlock childbearing, not death. Similarly, a divorced woman may have had a child after her divorce, so using cross-sectional data on living arrangements and marital status to determine the pathway into a mother-only family will misclassify some children's experiences.

2. Although divorce rates began rising as far back as the 1860s and could be argued to have been an increasingly important pathway since that time, it was not until the 1960s that there were real increases in the percentage of children living with one parent. This is because up until 1960, there was a substantial decline in parental mortality, and the two canceled one another out (Hernandez 1993).

3. Unfortunately, neither Andersson (2002) nor Heuveline and Timberlake (2001) provide life table estimates of United States children by race. Both authors use data from 1995 to estimate multistate life tables using the fertility and partnership histories of mothers aged fifteen to forty-four. Both treat nonresidence from the mother as a single and absorbing state that includes living with neither parent and living with the father only.

4. When we refer to a relationship that is not bivariate we specify which variables are included as controls.

5. Although those students whose parents separated prior to grade three were not significantly different on the academic self-concept scale from students who had lived continuously with both parents.

6. Guidubaldi and Cleminshaw (1985) showed that among children in the United States School Psychologists study, those from divorced families were reported to have poorer health than those in intact families. So physical health problems may begin early on.

7. In both cases, zero-order correlations are not reported and the relationships reflect regression coefficients holding constant age, father's

social class, parental education, size of community of origin, sibship size, religion, and maternal employment.

8. The way these authors measure time apart does not perfectly capture the timing, or indeed the cause, of father absence. If a child experienced a parental divorce at age 6 and then her father died at age fifteen, she will have been coded as having spent twelve years apart from her father and three years before the age of eighteen in a bereaved family even though bereavement was not the cause of her separation.

9. When they allow for the possibility of remarriage for divorced women, average income six years after a divorce is only 15 to 20 percent lower. When they allow for divorce after marriage to single mothers, income differences are also much lower.

REFERENCES

Acock, Alan C., and K. Jill Kiecolt. 1989. "Is it Family Structure or Socioeconomic Status? Family Structure During Adolescent and Adult Adjustment." *Social Forces* 68(2): 553–71.

Amato, Paul R. 1987. "Family Processes in One-parent, Stepparent, and Intact Families: The Child's Point of View." *Journal of Marriage and the Family* 49(2): 327–37.

———. 1988. "Parental Divorce and Attitudes Towards Marriage and Family Life." *Journal of Marriage and the Family* 50(2): 453–61.

———. 1993. "Children's Adjustment to Divorce: Theories, Hypotheses, and Empirical Support." *Journal of Marriage and the Family* 55(1): 23–38.

———. 1996. "Explaining the Intergenerational Transmission of Divorce." *Journal of Marriage and the Family* 58(3): 628–40.

Amato, Paul R. and Alan Booth. 1997. *A Generation at Risk: Growing Up in An Era of Family Upheaval.* Cambridge Mass.: Harvard University Press.

Amato, Paul R., and Joan Gilbreth. 1999. "Nonresident Fathers and Children's Well-Being: A Meta-Analysis." *Journal of Marriage and the Family* 61(3): 557–73.

Amato, Paul R., and Bruce Keith. 1991a. "Parental Divorce and the Well-Being of Children: A Meta-Analysis." *Psychological Bulletin* 110(1): 26–46.

———. 1991b. "Parental Divorce and Adult Well-being: A Meta-Analysis." *Journal of Marriage and the Family* 53(1): 43–58.

Amato, Paul R., L. Spencer Loomis, and Alan Booth. 1995. "Parental Divorce, Marital Conflict, and Off-Spring Well-Being during Early Adulthood." *Social Forces* 73(3): 895–915.

Andersson, Gunnar. 2002. "Children's Experience of Family Disruption and Family Formation: Evidence from 16 FFS Countries." *Demographic Research* 7(article 7): 343–64.

Antecol, Heather, Kelly Bellard, and Eric Helland. 2002. "Does Single Parenthood Increase the Probability of Teenage Promiscuity, Drug Use, and Crime? Evidence from Divorce Law Changes." Claremont College Working Paper in Economics, No. 106.

Astone, Nan Marie, and Sara S. McLanahan. 1991. "Family Structure, Parental Practices and High School Completion." *American Sociological Review* 56(3): 309–20.

Bane, Mary Jo, and David Ellwood. 1983. *The Dynamics of Dependence: The Routes to Self-Sufficiency.* Cambridge, Mass.: Urban Systems Research.

Bethke, Lynn, and Gary Sandefur. 1998. "Disruptive Events during High School Years and Educational Attainment." Unpublished paper. Institute for Research on Poverty, University of Wisconsin.

Biblarz, Timothy J., and Adrian Raftery. 1999. "Family Structure, Educational Attainment, and Socioeconomic Success: Rethinking the 'Pathology of the Matriarchy.'" *American Journal of Sociology* 105(2): 321–65.

Björklund, Anders, Donna K. Ginther, and Marianne Sundstrom. 2002. "Family Structure and Children's Educational Attainment: A Comparison of Outcomes in Sweden and the United States." Paper presented at the ESPE-meetings in Bilbao (June).

Boggess, Scott. 1998. "Family Structure, Economic Status, and Educational Attainment." *Journal of Population Economics* 11(2): 205–22.

Brown, Susan. 2001. "Child Well-being in Cohabiting Families." In *Just Living Together: Implications of Cohabitation on Families, Children, and Social Policy,* edited by Alan Booth and Ann Crouter. Mahwah, N.J.: Lawrence Erlbaum Associates.

Bumpass, Larry L, and Hsien-Hen Lu. 2000. "Trends in Cohabitation and Implications for Children's Family Contexts in the United States." *Population Studies* 54(1): 29–41.

Bumpass, Larry L., and Kelly Raley. 1995. "Redefining Single-Parent Families: Cohabitation and Changing Family Reality." *Demography* 32(1): 97–109.

Carlson, Marcia. 1999. "Do Fathers Really Matter?: Father Involvement and Social-Psychological Outcomes for Adolescents." Unpublished paper. Center for Research on Child Wellbeing, Princeton University.

Case, Anne, I-Fen Lin, and Sara S. McLanahan. 1999. "Household Resource Allocation in Step-Families: Darwin Reflects on the Plight of

Cinderella." *American Economic Review Papers and Proceedings* 89(2): 234–38.

———. 2001. "Educational Attainment of Siblings in Step-Families." *Evolution and Human Behavior* 22(4): 269–89.

Chase-Lansdale, P.L., Jeanne Brooks-Gunn, and E.S. Zamsky. 1994. "Young African American Multigenerational Families in Poverty: Quality of Mothering and Grandmothering." *Child Development* 65(2): 373–93.

Chase-Lansdale, P.L., Andrew J. Cherlin, and Kathleen E. Kiernan. 1995. "The Long-Term Effects of Parental Divorce on Mental Health of Young Adults: A Developmental Perspective." *Child Development* 66(6): 1614–34.

Cherlin, Andrew. 1978. "Remarriage As An Incomplete Institution." *American Journal of Sociology* 84(3): 634–50.

Cherlin, Andrew J., P. Lindsay Chase-Lansdale and C. McRae. 1998. "Effects of Parental Divorce on Mental Health Throughout the Life Course." *American Sociological Review* 63(2): 239–49.

Cherlin, Andrew J., Frank F. Furstenberg, P. Lindsay Chase-Lansdale, Kathleen E. Kiernan, Philip K. Robbins, Donna R. Morrison, and Julien O. Tietler. 1991. "Longitudinal Studies of Effects of Divorce on Children in Great Britain and the United States." *Science* 252(June): 1386–89.

Cherlin, Andrew J., Kathleen E. Kiernan, and P. Lindsay Chase-Lansdale. 1995. "Parental Divorce in Childhood and Demographic Outcomes in Young Adulthood." *Demography* 32(3): 299–318.

Coleman, James. 1988. "Social Capital in the Creation of Human Capital." *American Journal of Sociology* 94(supplement): S95–S120.

Comanor, William S., and Llad Phillips. 1998. "The Impact of Family Structure on Delinquency." Unpublished paper. University of California, Santa Barbara.

Covey, Lirio S., and Debbie Tam. 1990. "Depressive Mood, the Single-Parent Home, and Adolescent Cigarette Smoking." *American Journal of Public Health* 80(1): 1330–33.

Cowan, Philip A., Douglas Powell, and Carolyn P. Cowan. 1998. "Parenting Interventions: A Family Systems Perspective." In *Handbook of Child Psychology*, vol. 5, edited by William Damon. New York: John Wiley.

Daly, Martin, and Margo Wilson. 1998. *The Truth About Cinderella, A Darwinian View of Parental Love*. New Haven: Yale University Press.

DeLeire, Thomas, and Ariel Kalil. 2002. "Good Things Come in Threes: Single-Parent Multigenerational Family Structure and Adolescent Adjustment." *Demography* 39(2): 393–413.

Demo, David H., and Alan C. Acock. 1988. "The Impact of Divorce on Children." *Journal of Marriage and the Family* 50(3): 619–48.

Downey, Geraldine, and James C. Coyne. 1990. "Children of Depressed Parents: An Integrative Review." *Psychological Bulletin* 108(1): 50–76.

Dunifon, Rachel, and Lori Kowaleski-Jones. 2002. "Who's In the House? Race Differences in Cohabitation, Single Parenthood, and Child Development." *Child Development* 73(4): 1249–64.

Ely, Margaret, Martin P.M. Richards, Michael E.J. Wadsworth, and Bridget J. Elliot. 1999. Secular Changes in the Association of Parental Divorce and Childrens Educational Attainment—Evidence from Three British Cohorts. *Journal of Social Policy* 28(3): 437–55.

Emery, Robert E., Lisa Laumann-Billings, Mary C. Waldron, David A. Sbarra, and Peter Dillon. 2001. "Child Custody Mediation and Litigation: Custody, Contact, and Co-parenting 12 years after Initial Dispute Resolution." *Journal of Consulting and Clinical Psychology.* 69(2): 323–32

Entwisle, Doris R., and Karl L. Alexander. 1995. "A Parent's Economic Shadow: Family Structure Versus Family Resources as Influences on Early School Achievement." *Journal of Marriage and the Family* 57(2): 399–409.

———. 1996. "Family Type and Children's Growth in Reading and Math Over the Primary Grades." *Journal of Marriage and the Family* 58(2): 341–55.

Ermisch, John F., and Marco Francesconi. 2001. "Family Structure and Children's Achievements." *Journal of Population Economics* 14(2): 249–70.

Flewelling, Robert L., and Karl E. Bauman. 1990. "Family Structure as Predictor of Initial Substance Use and Sexual Intercourse in Early Adolescence." *Journal of Marriage and the Family* 52(1): 171–81.

Fronstin, Paul, David H. Greenberg, and Philip K. Robbins. 2001. "Parental Disruption and the Labor Market Performance of Children when They Reach Adulthood." *Journal of Population Economics* 14(1): 137–72.

Furstenberg, Frank F., S.P. Morgan, and P.D. Allison. 1987. "Paternal Participation and Children's Wellbeing After Marital Dissolution." *American Sociological Review* 52(5): 695–701.

Furstenberg, Frank F., and Christine W. Nord. 1985. "Parenting Apart: Patterns of Childrearing After Marital Disruption." *Journal of Marriage and the Family* 47(4): 893–904.

Furstenberg, Frank F., Christine W. Nord, James L. Peterson, and Nicholas Zill. 1983. "The Life Course of Children of Divorce." *American Sociological Review* 48(5): 656–68.

Garfinkel, Irwin, and Sara McLanahan. Forthcoming. "Strengthening Fragile Families." In *Breaking the Cycle: Nine Ideas for Improving Children's*

Futures, edited by Isabel Sawhill. Washington, D.C.: Brookings Institution Press.

Gennetian, Lisa. 2001. "One or Two Parents? Half or Step Siblings? The Effect of Family Composition on Young Children." Unpublished paper. Manpower Demonstration Research Corporation.

Ginther, Donna K., and Robert A. Pollak. 2000. "Does Family Structure Affect Children's Outcomes?" Unpublished paper. Department of Economics, Washington University.

Glenn, Norval D., and Kathryn D. Kramer. 1985. "The Psychological Well-Being of Adult Children of Divorce." *Journal of Marriage and the Family* 47(4): 905–12.

Glenn, Norval D., and B.A. Shelton. 1983. "Pre-Adult Background Characteristics and Divorce: A Note of Caution About Over-reliance on Explained Variance." *Journal of Marriage and the Family* 45(2): 405–10.

Goldscheider, Frances K., and Calvin Goldscheider. 1998. "The Effects of Childhood Family Structure on Leaving and Returning Home." *Journal of Marriage and the Family* 60(3): 745–56.

Gruber, Jonathan. 2000. "Is Making Divorce Easier Bad for Children? The Long Run Implications of Unilateral Divorce." NBER Working Paper, #7968. National Bureau of Economics.

Guidubaldi, John, and Helen K. Cleminshaw. 1985. "Divorce, Family Health, and Child Adjustment." *Family Relations* 34(1): 35–41.

Hampden-Thompson, Gillian, and Suet-Ling Pong. 2002. "Does Family Policy Environment Mediate the Effect of Single-Parenthood on Children's Academic Achievement? A Study of 14 European Countries." Unpublished paper. Population Research Institute. The Pennsylvania State University.

Hao, Lingxin, and Guihua Xie. 2002. "The Complexity and Endogeneity of Family Structure in Explaining Children's Misbehavior." *Social Science Research* 31(1): 1–28.

Harknett, Kristen, and Lisa A. Gennetian. 2001. "How an Earnings Supplement Can Affect the Marital Behaviour of Welfare Recipients: Evidence from the Self-Sufficiency Project." Working paper. Canada: Social Research and Demonstration Corporation.

Harper, Cynthia, and Sara McLanahan. 1999. "Father Absence and Youth Incarceration." Working Paper # 99-03. Center for Research on Child Wellbeing.

Haveman, Robert, and Barbara Wolfe. 1994. *Succeeding Generations.* New York: Russell Sage Foundation.

Hernandez, Donald J. 1993. *America's Children: Resources from Family, Government, and the Economy.* New York: Russell Sage Foundation.

————. 1996. *Trends in the Well Being of America's Children and Youth.* Department of Health and Human Services.

Hetherington, E. Mavis, Martha Cox, and Roger Cox. 1982. "Effects of Divorce on Parents and Children." In *Nontraditional Families: Parenting and Child Development,* edited by Michael E. Lamb, 233–285. Hillsdale, N.J.: Lawrence Erlbaum.

Hetherington, E. Mavis, and Margaret Stanley-Hagan. 1999. "The Adjustment of Children with Divorced Parents: A Risk and Resiliency Perspective." *Journal of Child Psychology and Psychiatry and Allied Disciplines* 40(1): 129–40.

Heuveline, Patrick, and Jeffrey M.Timberlake. 2001. "An International Comparison of Children's Experiences of Family Structures." Paper presented at the General Conference of the International Union for the Scientific Study of Population in Salvador, Brazil (August).

Hill, Martha S., Wei-Jun, Yeung, and Greg J. Duncan. 2001. "Childhood Family Structure and Young Adult Behaviors." *Journal of Population Economics* 14(2): 271–99.

Hobcraft, John. 1995. "Intergenerational and Life-Course Transmission of Social Exclusion: Influences and Childhood Poverty, Family Disruption and Contact with the Police." CASE paper 15. Center for the Analysis of Social Exclusion, London School of Economics.

Hofferth, Sandra L., and Kermyt G. Anderson. 2000. "Biological and Stepfather Investment in Children." Paper presented at Conference on Conflict and Cooperation in Families, sponsored by the MacArthur Network on Families and the Economy and the NICHD Family and Child Well-Being Research Network, Bethesda, Md. (March 3–4).

Hogan, Dennis P. 1980. "The Transition to Adulthood as a Career Contingency." *American Sociological Review* 45(2): 261–76.

Huston, Aletha, Robert Granger, Johannes Bos, Greg Duncan, Vonnie McLoyd, Rashmita Mistry, Danielle Crosby, Christina Gibson, Katherine Magnuson, Jennifer Romich, and Ana Ventura. 2001. "Work-based Anti-Poverty Programs for Parents Can Enhance the School Performance and Social Behavior of Children." *Child Development* 72(1): 318–36.

Jekielek, Susan M. 1998. "Parental Conflict, Marital Disruption, and Children's Emotional Well-Being." *Social Forces* 76(3): 905–35.

Johnson, John H., and Christopher J. Mazingo. 2000. "The Economic Consequences of Unilateral Divorce for Children." Social Science Research Network Electronic Paper Collection. Available at: http://papers.ssrn.com/paper.taf?abstract_id=236227 (accessed May 20, 2004).

Katz, Lawrence F., Jeffrey R. Kling, and Jeffrey B. Liebman. 2001. "Moving to Opportunity in Boston: Early Results of a Randomized Mobility Experiment." *Quarterly Journal of Economics* 116(2): 607–54.

Kiernan, Kathleen. 1997. "The Legacy of Parental Divorce: Social, Economic, and Demographic Experiences in Adulthood." CASE Paper 1, Center for the Analysis of Social Exclusion, London School of Economics.

Knox, Virginia, Cynthia Miller, and Lisa A. Gennetian. 2000. *Reforming Welfare and Rewarding Work: Final Report on the Minnesota Family Investment Program*. New York: Manpower Demonstration Research Corporation.

Krein, Sheila Fitzgerald, and Andrea H. Beller. 1988. "Educational Attainment of Children from Single-parent Families: Differences by Exposure, Gender, and Race." *Demography* 25(2): 221–234.

Kulka, R.A., and H. Weingarten. 1979. "The Long-Term Effects of Parental Divorce in Childhood on Adult Adjustment." *Journal of Social Issues* 35(4): 50–78.

Lang, Kevin, and Jay L. Zagorsky. 2001. "Does Growing Up With A Parent Absent Really Hurt?" *Journal of Human Resources* 36(2): 253–73.

Ludwig, Jens, Greg Duncan, and Paul Hirschfield. 2001. "Urban Poverty and Juvenile Crime: Evidence From A Randomized Housing-Mobility Experiment." *Quarterly Journal of Economics* 116(2): 665–79.

Ludwig, Jens, Helen Ladd, and Greg Duncan. 2001. "The Effects of Urban Poverty on Educational Outcomes: Evidence From a Randomized Experiment." In *Brookings-Wharton Papers on Urban Affairs*, edited by William Gale and Janet Rothenberg Pack. Washington, D.C.: Brookings Institution Press.

Maccoby, Eleanor E., and John A. Martin. 1983. "Socialization in the Context of the Family: Child-Parent Interaction." In *Handbook of Child Psychology*. 4th edition, vol. 4, edited by E. Mavis Hetherington, 1–101. New York: John Wiley.

Manski, Charles F., Gary D. Sandfeur, Sara S. McLanahan, and Daniel Powers. 1992. "Alternative Estimates of the Effect of Family Structure During Adolescence on High School Graduation." *Journal of the American Statistical Association* 87(417): 25–37.

Matsueda, Ross L., and Karen Heimer. 1987. "Race, Family Structure and Delinquency: A Test of Differential Association and Control Theories." *American Sociological Review* 52(6): 826–40.

McLanahan, Sara S. 1985. "Family Structure and the Reproduction of Poverty." *American Journal of Sociology* 90(4): 873–901.

———. 2002. "Life Without Father: What Happens to Children? *Context* 1(1): 35–44.

McLanahan, Sara S., and Karen Booth. 1989. "Mother-Only Families: Problems, Prospects, and Politics." *Journal of Marriage and the Family* 51(3): 557–80.

McLanahan, Sara S., and Larry L. Bumpass. 1988. "Intergenerational Consequences of Family Disruption." *American Journal of Sociology* 94(1): 130–52.

McLanahan, Sara S., and Gary Sandefur. 1994. *Growing Up with a Single Parent: What Hurts, What Helps?* Cambridge, Mass.: Harvard University Press.

Morrison, Donna R., and Andrew J. Cherlin. 1995. "The Divorce Process and Young Children's Well-Being: A Prospective Analysis." *Journal of Marriage and the Family* 57(3): 800–12.

Nelson, Sandi, Rebecca L. Clark, and Gregory Acs. 2001. "Beyond the Two-parent Family: How Teenagers Fare in Cohabiting Couple and Blended Families." *Assessing the New Federalism,* Policy Brief B-31. Washington, D.C.: Urban Institute Press.

Ni Bhrolchain, Maire, Roma Chappell, Ian Diamond, and C. Jameson. 2000. "Parental Divorce and Outcomes for Children: Evidence and Interpretation." *European Sociological Review* 16(1): 67–91.

Nock, Steven. 1988. "The Family and Hierarchy." *Journal of Marriage and the Family* 50(4): 957–66.

———. 1995. "A Comparison of Marriages and Cohabiting Relationships." *Journal of Family Issues* 16(1): 53–76.

Osborne, Cynthia, Sara McLanahan, and Jeanne Brooks-Gunn. 2003. "Is There An Advantage to Being Born to Married Versus Cohabiting Parents? Differences In Child Behavior." Center for Research on Child Wellbeing Working Paper #03-09-FF, Princeton University.

Page, Marianne E., and Ann H. Stevens. 2004. "Will You Miss Me When I Am Gone? The Economic Consequences of Absent Parents." *Journal of Human Resources* 39(1): 80–107.

Painter, Gary, and David I. Levine. 1999. "Daddies, Dedication, and Dollars: What About Family Structure Matters for Youth?" Unpublished paper. Institute for Industrial Relations, Paper No. 73.

———. 2000. "Family Structure and Youths' Outcomes. Which Correlations are Causal?" *Journal of Human Resources* 35(3): 524–49.

Peterson, James L. and Nicholas Zill. 1986. "Marital Disruption, Parent-Child Relationships, and Behavioral Problems in Children." *Journal of Marriage and the Family* 48(2): 295–307.

Pong, Suet-Ling, Jaap Dronkers, and Gillian Hampden-Thompson. 2002. "Family Policies and Academic Achievement by Young Children in Single-Parent Families: An International Comparison." Unpublished paper. Population Research Institute, The Pennsylvania State University.

Powell, Mary Ann, and Toby L. Parcel. 1997. "Effects of Family Structure on the Earnings Attainment Process: Differences by Gender." *Journal of Marriage and the Family* 59(2): 419–33.

Rogers, Bryan, and Jan Pryor. 1998. *Divorce and Separation: The Outcomes for Children.* York, U.K.: Joseph Rowntree Foundation.

Sandefur, Gary D., Sara McLanahan, and Roger A. Wojtkiewicz. 1992. "The Effects of Parental Marital Status During Adolescence on High School Graduation." *Social Forces* 71(1): 103–121.

Sandefur, Gary D., and Thomas Wells. 1997. "Using Siblings to Investigate the Effects of Family Structure on Educational Attainment." Unpublished paper. University of Wisconsin.

Seltzer, Judith. 1991. "Relationships between Fathers and Children Who Live Apart: The Father's Role After Separation." *Journal of Marriage and the Family* 53(1): 79–101.

Sigle-Rushton, Wendy, and Sara S. McLanahan. 2002. "The Living Arrangements of New, Unmarried Mothers." *Demography* 39(3): 415–33.

Simons, Ronald L., Kuei-Hsiu Lin, Leslie C. Gordon, Rand D. Conger, and Frederick O. Lorenz. 1999. "Explaining the Higher Incidence of Adjustment Problems Among Children of Divorce Compared with Those in Two-Parent Families." *Journal of Marriage and the Family* 61(4): 1020–33.

Smith, Thomas E. 1990. "Parental Separation and the Academic Self-Concepts of Adolescents: An Effort to Solve the Puzzle of Separation Effects." *Journal of Marriage and the Family* 52(1): 107–18.

Stanley, Scott M., S.L. Blumberg, and Howard J. Markman. 1999. "Helping Couples Fight for Their Marriages: The PREP Approach." In *Handbook of Preventive Approaches in Couples' Therapy*, edited by R. Berger and M.T. Hannah. New York: Brunner/Mazel.

Thomson, Elizabeth, Thomas L. Hanson, and Sara S. McLanahan. 1994. "Family Structure and Child Well-Being: Economic Resources vs. Parental Behaviors." *Social Forces* 73(1): 221–42.

Thomson, Elizabeth, Sara S. McLanahan, and Roberta B. Curtin. 1992. "Family Structure and Parental Socialization." *Journal of Marriage and the Family* 54(2): 368–78.

Tucker, Joan S., Howard S. Friedman, Joseph E. Schwartz, Michael H. Criqui, Carol Tomlinson-Keasey, Deborah L. Wingard, and Leslie R. Martin. 1997. "Parental Divorce: Effects on Individual Behavior and Longevity." *Journal of Personality and Social Psychology* 73(2): 381–91.

Ventura, Stephanie J., and Christine A. Bachrach. 2000. "Nonmarital Childbearing in the United States, 1940–99." *National Vital Statistics Reports* 48(16). Hyattsville, Md.: National Center for Health Statistics.

Webster, Pamela S., Terri L. Orbuch, and James House. 1995. "Effects of Childhood Family Background on Adult Marital Quality and Perceived Stability" *American Journal of Sociology* 101(2): 404–32.

Wojtkiewicz, Roger A. 1993. "Simplicity and Complexity in the Effects of Parental Structure on High School Graduation." *Demography* 30(4): 701–17.

Wolchik, Sharlene A., Irwin N. Sandler, Roger E. Millsap, Brett A.

Plummer, Shannon M. Greene, Edward R. Anderson, Spring R. Dawson-McClure, Kathleen Hipke, and Rachel A. Haine. 2002. "Six Year Follow-up of Preventive Interventions for Children of Divorce." *JAMA* 288(15): 1874–81.

Wolfinger, Nicholas H. 1999. "Trends in the Intergenerational Transmission of Divorce." *Demography* 36(3): 415–20.

———. 2003. "Parental Divorce and Offspring Marriage: Early or Late." *Social Forces* 82(1): 337–354.

Wu, Lawrence L. 1996. "Effects of Family Structure and Income on the Risks of a Premarital Birth." *American Sociological Review* 61(3): 386–406.

Wu, Lawrence L., and Brian C. Martinson. 1993. "Family Structure and the Risk of a Premarital Birth." *American Sociological Review* 58(2): 210–32.

Yeung, Jean W., Greg J. Duncan, and Martha Hill. 1995. "A Sibling-Based Analysis of the Effects of Family Structure on Children's Achievement." Paper presented at the 1995 Meeting of the Population Association of America, San Francisco (April 6–8).

PART II

Commentary on the Family

CHAPTER SIX

Fatherlessness in Non-Intact Families and Gender Inequality in Intact Families: Two Sides of the Same Coin?

Janet C. Gornick

THIS CHAPTER raises three interrelated questions about contemporary American families that should be integrated into research agendas on single parenting. The first concerns the link between single parenting and fatherlessness. The second relates to gender divisions of labor within contemporary American marriages. The third concerns the possible effect of gender inequality in intact families on the prevalence of female-headed, single-parent families. These questions are posed in relation to the United States, but they could be asked with respect to all industrialized countries with similar patterns and trends in family formation.

SOLO PARENTING AND FATHERLESSNESS IN THE UNITED STATES

Why is it that in the United States, in practice, there is such a tight link between single parenting and fatherlessness? Why is it that when biological parents split up—whenever it is during a child's lifecycle—that the great majority of children go with their mothers? This fact is evident among never-married parents, and it is also evident among separated and divorced parents.

Among researchers and the public alike, the fact that most children of separated, divorced, and never-married parents live with their mothers is taken as so inevitable, so immutable—and perhaps so preferable—that we virtually never ask why. Yet it is clear that our concerns about single parenthood and about fatherlessness are, in fact, distinct (see chapters 2, 3, and 5).

On the one hand, we are concerned with single parenthood, largely because having an absent parent places children at risk. The problematic consequences, and the transmission mechanisms underlying those consequences, have been especially well clarified (see chapter 5). On the other hand, we are also concerned with fatherlessness. Separate from the fact that living with a single parent places children at risk is that residing with a single mother—that is, being fatherless—places children at even more risk, certainly economically. Why? Because women's earnings are substantially less than men's. And why is that? A major reason is that, across all family structures, women (on average) are the primary caregivers of children. An extensive body of empirical research establishes that much gender inequality in the labor market is explained by women's and men's differential engagement in caregiving.

We can play this idea out further, by hypothesizing: if we lived in a world in which the rate of single parenting remained the same as it is today, but single parents were 50 percent fathers, it seems likely that single parenting would be considerably less problematic; it would surely be less economically hazardous for children, at least in the short term. And, political scientists would argue, institutional supports for single parents would likely be greater, and stigma less, both further reducing the consequent risks.

To reiterate: is it possible that, if single parenting cannot be reduced, or will not be reduced, that we might aim to decouple single parenting and fatherlessness? Why might we aim to do that? Why not? And, if achieved, what would be the consequences?

CONTEMPORARY MARRIAGE PATTERNS

A second question to raise extends the first: Are there characteristics of contemporary American marriages that might be implicated in the tight link between single parenting and fatherlessness?

I recently reviewed the literature on gender inequality within marriages, in particular in marriages where there are children (Gornick and Meyers 2003). Note that I refer here to inequality and not inequity; I am addressing gendered patterns of difference and leaving aside questions of fairness. Here is a summary of what I found:

As of 2000, in the United States, divisions of labor within marriage remain deeply gendered. When married couples have children, most mothers reduce their level of paid work—whether through temporary leaves, intermittent employment, and/or part-time employment—and their hourly wages and annual earnings fall. Most fathers increase their level of paid work and their hourly wages rise. Married mothers, employed or not, spend substantially more time than their husbands in caregiving, especially during the infant and toddler years, but also throughout the child's life. Furthermore, as much research establishes, in most intact families with children, mothers are the primary managers of the daily organization of child caregiving. Their greater time commitment is often dwarfed by their greater psychological engagement.

In short, while total specialization is increasingly rare, partial specialization is very much the norm in contemporary American marriages. In 2000, married mothers work for pay, on average, thirteen to twenty-four fewer hours per week than married fathers. According to data from the 2000 Current Population Survey (CPS), that is true with respect to children of all ages—and across the income spectrum (see table 6.1). Upper-income couples have no monopoly on gendered divisions of labor.

Why do married mothers continue to specialize, albeit partially, in caregiving, and married fathers continue to specialize in paid work? In fact, there is little consensus on this, and not surprisingly most analyses are embedded in ideology. Many feminists point to socially constructed and highly constraining gender systems. Many liberals highlight the structure of the labor market, combined with social policies that create incentives for partial specialization—for example, joint income taxation, weak limits on weekly work hours, inadequate child care, and the absence of paid family leave. Economists typically point to the economic benefits of specialization for the family, generally sidestepping why it is, or should be, gendered. And many conservatives—a recent high-profile example is James Q. Wilson in his book *The Marriage Problem* (2002)—emphasize biological determinism or the processes and consequences of evolutionary psychology, or both.

We really do not know, in fact, why so much gendered specialization remains. We do not know how much is due to unconstrained differences in women's and men's preferences, and how much is due to institutional and social barriers. Nor do we know how much, nor how quickly, gender inequality within marriage might erode in the future.

What we do know is that we live in a world in which partial specialization is consistent with social expectations and, to a large degree, with prevailing notions of what is both natural and, in the eyes of many, ideal.

Table 6.1   Average Weekly Hours in Paid Work, Two-Parent Families, 2000

Families	Mothers	Fathers	Total	Difference
	All Two-Parent Families			
With youngest child age zero to two	24	44	68	20
With youngest child age three to five	24	44	68	20
With youngest child age six to twelve	28	44	72	16
With youngest child age thirteen to seventeen	31	44	75	13
	Low-Income Families (Bottom Quartile)			
With youngest child age zero to two	16	40	56	24
With youngest child age three to five	19	39	58	20
With youngest child age six to twelve	21	38	59	17
With youngest child age thirteen to seventeen	22	35	57	13
	High-Income Families (Top Quartile)			
With youngest child age zero to two	27	47	74	20
With youngest child age three to five	27	47	74	20
With youngest child age six to twelve	30	47	77	17
With youngest child age thirteen to seventeen	34	48	82	14

Source: Results based on author's calculations, using the Current Population Survey (CPS).
Notes: Data refer to parents aged twenty-five to fifty. Hours refer to "usual hours worked per week," exclusive of commuting time and lunch breaks. Average hours include persons spending zero hours in market work.

The most casual look at popular culture, political discourse, and even a considerable amount of academic research will reveal that, in the United States today, it is considered natural that mothers of newborns withdraw from paid work for a year while fathers stay home less than a week; it is considered natural that mothers work part-time during their children's early years if not until they leave home, while fathers are expected to work full-time and full-year throughout their children's entire lives; it is considered natural that mothers know the names of their daughters' friends, their sons' shoe sizes, and the pediatrician's phone number, while good fathers in intact homes are, for the most part, not expected to know any of these.

And there is a corollary. What is considered extremely unnatural is for any mother to allow herself to be separated from her biological children.

Conservatives and liberals alike, men and women, will say of a divorcing mother who does not seek custody, "She what? She gave away her children?" A mother who voluntarily relinquishes custody of her biological children is, for the most part, viewed as an atrocity. Not surprisingly, a recent study concluded that in contested cases, 70 percent of mothers seek sole custody, compared to 15 percent of fathers (Braver 1998). Given the way that marital divisions of labor are arranged in the United States today, it seems overdetermined that most children of separated and divorced parents will live without their fathers, and that many non-resident fathers will recede from their children's lives.

To reiterate: To what extent are widely accepted social norms about gendered divisions of labor in intact families undermining our efforts to strengthen fathering in non-intact families? Is it possible that we as a society are working at cross purposes, revering the supremacy of motherhood in intact families, while mourning the weakness of fatherhood in non-intact families?

GENDER CONFLICT

A third question arises from the second: Is gender inequality in intact families, combined with unsupportive social policy, causing some share of women—and perhaps men—to opt out of marital fertility (see chapter 2)?

The Australian demographer Peter McDonald provides an excellent framework for considering the relationship between gender conflict and changing family forms. His core concern is low fertility, driven by both rising childlessness and shrinking family size, especially in wealthy countries. With the exception of the United States and—for the most part—Australia, France, Ireland, New Zealand, and the Nordic countries, many industrialized countries now have total fertility rates that are substantially below replacement level. In some countries, the magnitude of the ongoing fertility decline is extreme. McDonald points, for example, to the Italian case: if 1995 fertility and longevity are projected forward 100 years, Italy's population size will drop to 14 percent of its current level (McDonald 2000a).

In contrast to McDonald's emphasis—on low fertility and, by extension, low marital fertility—the concern at the heart of this volume is different; it is with high out-of-wedlock fertility and/or family formation. But the determinants surely overlap. At the very least, low marital fertility directly drives up the ratio of nonmarital to marital fertility. Furthermore, to the extent that the factors that suppress fertility within marriage also suppress marriage, there will be substantial overlap in causality.

McDonald's thesis is as follows: "Very low fertility in advanced countries today is the outcome of a conflict or inconsistency between high gender equity in individual-oriented institutions and sustained gender inequity in family-oriented institutions. The implication is that higher levels of gender equity in family institutions are necessary to avoid very low fertility" (McDonald 2000b, 427).

McDonald's claim, then, is that in countries where women's individual opportunities are limited, meaning opportunities for education and employment, there is little impetus for them to resist high marital fertility. In contrast, in countries where women have ample opportunities in these individual-oriented institutions but where conventional divisions of labor in the home persist, or social policy supports for maternal employment are weak, many women will limit their childbearing or opt out of parenthood altogether. And some men will as well to the extent that they wish to avoid struggles over family roles.

McDonald finds historical evidence for this perspective. In a number of countries, in "the old days"—the days of the family wage—women's opportunities outside the home were limited, providing incentives for most women to marry and bear children within their marriages. When their educational and economic opportunities opened up, but their families did not adjust accordingly, many women opted out of marriage, or at least out of childbearing. McDonald argues that the mismatch between individual and family-based opportunities underlies the long fertility transition underway in many economically developed countries.

Contemporary cross-national variation provides additional compelling evidence. McDonald reports that in countries where women's educational and labor market opportunities remain limited—generally, poorer countries—fertility typically remains at or above replacement. In contrast, in countries where women's public opportunities have expanded and where family behavior and family policy most support women's education and employment—notably, the Nordic countries—fertility has not plummeted. Finally, and somewhat paradoxically, in countries with the most conservative family expectations—in Italy and Japan, for example—fertility has dropped the most drastically. McDonald's interpretation is persuasive. On reflection, the plunging fertility in these conservative countries should not surprise us: any rational Italian or Japanese woman with her eye on a future career (now a realistic option) would do well to forgo childbearing, whether she is single or coupled.

We can extend the McDonald story of "gender opportunity mismatch" to an analysis of outcomes in the United States and the other English-speaking countries, including the United Kingdom, which has a higher percentage of out-of-wedlock births than the United States (see chapter 3). In these countries, we see widespread opportunities for women in education and in paid work, albeit side-by-side with unsupportive family environments. Family environments are unsupportive not because of especially conservative ideologies but because of dramatically lacking social policy. The English-speaking welfare states provide extremely little support for employed mothers, compared to the rest of the industrialized world, and public child care and paid family leave are especially meager (see Gornick, Meyers, and Ross 1997; and Gornick and Meyers 2003). And the family formation outcomes? Unlike Italy and Japan, the English-speaking countries have not seen a massive plummeting of aggregate fertility, but like Italy and Japan, they have experienced a decline in marital fertility.

So, in closing, is gender inequality in intact families pushing some of those who choose not to marry and have children to have those children outside of marriage instead? In my view, we would do well to take a hard look at both gender inequality in intact American families and at U.S. social policy, and consider the ways in which each may spill over onto single parenting and fatherlessness.

REFERENCES

Braver, Sanford. 1998. *Divorced Dads: Shattering the Myths.* New York: Penguin Putnam.

Gornick, Janet C., and Marcia K. Meyers. 2003. *FamiliesThat Work: Policies for Reconciling Parenthood and Employment.* New York: Russell Sage Foundation.

Gornick, Janet C., Marcia K. Meyers, and Katherin E. Ross. 1997. "Supporting the Employment of Mothers: Policy Variation Across Fourteen Welfare States." *Journal of European Social Policy* 7(1): 45–70.

McDonald, Peter. 2000a. "Gender Equity, Social Institutions and the Future of Fertility," *Journal of Population Research* 17(1): 1–16.

————. 2000b. "Gender Equity in Theories of Fertility Transition," *Population Development Review* 26(3): 427–439.

Wilson, James Q. 2002. *The Marriage Problem: How Culture Has Weakened Our Families.* New York: HarperCollins.

CHAPTER SEVEN

The Developmentalist Perspective: A Missing Voice

P. Lindsay Chase-Lansdale

THE VOICE OF developmental psychology—the people, the humans, the families, the children, and a focus on relationships from an emotional perspective—is critical in this debate. Most people want partners, they want spouses; they are seeking love and connectedness, which are essential for healthy functioning. Most people do not wish to get divorced or to be single parents. What do people think about relationships? How do they form them? What are their expectations for marriage? How do they behave within marriages? What are the consequences of their behavior? The answers to these questions cannot be completely covered by demographic or economic approaches.

For example, a key point is that conflict between genders is occurring in the United States (see chapter 2). Ellwood and Jencks argue that women are "no longer willing to put up with the way men treat them." Their focus on gender needs more exploration. Psychological data from family process studies can shed some light on these issues. A wealth of observational research on marital interaction, using videotapes of couples' problem solving in the laboratory, reveals that a prominent pattern of problematic marital interaction is called "demand/withdraw," in which wives start an interaction sequence with criticism and negative emotions, and husbands often withdraw and avoid the conflict (Bradbury, Fincham, and Beach 2000). In these distressed marriages, men typically seek to escape marital conflict because it causes physiological arousal and distress, while women are seeking change in the relationship, but requesting it in aversive, difficult ways. Marriages improve when husbands are able to remain open to their wives' critiques and stay even-keeled, and wives, in turn, begin their discussions in a less confrontational manner (Carrere and Gottman 1999).

Marital conflict that involves contempt, criticism, and stonewalling is likely to lead to divorce. But anger and disagreements, especially when combined with humor, friendship, love, and connectedness, are not risk factors for marital dissolution (Carrere and Gottman 1999; Fincham 2003). Marital discord, especially when it is acrimonious and hostile, is detrimental to children. When children witness marital conflict, they experience physiological arousal, fearfulness, and a general disequilibrium that interferes with their ability to interpret social cues and internal emotions (Friedman and Chase-Lansdale 2002). Marital conflict is also linked with problematic parenting, which is more likely to be harsh or abusive at times, inconsistent, or disengaged. Children who experience marital conflict and difficult parenting have problems with their own self-regulation and are likely to develop psychological problems. Moreover, they do not have effective models of how to deal with conflict. How couples develop constructive ways of resolving conflict in addition to forging bonds of friendship, respect, and intimacy is what matters in terms of promoting healthy relationships and healthy children.

I therefore commend the initiative coming from the U.S. Department of Health and Human Services to try to work with couples along these lines, specifically marriage strengthening programs (see chapter 9). This new policy initiative could be a factor in promoting healthy marriages in the United States, without stigmatizing or withdrawing support from other family forms (Chase-Lansdale 1994). A focus on low-income couples is important, because these couples face many economic and structural stressors, all of which can contribute to marital distress, and because most of the existing interventions target middle-income families.

I would also like to argue that a focus on healthy relationships needs to begin earlier. And here, I mean with adolescents and college students, especially those in community colleges—the education level of individuals who are more likely to experience divorce (see chapter 2). For example, pathbreaking work is occurring that studies the origins of romantic relationships among adolescents, as well as the quality of those relationships and their role in adolescent adjustment (Collins 2003). Similarly, the little work being done with college students finds a hunger and thirst for learning more about relationships, marriage, and conflict. Young people of this age need a combination of information, expectations, and exposure to modeling of long-term successful relationships.

I must also mention domestic violence and how serious a force it may be, another dimension too often absent in policy discussions about marriage. For example, in the "Three-City Study of Children, Families, and Welfare" I am conducting with a number of colleagues, we have used both survey and ethnographic methods regarding domestic violence in relationships (Chase-Lansdale 2002; Winston et al. 1999). In our survey interviews of about 2,400 mothers in Boston, Chicago, and San Antonio, all of whom are in low-income families in low-income neighborhoods, we asked about moderate violence (being slapped) as well as extreme violence (being choked, beaten, threatened with a weapon), and mothers reported on these experiences in the past twelve months. Fully, 30 percent reported that they had experienced some domestic violence in the prior year, a high rate (Votruba-Drzal, Lohman, and Chase-Lansdale 2003). Similarly, the ethnography of approximately 256 families, followed extensively once or twice a month for about eighteen months, shows high levels of domestic abuse (Cherlin, Burton, Hurt, and Purvin 2003). Clearly, this is an important phenomenon that needs to be addressed in studies and policy decisions.

This leads to my final point. Absent in the debates on marriage is a focus on the mental health of adults and children. Adults with mental health problems—anxiety, depression, or antisocial behavior—have extraordinary difficulties in developing and maintaining healthy friendships, partnerships, and marriages (Hahlweg 2004). We know that a variety of mental health problems have increased among adolescents and young adults in the past several decades (Rutter 2004). Moreover, mental health problems are not evenly distributed across all income levels, and are overrepresented among families with low socioeconomic status (Gallo and Matthews 2003). This may be one explanation for why Ellwood and Jencks find an increase in divorce and single parenthood in the group of women with eleven to fifteen years of education.

What can be done? There are currently many intervention efforts to address mental health issues and relationship problems. But many mental health problems can be treated more effectively if the intervention occurs when the individual is young. We have experienced significant advances in identifying these problems in young children (Shonkoff and Phillips 2000). While mental health problems, along with other human characteristics, have a strong genetic component, we have key scientific evidence that genetic predispositions toward depression, aggression, and anxiety do not actually express themselves unless children experience certain environmental conditions, namely, difficult family systems such as a lack of responsiveness or heightened harshness and unpredictability (Chase-Lansdale and Votruba-Drzal 2004; Friedman and Chase-Lansdale 2002).

I end with a plea to focus even earlier on young children. Ellwood and Jencks have made key arguments that perhaps early pregnancy and parenthood give young people another way to feel effective and in control. I would counter that we have strong evidence that a true sense of mastery and ability to make a difference develops at a very young age. In the first year of life and in the early preschool years, children learn at home what it is like to be cherished and what trust feels like. Infants and toddlers who experience sensitive, responsive, and appropriate parenting develop internal working models of themselves as loved and masterful. They explore the environment better, they are curious and engaged, and they learn to regulate their emotions and to deal with conflict appropriately. They then go on to apply this to peer relations in childhood and to romantic relationships in adolescence. These are key dimensions for successful adult relationships as well (Sroufe 2002; Waters, Hamilton, and Weinfield 2000).

REFERENCES

Bradbury, Thomas N., Frank D. Fincham, and Steven R.H. Beach. 2000. "Research on the Nature and Determinants of Marital Satisfaction: A Decade in Review." *Journal of Marriage and the Family* 62(4): 964–80.

Carrere, Sybil, and John M. Gottman. 1999. "Predicting the Future of Marriages." In *Coping with Divorce, Single Parenting, and Remarriage*, edited by E.M. Hetherington. Mahwah, N.J.: Erlbaum.

Chase-Lansdale, P. Lindsay. 1994. "Policies for Stepfamilies: Crosswalking Private and Public Domains. In *Stepparent Families with Children: Who Benefits and Who Does Not?* edited by A. Booth and J. Dunn. Mahwah, N.J.: Erlbaum.

———. 2002. Co Principal Investigator of *Welfare, Children, and Families: A Three-City Study*. Congressional Briefing, Consortium of Social Science Associations, Washington, D.C. (May 17).

Chase-Lansdale, P. Lindsay, and Elizabeth Votruba Drzal. 2004. "Human Development and the Potential for Change from the Perspective of Multiple Disciplines: What Have We Learned?" In *Human Development Across Lives and Generations: The Potential for Change*, edited by P. Lindsay Chase Lansdale, Kathleen Kiernan, and Ruth J. Friedman. New York: Cambridge University Press.

Cherlin, Andrew J., Linda M. Burton, Tera Hurt, and Diane Purvin. 2003. "Domestic Abuse and Patterns of Marriage and Cohabitation: Evidence from a Multi-method Study." Paper presented at the conference on "Marriage and Family Formation among Low-Income Couples: What Do We Know from Research?" National Poverty Center, Washington, D.C. (September 4–5).

Collins, W. Andrew. 2003. "More than Myth: The Developmental Significance of Romantic Relationships During Adolescence." *Journal of Research on Adolescence* 13(1): 1–24.

Fincham, Frank D. 2003. "Marital Conflict: Correlates, Structure, and Context." *Current Directions in Psychological Science* 12(1): 23–27.

Friedman, Ruth J., and P. Lindsay Chase-Lansdale. 2002. "Chronic Adversities." In *Child and Adolescent Psychiatry, Fourth Edition,* edited by Michael Rutter, and Eric Taylor. London: Blackwell Publishing.

Gallo, Linda C., and Karen A. Matthews. 2003. "Understanding the Association Between Socioeconomic Status and Physical Health: Do Negative Emotions Play a Role?" *Psychological Bulletin,* 129(1): 10–51.

Hahlweg, Kurt. 2004. "Strengthening Partnerships and Families." In *Human Development Across Lives and Generations: The Potential for Change,* edited by P. Lindsay Chase-Lansdale, Kathleen Kiernan, and Ruth J. Friedman. New York: Cambridge University Press.

Rutter, Michael. 2004. "Intergenerational Continuities and Discontinuities in Psychological Problems." In *Human Development Across Lives and Generations: The Potential for Change,* edited by P. Lindsay Chase-Lansdale, Kathleen Kiernan, and Ruth J. Friedman. New York: Cambridge University Press.

Shonkoff, Jack P., and Deborah A. Phillips, eds. 2000. *From Neurons to Neighborhoods: The Science of Early Childhood Development.* Washington, D.C.: National Academy Press.

Sroufe, L. Alan. 2002. "From Infant Attachment to Promotion of Adolescent Autonomy: Prospective, Longitudinal Data on the Role of Parents in Development." In *Parenting and the Child's World: Influences on Academic, Intellectual, and Social-Emotional Development,* edited by J. Borkowski, Sharon Ramey, and Marie Bristol-Power. Hillsdale, N.J.: Erlbaum.

Votruba-Drzal, Elizabeth, Brenda J. Lohman, and P. Lindsay Chase-Lansdale. 2003. "Violence in Intimate Relationships as Women Transition from Welfare to Work." Manuscript under review.

Waters, Everett, Claire E. Hamilton, and Nancy S. Weinfield. 2000. "The Stability of Attachment Security from Infancy to Adolescence and Early Adulthood: General Introduction." *Child Development* 71(3): 678–83.

Winston, Pamela, Ronald J. Angel, Linda M. Burton, P. Lindsay Chase-Lansdale, Andrew J. Cherlin, Robert A. Moffitt, and William Julius Wilson. 1999. *Welfare, Children, and Families: A Three-City Study. Overview and Design Report.* Baltimore, Md.: Johns Hopkins University. Available at: http://www.jhu.edu/~welfare (accessed May 20, 2004).

CHAPTER EIGHT

Demography, Public Policy, and "Problem" Families

Douglas A. Wolf

WE HAVE DISCUSSED two aspects of family change, namely the growth in nonmarital unions and the phenomenon of children being raised by just one, often an unmarried, parent. There have been, however, other substantial changes in family patterns in recent decades, and some of them have implications for the issues raised in these other chapters.

GROWTH IN CHILDLESSNESS

Attention has been focused on children growing up in single-parent families and the problems associated with a group being born in—or in some cases raised in—a particular set of circumstances. But it is also instructive to consider another set of children, namely those that are increasingly not being born at all.

Available data on the fertility of women forty- to forty-four-years-old permit trend analysis over a sixty-year period (see figure 8.1). These data provide a reasonably accurate source for trends in completed fertility, given that women in this age group will have very few additional children. There is a clear change in trends in 1975: women aged forty to forty-four in that year lived their peak childbearing years—twenty to twenty-four years old—during the peak years of the baby boom—1955 to 1959 (NCHS 1983). Accordingly, they are the cohort of women

Figure 8.1   Indicators of Completed Fertility, Women Age Forty to
Forty-Four

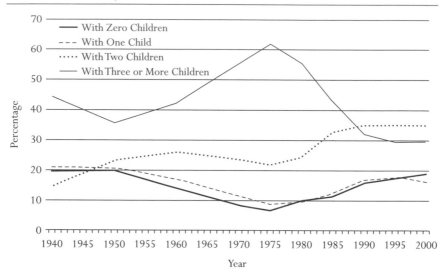

Source: Author's compilation of Census and Current Population Survey data.

among whom the percentage with large families (three or more children) was greatest—nearly two-thirds of that cohort—while the percent remaining childless reached a sixty-year low of only 7 percent. Since 1975, the percentages of women ending up with two, one, or no children have generally grown, while the percentage with three or more has fallen. Being the mother of two children has become the norm, and having fewer than two has become more common than having more (see figure 8.1).

Although the rise in childlessness has not gone unnoticed, less attention has been paid to racial and ethnic differences in childlessness. With respect to out-of-wedlock childbearing, one of our principal themes, there has been a convergence of racial patterns. For example, in 1970, 37.6 percent of births to black women were to unmarried black women, while only 5.7 percent of births among whites were to unmarried women, a 6.6-to-1 ratio (calculations based on data found in Child Trends 2003, table 1). By 2002 this ratio had fallen to 2.4. For Hispanic women the available data cover fewer years, and the relative prevalence of out-of-wedlock births is less dramatic, but the same pattern of convergence holds: in 1980 the ratio for Hispanic relative to white women was 2.1, a ratio that fell to 1.5 by 2002.

In marked contrast, there has been a divergence across racial and ethnic

Figure 8.2   Childless Families

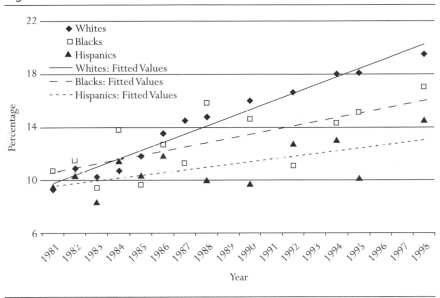

Source: U.S. Census Bureau (1984–2000).

groups in the prevalence of childlessness. Figure 8.2 illustrates this divergence, showing (with symbols) the data on childlessness by race for the 1981 to 1998 period (and using the same measure of childlessness as used in figure 8.1). Also shown are fitted trend lines for each group of women. Remarkably, the average annual increase in childlessness among white women is 0.62 percentage points, and for black 0.32, and for Hispanic 0.21. As the figure makes clear, the three groups exhibit roughly equal levels of childlessness when this series begins, but diverge steadily thereafter.

Particularly noteworthy is the overall growth of childlessness. Childless women have become slightly more prevalent than women with one child in the past few years. Childbearing is obviously important to society at large, for many reasons, not the least of which is the anticipated future contributions of today's children towards maintaining our pay-as-you-go retirement income system, as well as their providing care and assistance to their elderly parents. Indeed, from a purely fiscal standpoint it has been estimated that the average newborn child conveys substantial economic benefits to society. A recent National Academy of Sciences (NAS) study of the fiscal impacts of immigration (Smith and Edmonston 1997) employs an intergenerational accounting framework that generates estimates of the fiscal impacts—the dollar value to society—of a newborn child. These calculations take into account the expected fiscal impacts of the descendants that may follow a given newborn child. The estimates, which condition on the educational achievement of the parent, are striking, ranging from $92,000 for the child of a parent with less than a high school education to $245,000 for one with at least some college.

The problems associated with out-of-wedlock childbearing—and by implication the social costs attributable to that childbearing—should be viewed in the context of overall fertility behavior, including growing childlessness. It is widely acknowledged that the private costs of raising children are high, and some commentators suggest that there is a connection between those high costs and increasing childlessness (see Crittenden 2001). Yet the NAS findings and other results (Folbre 1994) suggest that substantial positive public benefits—positive externalities—to childbearing accompany these private costs. If so, then policies that "reward" childbearing or lower its costs—such as tax reductions, child allowances, or low-cost child care—may be warranted. Such policies already exist, of course, although many argue that further reductions in the cost of childbearing are needed (see England and Folbre 1999). The diverging racial patterns in childlessness illustrated in figure 8.2 complicate this policy discussion considerably. For example, a greater relative prevalence of childlessness among future cohorts of elderly white women implies racial differences in the extent to which disabled individuals will look to the state for sources of personal assistance. Alternatively, a policy intended to reward childbearing may convey a disproportionate share of those rewards to white women, raising equity concerns.

Policies that lower the private costs of raising a child may encourage both nonmarital and marital fertility. It therefore is important to be very clear about the goals of policy as well as the design of the tools to promote those goals. Is the goal to reduce or even eliminate teenage motherhood? Or, is it to delay the births that would otherwise come to teenage mothers? Is the goal to reduce out-of-wedlock childbirth more generally? Can we afford to forgo the potential social benefits associated with the birth of "average" children, including those born in modest circumstances? And, if the goal is to reduce the negative externalities associated with problematic childbearing, then—recognizing the obvious facts that many children born in arguably adverse circumstances, that is, to unmarried teenage women, are not problematic, while many children born in "ideal" circumstances nonetheless are—can we be at all optimistic about our ability to effectively target social policies to encourage the childbearing essential to the maintenance of the social, economic, and elder care systems, while discouraging "problematic" childbearing?

Figure 8.3   U.S. Trends in Fertility, Population Composition, and Household Size, 1890 to 1973

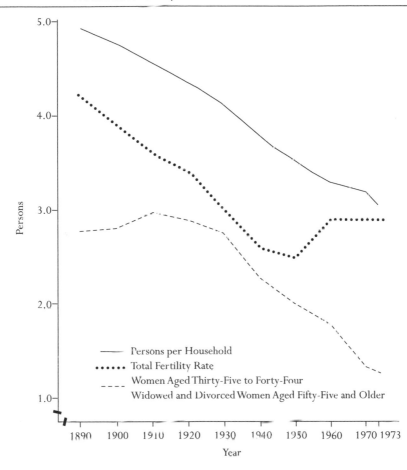

Source: Kobrin (1976, 135).

GROWTH IN SOLITARY LIVING

For many years demographers and other social scientists have been studying household size and structure, pointing out two mirror-image trends: a fall in the average size of households, and a rise in the percentage of persons living alone (see figure 8.3). One reason for smaller households is falling fertility, and overall fertility trends do track household size reasonably well, at least up to 1950 (see figure 8.3). But just as reduced fertility reduces the average size of households containing young children, it encourages smaller households—and solitary living—late in life, when older people are confronted with having comparatively few grown children with whom to live (see figure 8.3 for the average number of adult females relative to divorced or widowed women one generation older, a rough ratio of adult "daughters" to older "mothers").

The rise in solitary living among the older population has received particular attention. However, the phenomenon is not confined to those sixty-five or older: from 1960 to 1999, the percentage living alone among people aged twenty-five to forty-four rose from under 3 percent to over 12 percent, while for those aged forty-five to sixty-four it rose from 7.5 percent to over 13 percent (calculations based on data taken from the *Statistical Abstract of the United States*, various years). The growth in single-person households is widely interpreted as the result of rising incomes (Beresford and Rivlin 1966; Michael, Fuchs, and Scott 1980; McGarry and Schoeni 2000). That is, people have been willing to use some of their incomes to purchase what is interpreted as "privacy," or "autonomy" (Burch and Matthews 1987). Moreover, when people choose to live independently, they forgo some of the economies of scale available through shared living arrangements, and, possibly, some benefits from income pooling as well (Waehrer and Crystal 1995). Indeed, one study pointed out that downward trends in the prevalence of poverty among older women would have been more pronounced were it not for the growing propensity of such women to spend their rising incomes on independent living (Holden 1988).

These trends in living arrangements are relevant because they remind us of how strongly norms of individual autonomy and privacy are held. People will sacrifice a degree of economic well-being—even, in the extreme, cause themselves to be classified as "poor"—to achieve the autonomy and privacy that accompany independent living. Among the domains of behavior held by Americans to be largely a private matter, in which a great deal of autonomy should prevail, are marital relationships, domestic life, and childraising. All are, of course, subject to some degree of government regulation, but that regulatory apparatus leaves room for a great deal of heterogeneity in the conduct of private life.

Against that backdrop of strongly held norms of privacy and domestic autonomy, the current administration's marriage initiatives merit some critical scrutiny. The program's goals are unassailable: "[t]he healthy marriage initiative is about helping couples, who choose marriage for themselves, develop the skills and knowledge necessary to form and sustain healthy marriages" (Administration for Children and Families 2002, attachment A). States are encouraged to direct funds so as to promote the Healthy Marriage Initiative. Among the many specific programmatic suggestions for how those funds might be used are:

- training for program participants and clients in why marriage matters, what to expect in marriage, and the knowledge and skills to make a healthy marriage a reality;
- providing vouchers for registration and materials to program staff and participants who attend marriage education activities; and
- providing vouchers for mediation services or marriage education programs designed for those having serious marital problems, prior to separation or divorce.

These examples, and the other twenty-three on the list from which they were selected, share the virtue of appearing to be potentially helpful to some couples whose marriages might otherwise fail, while having little or no potential for doing any harm. The problem, however, lies in the inevitable tendency of government-sponsored healthy marriage training or mediation services to adopt or endorse a far narrower range of tools, techniques, or therapies than the very heterogeneous public-at-large is prepared to find acceptable. We must be wary of a narrow set of "government approved" marital-relationship styles. We should be wary of even subtly coercive requirements imposed on social-service clients to adopt such requirements.

I am grateful to Alison Louie for assistance with the data used in this chapter.

REFERENCES

Administration for Children and Families, U.S. Department of Health and Human Services, *Program Instructions* (OMB Approval #0980-0047), issued May 10, 2002. Available at: http://www.acf.hhs.gov/programs/cb/laws/pi/pi0205.pdf (accessed May 20, 2004).

Beresford, John, and Alice Rivlin. 1966. "Privacy, Poverty, and Old Age." *Demography* 3(1): 247–58.

Burch, Thomas K., and Beverly J. Matthews. 1987. "Household Formation in Developed Societies." *Population and Development Review* 13(3): 495–511.

Child Trends (Washington, D.C.). 2003. "Data Bank: Percentage of

Births to Unmarried Women." Available at: http://www.childtrends-databank.org/indicators/75UnmarriedBirths.cfm (accessed October 21, 2003).

Crittenden, Ann. 2001. *The Price of Motherhood*. New York: Henry Holt/Metropolitan Books.

England, Paula, and Nancy Folbre. 1999. "Who Should Pay For the Kids?" *Annals of the American Academy of Political and Social Sciences* 563(May): 194–207.

Folbre, Nancy. 1994. "Children as Public Goods." *American Economic Review* 84(2): 86–90.

Holden, Karen. 1988. "Poverty and Living Arrangements Among Older Women: Are Chances in Economic Well-Being Underestimated?" *Journal of Gerontology: Social Sciences* 43(1): S22–27.

Kobrin, Frances E. 1976. "The Fall in Household Size and the Rise of the Primary Individual in the United States." *Demography* 13(1): 127–38.

McGarry, Kathleen, and Robert F. Schoeni. 2000. "Social Security, Economic Growth, and the Rise in Elderly Widows' Independence in the Twentieth Century." *Demography* 37(2): 221–36.

Michael, Robert T., Victor R. Fuchs, and Sharon R. Scott. 1980. "Changes in the Propensity to Live Alone: 1950–1976." *Demography* 17(1): 39–56.

National Center for Health Statistics. 1983. "Advance Report of Final Natality Statistics, 1983." *Monthly Vital Statistics Report* 34(6): Supplement. Hyattsville, Md.: Public Health Service.

Smith, James P., and Barry Edmonston, eds. 1997. *The New Americans: Economic, Demographic, and Fiscal Effects of Immigration*. Washington, D.C.: National Academy Press.

U.S. Census Bureau. 1984–2000. "Fertility of American Women." Current Population Reports, Series P-20, Nos. 378, 387, 395, 401, 406, 421, 427, 436, 454, 470, 482, 499, and 526. Washington: U.S. Government Printing Office.

Waehrer, Keith, and Stephen Crystal. 1995. "The Impact of Coresidence on Economic Well-Being of Elderly Widows." *Journal of Gerontology: Social Sciences* 50B(4): S250–S258.

PART III

Policy Perspectives

CHAPTER NINE

Marriage, Family, and the Welfare of Children: A Call for Action

Wade F. Horn

No one has yet found a satisfactory substitute for a good mother and father. As the lawyers say, we can stipulate that. And if evidence is needed, we have that, too.

But children do not grow up only within the shelter of the family: the family functions in a social setting. Just as the health of the child affects the health of the family, the health of the family affects the health of society—and vice versa. The "vice versa"—the immense pressure for good or ill that society brings to bear—has a far more profound effect on the family and its members than the pressure any single family or individual can apply in return. Society is a living organism and the family is its nucleus: the one cannot survive without the other.

Society has a vital interest in the civic development and future productivity of the next generation. To sustain the culture and the values it upholds, society must protect the most vulnerable of its members, its children, by nurturing the family that nurtures them. In a nutshell, the survival of our society depends on the survival of the family. When the family is in peril, so are we.

Government is an instrument of society. Its most important function, its raison d'être, is to protect its citizens from both external and internal threats. Al Qaeda is an obvious example of an external threat, a clear and present danger to the safety of the state and its citizens. But there is another threat that bores from within and undermines our society more insidiously, and that is the breakdown of families and the consequent danger to our children. Its effects are not as shockingly immediate and unquestionable as al Qaeda's attacks on the World Trade Center and the Pentagon, but in the long run they could be as devastating.

Dramatic changes with dramatic consequences for both children and parents have taken place in the structure of the American family over the past thirty years. In 1970, less than 30 percent of all marriages ended in divorce, 13 percent of children lived in single-parent families, and only 11 percent of all births occurred outside marriage (Ventura and Bachrach 2000). Today, almost 50 percent of all marriages are expected to end in divorce, 28 percent of all children live in single-parent homes, and 33 percent of all births are to unmarried women (Ventura and Bachrach 2000). Although both the percentage of births to unmarried mothers and the divorce rate have leveled off in recent years, and teenage birth rates have been declining since 1991, the weakening of marriage is a long-term trend.

The decline of marriage and the rise of single parenthood have had a particularly baleful effect on the lives of poor families. The decreased propensity to marry has caused substantially higher child poverty rates. In 2001, 39 percent of children in single-parent households were living in poverty, compared with only 8 percent of children in married-parent families. Indeed, research has found that if the proportion of children living in single-parent families had remained constant since 1970, the child poverty rate would have been considerably lower than it was in 1998 (Thomas and Sawhill 2001).

I have spent my professional life moving between stints in government and stints as a practicing clinical child psychologist. For seven years, until I resigned to head the Administration for Children and Families, I directed the National Fatherhood Initiative, a nonprofit organization promoting responsible fatherhood. But whether I was working inside the government or outside the government, whether I was dealing with issues of welfare, fatherhood, or marriage, I always asked myself the same question: "Will the choices I make promote the well-being of children?" From that perspective, the right choice is always strategic and always based on the best available evidence of what works. Common sense and numerous empirical studies tell us that a healthy, stable family works better for children—and for their parents—than an unstable, abusive, or simply nonexistent one. A healthy family is the single most important asset we have for ensuring the well-being of our children.

The president shares that conviction. In this paper I will discuss several administration initiatives to support marriage and family and thereby improve the well-being of our children. Because a healthy marriage is so important to a healthy family, I will devote most of my efforts to the ways government can help support it.

SUCCESS STORY

In 1996 a historic change took place in our country's welfare policy. Congress passed and the president signed into law the Personal Responsibility and Work Opportunity Reconciliation Act (PRWORA). This sweeping welfare reform act shifted the emphasis from passive entitlement to independence and self-sufficiency. Despite predictions to the contrary, the evidence shows that the law has been a striking success.

Nationwide, welfare caseloads are less than half their levels of six years ago. According to the latest figures released by the Department of Health and Human Services, 7.3 million fewer Americans depend on welfare. From a peak of 14.4 million welfare recipients in March 1994, the number had declined by 65 percent in 2002. More important, poverty declined for seven straight years between 1994 and 2001. Although overall it increased slightly in 2002, the percentage of children living in poverty did not. These most recent trends support the position that welfare reform, not simply the economic expansion of the 1990s, played a key role in bringing about simultaneous reductions in welfare dependency and child poverty.

The movement of mothers from dependence on welfare to independence through work has surely been central to that decrease. Data from the Current Population Survey (Temporary Assistance for Needy Families Program 2002) reveal that earnings for the group most likely to receive welfare, low-income women heading families, increased significantly between 1996 and 2000, particularly for the two quintiles at the bottom of the income scale. In 1996 only 26 percent of all families in the bottom income quintile of female-headed families with children earned any money at all.[1] In 2000 almost half (48 percent) did. Where in 1996 the average annual earnings of female-headed households in the bottom quintile was $315, in 2000 it was $1,646 (both in constant 2000 dollars and averaged over all families in the quintile). For families in the second quintile, real annual earnings almost doubled, from an average of $6,304 in 1996 to $11,509 in 2000 (Temporary Assistance for Needy Families Program 2002).

Six years after the passage of PRWORA, the entire climate around welfare has changed. Secretary of Health and Human Services Tommy Thompson summed it up before the House Education and Workforce Committee in April 2002: welfare reform "has exceeded our most optimistic expectations."

LOOKING AHEAD

Despite these successes, much more remains to be done if we are to achieve the goals laid down by PRWORA. The welfare reform act of 1996 envisioned considerably more than simply moving families from welfare to work. We have made great progress toward that particular goal, but our success in reducing the incidence of out-of-wedlock pregnancies and encouraging the formation and maintenance of married, two-parent families has been much more modest. These concerns, which helped motivate policy makers to reform welfare in 1996, remain critical issues today. They lie behind the Bush administration's proposal to strengthen the Temporary Assistance to Needy Families (TANF) program by explicitly linking marriage to improving child well-being in reauthorizing legislation.

Families are greatly strengthened by stable employment, but promoting work alone will not overcome the impediments to healthy development that many children experience. We must support positive changes in family structure as well and, in the next phase of welfare, we must focus more explicitly on fostering healthy marriages and allocate more resources to promoting it.

A healthy marriage is not only an end in itself. It is also the most successful mechanism we have to support the healthy development of our children. The overwhelming weight of scientific research finds that children who grow up with two continuously married parents fare better, on average, than those raised in other family structures. These children are more likely to be physically healthy, to finish school, and to become economically self-sufficient adults; they are less likely to abuse drugs and alcohol, to get in trouble with the law, or to become parents when they are still adolescents (Amato 1991; Wallerstein, Lewis, and Blakeslee 2000). As marriage experts Barbara Dafoe Whitehead and David Popenoe note, "throughout the history of the world and in much of the world today, marriage is first and foremost an institution for bearing and raising children" (Whitehead and Popenoe 2001). If the enhancement of children's well-being is our goal, then helping couples form and sustain healthy marriages must be part of any child-centered public policy effort.

The administration's welfare reauthorization proposal directly links the receipt of financial aid with the efforts of participants to improve their employment prospects and to strengthen their roles as parents. It does this by requiring that families receiving welfare benefits be fully and constructively engaged in work and other meaningful activities. This requirement, often mentioned, but seldom completely explained in the Congressional debate and in the media, demands full participation in the program for forty hours each week, but only twenty-four of those hours need be spent working at a job for money. (Community service and on-the-job training also count as employment.) The sixteen remaining hours can be spent not only in activities to increase the employment prospects of welfare recipients, such as education, but also in structured activities aimed at improving family life and aiding child development. These activities could include parent-child participation in after-school activities, for example, or in Head Start. The hours could also be spent engaged in educational activities designed to enhance relationship skills for couples who have chosen marriage for themselves.

A LOOK AT THE EVIDENCE

Although many single parents and their children do well, the best available evidence shows that marriage can make a dramatic difference in the health, financial well-being, mortality, and happiness of adults, as well as in the achievement and well-being of children. For children, growing up in a household with two married parents is associated with better school performance, fewer emotional and behavioral problems, less substance abuse, less abuse or neglect, less criminal activity, less early sexual activity, and fewer out-of-wedlock births.

The research-based consensus is now clear on what common sense has long taught us: all else being equal, children in stable, healthy families with two married parents fare better, on average, than children who grow up in dysfunctional married households or with only one parent. Although it is uncertain what proportion of the better outcomes can be attributed to marriage and how much simply to an artifact of selection, the effects of good marriages on the well-being of children persist, even after controlling for levels of education, income, and other observed factors such as parent-child interaction. For example, Sara McLanahan and Gary Sandefur found that children who lived with two married parents through age sixteen had higher grades, higher college aspirations, and better attendance records than children who lived with one parent or whose family had broken up. These children also were half as likely to drop out of high school (McLanahan and Sandefur 1994). Robert A. Johnson and others found that children in two-parent families are less than half as likely to have emotional or behavioral problems as children in single-parent families (National Center for Health Statistics 1988). Also, they are about 33 percent less likely to use illegal drugs, alcohol, or tobacco (Johnson, Haffman, and Gerstain 1996). Children growing up in intact, married households also are 44 percent less likely to be physically abused than children living with single parents, 47 percent less likely to suffer physical neglect, and 43 percent less likely to suffer emotional neglect. Altogether they are 55 percent less likely to suffer some form of child abuse than children living with a single parent (Sedlak and Broadhurst 1996). Moreover, Cynthia Harper and Sara McLanahan observed that boys raised in two-parent families are, by their early thirties, about half as likely to commit a crime leading to incarceration. This comparison holds true even after controlling for race, mother's education, neighborhood quality, and cognitive ability (Harper and McLanahan 1998).

Finally, and perhaps most important, children growing up in a traditional married family can break the cycle of single-parenthood. According to Cherlin, Kiernan, and Chase-Lansdale, young women from married families are about 33 percent as likely to have children out of wedlock as are those from families headed by a single parent (Cherlin, Kiernan, and Chase-Lansdale 1995).[2]

WHAT'S SAUCE FOR THE GOOSE

What is good for children is good for their parents. Mortality rates for married men are two-thirds the rate for single men, and mortality rates for married women are one-third the rate for single women (Berkman and Breslow 1983; Litwac and Messeri 1989). Married people are less likely to suffer long-term chronic illnesses or disabilities than single people of the same age (Murphy, Glaser, and Grundy 1997). Married women are 30 percent more likely to rate their health excellent or good than single women of the same age.[3]

Married people also tend to be happier than their single counterparts. Ronald Kessler and others determined that married men and women are less than half as likely as their divorced counterparts to attempt suicide (Kessler, Borges, and Walters 1999; Smith, Mercy, and Conn 1988). Researcher Linda Waite found that 40 percent of married people say they are very happy, compared with less than 25 percent of unmarried.[4] Finally, a U.S. Department of Justice statistical analysis showed that married women are less likely to be victims of violent domestic abuse than divorced, separated, or never-married women (Rennison and Welchans 2000). It should go without saying, however, that just getting married does not in itself turn a violent and abusive partner into a loving one.

The association of marriage with positive social, educational, economic, and health outcomes for both adults and children has been demonstrated repeatedly in both relatively simple and more complex analytical studies. Across these studies, even after controlling for observable characteristics such as race, income, and education level of the mother, the striking differences between two-parent, continuously married households and single-parent families persist, and the advantages of growing up in a traditional household where both parents are married to each other, remain. These studies contribute to a body of evidence that supports the notion that marriage, in and of itself, has an independent effect on well-being that continues to appear, even after attempts to control for observable characteristics.

The evidence concerning the effect of unobservable characteristics of marriage and family structure on positive outcomes for children is more limited, although some studies conclude that the differences between growing up with one parent and growing up with two continuously married parents persist even after controlling for these circumstances.[5] A recent review of the literature finds that after controlling for observed and unobserved factors, a positive relationship between marital status and child well-being and paternal earnings often remain, consistent with causal effects of marriage (Ribar 2003).

In terms of selection, biased estimates of the effects of growing up with two married parents would be more problematic if the president and the department were concerned primarily with increasing the rates of marriage and not the *quality* of the unions taking place. In addition to a wide body of literature finding that growing up with two parents is associated with better outcomes than growing up with a single parent, a corresponding body of research has found that it matters not just that parents be married, but also that the quality of the marital relationship be good. For this reason, the government is interested not simply in promoting marriage per se, but promoting healthy, safe, and stable marital unions.

Of course, given the substantial potential for unobserved heterogeneity and the possibility of numerous causal paths, even the best empirical analyses of the effect of family structure on the lives of children cannot be entirely conclusive. Nevertheless, it is important to keep in mind that there has never been a study indicating that growing up in a single-parent household is, on average, associated with better outcomes for children when compared to growing up in a two-parent, continuously married household, nor that single adults are, on average, better off than their married counterparts.

Despite these caveats, it is important to remember that imperfect information should not be an impediment to policy action. Even if there are some elements of the effects of marriage that are due to unobserved characteristics, it is more important, from a policy standpoint, to consider the total effects of marriage on improving the well-being of children and adults, even if the direct effect is smaller. In this light, the totality of the evidence supports the notion that all things being equal, it is better for children and adults to develop in a stable, two-parent married household.

FROM "WHETHER" TO "HOW" (AND HOW NOT)

In my view, moving the public conversation about marriage from whether we should support it (or even if it matters) to how we can support it (because it does matter) is a great leap forward. Nonetheless, I am aware that there are those who suggest we do not know enough about how to support healthy marriages to warrant government action in this area. To some extent, these critics have a point: there is still much we need to know. But we should also acknowledge that there is much we do know. We know, for example, that healthy marriages are a result, not of luck or chance, but of hard work and skills, and that these skills can be taught. We also know that premarital education programs can help couples form and sustain a healthy marriage by teaching communication and problem-solving skills. We also know that programs that assign mentoring couples to newlyweds can help young couples adjust to their new marriage in healthy ways. Finally, we know that programs designed to save even the most troubled marriages can work. Yes, there is much we need to learn about supporting healthy marriages, but we already know more than enough to get started. As the Russian novelist Ivan Turgenev observed, "If we wait for the moment when everything, absolutely everything is ready, we shall never begin" (2000, 181).

The case for acting now is clearer when one acknowledges that the decline in marriage is a public health crisis in much the same way as increases in smoking and drunk driving were public health crises in previous decades. Each of these involves an individual decision, with certain choices, such as the decision to smoke or to drink and drive, leading to negative consequences for the individual and for the public at large, which the government, with a vested interest in the health of its citizenry and in a more civil and productive society, cannot ignore. The same is true for marriage. As Rhode Island psychiatrist Scott Haltzman, writing in March 2002 in *The Providence Journal*, noted: "A citizen's decision to marry is like the decision to put on a seat belt—private, yes, but society has something at stake, so the government is justified in exerting some influence. The decision not to marry or to end a marriage, especially if there are children, is a bit like deciding to drink before driving. Again, it's a personal choice, but society bears its effects" (Scott Haltzman, "Uncle Sam's Role Nudging, Not Forcing, Parents to Wed," *The Providence Journal*, March 11, 2002, n.p.).[6]

There are, of course, limits on government action even when seeking to improve the welfare of children. Choosing to marry is a private decision. Only in support of couples' own decisions does government have a legitimate interest in helping them acquire the skills and knowledge necessary to form and sustain a healthy marriage. No one—and certainly not the Bush administration—believes that the proper role of government in this arena should include the creation of a Federal Dating Service to pair up men and women and herd them into marriage.

Rather, the Bush administration is concerned with improving the quality of marriage, not just increasing the number of them. It goes without saying—but perhaps I should say it anyway: healthy marriages are good for children and adults, whereas abusive ones obviously are not. The government has no interest in encouraging couples to remain in marriages that are good for no one, neither adults nor children—nor society, for that matter.

Nor should withdrawing supports for single-parent families be equated with the promotion of healthy marriages. Government should encourage and support healthy marriages because of the overwhelming empirical evidence that supports the conclusion that an intact, married household is, on average, the best environment in which to raise a child. In contrast, there are no data to suggest that taking away supports from single mothers helps children. Indeed, the reverse would be true. The fact is that many single parents make heroic efforts, often with great success, to raise their children well. President Bush acknowledged this when he said in his 2001 proclamation for National Family Week that "many one parent families are . . . a source of comfort and reassurance." Promoting healthy marriage and supporting single parents are not, and must not, be mutually exclusive. Together, they are part of an integrated effort to promote child well-being.

From tax policy to housing policy, the government is already involved in decisions that affect the formation of marital unions. But it can do more. I believe the following four principles should guide policy making in this area.

First, government ought to make clear that it is in the business of promoting healthy marriages and not just in increasing marriage rates. That's because healthy marriages are an effective strategy for improving the well-being of children, whereas unhealthy marriages are not. Government has no interest in encouraging couples to enter into or remain in marriages that are violent or abusive. The goal ought to be to increase the percentage of children growing up in married households where the marriage is a healthy one.

Second, government should not merely strive for neutrality in this matter, but should positively support healthy marriages. Government is neutral about many things. For example, government is neutral about what flavor of ice cream we buy because there is no evidence that one choice is better for us than another. But it is not neutral about other things—home ownership or charitable giving, for example—because home ownership and charitable giving contribute to the common good.

For that reason, the government makes it easier for us to buy a house or to give to charities by providing tax incentives. In much the same way, government can—and should—provide support for healthy marriages precisely because it can be shown that healthy marriages contribute to the common good.

Third, whatever the government does in this area ought to be carefully evaluated to determine what actually does work and what doesn't, and evaluated not only for the intended effects but for any unintended consequences as well. Imperfect knowledge in this area should not paralyze government action, but it should emphasize the need to carefully evaluate whatever innovative work government chooses to undertake.

Finally, government ought not seek to promote marriage by being afraid to speak its name. There is no evidence that cohabitation confers the same benefits on children, adults, or communities as marriage. In fact, much of the evidence indicates that cohabitation may be no different than living with only one parent. For example, Moore and Chase-Lansdale (2001, 1154) found that "the presence of a cohabiting partner did not significantly affect the likelihood of intercourse or pregnancy [in the children of the household], suggesting that it is the marital union rather than the added household adult that acts as a protective factor against early sexual intercourse for adolescents in two-parent households." If the policy objective is the betterment of the lives of children, there is no evidence to suggest we will be able to do so by equating cohabitation with marriage.

With these principles and constraints as guides for action, the Bush administration has put forward a proposal within the context of TANF reauthorization that would provide those individuals who freely choose to marry greater access to services where they can acquire the skills and knowledge necessary to form and maintain a happy and healthy marital union.

THE PRESIDENT'S PROPOSALS

Improving the well-being of the nation's children is the overarching purpose of the Bush administration's welfare reauthorization plan. To achieve that purpose it proposes to strengthen both work- and family-based programs. The president's program has six goals: to maximize self-sufficiency through work, to promote healthy marriages, to encourage abstinence and prevent teen pregnancy, to improve program performance with a new emphasis on information systems and accountability, to enhance child support enforcement, and to facilitate program integration. While each of these aspects of reauthorization is important, I will focus here on the administration's proposals for promoting healthy marriages.

Both in its preamble and throughout the act, the 1996 legislation reauthorizing TANF explicitly states that the promotion and encouragement of marriage is national policy. To help achieve this, President Bush proposes to create a $120 million annual fund for supporting healthy marriage demonstration projects, research, and technical assistance. The proposal also creates a competitive $120 million matching-grant program for states, territories and tribal organizations interested in implementing innovative approaches to promoting healthy marriage and reducing out-of-wedlock births. States would be required to describe in their state plan how they are addressing each of the TANF purposes, and how these will help to improve the well-being of children. States also would be encouraged to provide equitable treatment of two-parent married families under state TANF programs.

These funds could be used for a variety of innovative activities. Although it would be up to states and communities to decide exactly what they would like to support, money might be used to help low-income couples gain access, perhaps through vouchers, to pre- and postmarital education services that have been shown to work. The Prevention and Relationship Enhancement Program (PREP) is one of them. PREP consists of a twelve-hour sequence of mini-lectures and discussions on topics that include communication, conflict management, forgiveness, religious beliefs and practices, expectations, fun, and friendship. It emphasizes strategies for enhancing and maintaining commitment. Three years after intervention, published empirical evidence showed PREP couples expressed more satisfaction with their marriages, were communicating more effectively, and reported fewer conflicts than did matched control couples. Also, fewer instances of physical violence were reported in three- to five-year follow-ups (Markman, Floyd et al. 1988; Markman, Renick et al. 1993). Eighty-five percent of couples who went through the program came out of it highly satisfied (Hahlweg and Klann, 1997; Stanley et al. 2001).

Funding could also be used to increase access to such well-documented marital enrichment programs as Relationship Enhancement (RE), a weekend course that teaches couples how to communicate effectively, respond empathetically, and resolve conflicts more easily. A recent review of the literature states, "Numerous studies have evaluated the impact of RE enrichment programs for couples. These studies have typically found couples make significant gains in the areas of communication, self-disclosure, empathy, and relationship adjustment" (Christensen and Heavey 1999).

There are, of course, critics of the president's proposals. First, they maintain there is no evidence that the behavior of low-income individuals is influenced by welfare policies. Second, they claim there is no evidence that Americans think it is a good idea for the government to get involved with the marriage issue, nor that low-income couples, in particular, are interested in accessing services to help them build strong and healthy marriages. Third, they claim there is no evidence that we know how to promote the formation of healthy marriages.

New evidence refutes each of these claims. In the first survey of its kind, researchers working with the Oklahoma Marriage Initiative found that 63 percent of current or former welfare recipients believed that, if they were to marry, they would lose some or all of their assistance (Johnson et al. 2002). The tragedy is not that this is their belief; the tragedy is that they are correct. As Adam Carasso and Eugene Steuerle of the Urban Institute have demonstrated, there are substantial financial penalties in our current welfare system when low- to moderate-income families choose to marry.[7]

The Oklahoma survey also found that 85 percent of all Oklahomans, including large majorities of low-income adults, believe that a statewide initiative to "promote marriage and reduce divorce" is a good or very good idea. This parallels a national survey, conducted by the Opinion Research Corporation, which found that 67 percent of Americans thought it was a good idea to use surplus welfare funds for programs to strengthen marriage and reduce divorce and out-of-wedlock births.[8] Indeed, the Oklahoma survey found that 72 percent of low-income persons would consider using relationship education workshops or classes to strengthen their relationships if they were made available.

Finally, contrary to claims that we don't know anything, we know quite a bit—from theory, field experience, and empirical research—about how to promote healthy marriages. For over twenty-five years, leading researchers in psychology, sociology, and other fields have been focusing on the knowledge and skills good marriages require. This knowledge base is fertile ground on which to build solid, well-researched demonstrations using existing insight into the operations of marital relationships. Moreover, the entire purpose of the healthy marriage initiative is to promote innovations in order to evaluate them. As such, while our knowledge of successful interventions is incomplete and, for the most part, has not been based on samples of low-income individuals, the president's proposals are aimed at building on our existing knowledge by trying and testing new ideas.

In addition to the president's proposals for reauthorization of TANF, the Administration for Children and Families (ACF) is engaged in a number of research projects to investigate the effects of government efforts to strengthen healthy marriages. For example, we have already begun work on the Building Strong Families Evaluation. Building Strong Families will target low-income couples around the time of the birth of a child out of wedlock. It will assess the effectiveness of programs—designed to help parents who wish to marry—to enter and sustain healthy marriages, to help all parents develop positive functioning family relationships, and to address varied needs for service. The specific goal of this project is to increase knowledge of programs, policies, services, and delivery of services that offer promise for improving parent and child well-being. This will be accomplished by identifying and recruiting six study sites, providing technical assistance on program and evaluation issues, closely monitoring program performance and feedback, and by conducting an impact evaluation based on large samples of individuals randomly assigned to treatment and control groups.

The state of knowledge about how to promote healthy marriages today is similar in many ways to the state of knowledge about promoting work twenty years ago. At that time there were many competing theories about how to help recipients move from welfare into work. A few states had moved aggressively with experiments, but many had not. Over the last two decades, state activities paired with high quality research and evaluations have dramatically increased knowledge about what works best. This laid a foundation for implementing work programs nationwide with stunning success. The president's proposals, and efforts such as the Building Strong Families evaluation, are intended to generate the same kind of creative explosion in the area of promoting healthy marriage.

OTHER IMPORTANT INITIATIVES

The administration's efforts to create family policies that improve child well-being are not limited to simply promoting marriage. I briefly describe three others.

The administration is undertaking a major initiative, Good Start, Grow Smart, to improve the quality and delivery of early childhood programs, including Head Start, with an emphasis on teaching early literacy skills. Every Head Start program will assess the early literacy, language, and numeric skills of every Head Start child as part of a national reporting system. Head Start will use the data to help target programs for additional training and technical assistance efforts, and to strengthen accountability for results. But our efforts will not be limited to Head Start programs. Steps are being taken to enhance the capabilities of pre-kindergarten teachers, child care providers, and parents so that they can help realize the president's goal of ensuring that all children entering school are ready to learn and succeed. By making investments to improve teacher qualifications, enhancing training for using evidence-based teaching practices, and developing policies to support early childhood literacy, we will strengthen the ability of pre-kindergarten teachers and child care providers to teach early literacy skills.

Strongly enforcing child-support payments is another important Bush administration initiative to promote child well-being. The administration has proposed legislation that would not only increase financial support from noncustodial parents, but would also send more of what is collected directly to the support of the children involved. This will move the program further away from its historical focus on recouping welfare costs for the government and more toward assisting families in meeting their needs. The proposal would provide financial incentives to the states to encourage them to pass through more child support directly to families of both current and former TANF recipients.

The administration has also proposed the creation of a new program to promote responsible fatherhood. This program would make grants to community and faith-based organizations, American Indian tribes and tribal organizations for projects designed to test the effectiveness of alternative approaches for helping parents be more responsible, caring, and effective, for improving the ability of low-income fathers to manage their finances and support their families, and for encouraging and supporting healthy married fatherhood.

CONCLUSION

The president's proposals for welfare reform and child well-being grew out of his commitment to improve the lives of children by working to ensure that more of them are raised within the context of stable, healthy, two-parent married families. To promote conditions that strengthen and support healthy marriages, and thus better lives for parents and their children, government must act as a catalyst for local faith-based and other community organizations. Federal action is essential to this vital effort, but the action cannot come from government alone. All society benefits from stable marriages, stable families, and children who are cared for. All society must support the effort.

The views expressed in this chapter do not necessarily represent the views of the Administration for Children and Families, the U.S. Department of Health and Human Services, or the U.S. Government.

NOTES

1. Only money actually earned is included, government transfers and taxes are not.

2. The study cited controlled for children's emotional problems, cogni-

tive achievement, and parents' socioeconomic status prior to divorce.

3. Linda J. Waite's tabulations from the Health and Retirement Survey, wave 1. See Thomas F. Juster and Richard Suzman (1995).

4. Tabulations by Linda J. Waite from the General Social Survey, 1990 to 1996 waves, in Waite (2000).

5. See, for example, Sandefur et al. (1992).

6. Available at http://listarchives.his.com/smartmarriages/smartmarriages. 0203/msg00055.html (accessed May 20, 2004).

7. See Adam Carasso and C. Eugene Steuerle (2002).

8. Opinion Research Corporation poll for the Coalition for Marriage, Families and Couples Education, www.smartmarriages.com, May 3–6, 2002.

REFERENCES

Amato, Paul R. 1991. "Children of Divorce in the 1990s: An Update of the Amato and Keith (1991) Meta-Analysis." *Journal of Family Psychology* 13(3): 355–370.

Berkman, Lisa F., and Lester Breslow. 1983. *Health and Ways of Living, the Alameda County Study*. Oxford/New York: Oxford University Press.

Carasso, Adam, and C. Eugene Steuerle. 2002. "Saying 'I Do' After The 2001 Tax Cuts." *Tax Policy Issues and Options* 4. Washington, D.C.: Urban Institute Press.

Cherlin, Andrew J., Kathleen E. Kiernan, and P. Lindsay Chase-Lansdale. 1995. "Parental Divorce in Childhood and Demographic Outcomes in Young Adulthood." *Demography* 32(3): 299–318.

Christensen, Andrew, and Christopher L. Heavey. 1999. "Interventions for Couples." *Annual Review of Psychology* 50(1): 65–190.

Hahlweg, Kurt, and Notker Klann. 1997. "The Effectiveness of Marital Counseling in Germany: A Contribution to Health Services Research." *Journal of Family Psychology* 11(4): 410–21.

Harper, Cynthia, and Sara McLanahan. 1998. "Father Absence and Youth Incarceration." Paper presented at the Annual Meeting of the American Sociological Association. San Francisco, Calif. (August).

Johnson, Christine A., Scott M. Stanley, Norval D. Glenn, Paul R. Amato, Steve L. Nock, Howard J. Markman, and M. Robin Dion. 2002. *Marriage in Oklahoma: 2001 Baseline Statewide Survey on Marriage and Divorce (S02096 OKDHS)*. Oklahoma City: Oklahoma Department of Human Services.

Johnson, Robert A., John P. Haffman, and Dean R. Gerstain. 1996. "The Relationship Between Family Structure and Adolescent Substance Use." National Opinion Research Center for the U.S. Department of Health and Human Services, Washington, D.C.

Juster, Thomas F., and Richard Suzman. 1995. "An Overview of the Health and Retirement Survey." *Journal of Human Resources* 30(supplement): S7–S56.

Kessler, Ronald C., Guilherme Borges, and Ellen E. Walters. 1999. "Prevalence of and Risk Factors for Lifetime Suicide Attempts In The National Comorbidity Survey." *Archives of General Psychiatry* 56(7): 617–26.

Litwac, Eugene, and Peter Messeri. 1989. "Organizational Theory, Social Supports, and Mortality Rates: A Theoretical Convergence." *American Sociological Review* 54(1): 49–66.

Markman, Howard J., Frank J. Floyd, Scott M. Stanley, and Ragnar D. Storaasli. 1988. "Prevention of Marital Distress: A Longitudinal Investigation." *Journal of Consulting and Clinical Psychology* 56(2): (S)210–17.

Markman, Howard J., M. J. Renick, Frank J. Floyd, Scott M. Stanley, and M. Clements. 1993. "Preventing Marital Distress through Communication and Conflict Management Training: A 4- and 5-Year Follow-Up." *Journal of Consulting and Clinical Psychology* 61(1): 70–77.

McLanahan, Sara, and Gary Sandefur. 1994. *Growing Up With a Single Parent: What Hurts, What Helps.* Cambridge, Mass.: Harvard University Press.

Moore, Mignon R., and P. Lindsay Chase-Lansdale. 2001. "Sexual Intercourse and Pregnancy Among African-American Adolescent Girls in High Poverty Neighborhoods: The Role of Family and Perceived Community Involvement." *Journal of Marriage and Family* 63(4): 1146–1157.

Murphy, Michael, Karen Glaser, and Emily Grundy. 1997. "Marital Status and Long-Term Illness in Great Britain." *Journal of Marriage and the Family* 59(1): 156–64.

National Center for Health Statistics. 1988. *National Health Interview Survey.* Washington: U.S. Department of Health and Human Services, National Center for Health Statistics.

Rennison, Callie Marie, and Sarah Welchans. 2000. "Intimate Partner Violence." Bureau of Justice Statistics Special Report. (May): NCJ 178247.

Ribar, David C. 2003. "What Do Social Scientists Know About The Benefits of Marriage? A Review of Quantitative Methodologies." Unpublished manuscript.

Sandefur, Gary D., Charles F. Manski, Sara McLanahan, and Daniel A. Powers. 1992. "Alternative Estimates of the Effect of Family Structure during Adolescence on High School Graduation." *Journal of the American Statistical Association* 87(417): 25–37.

Sedlak, Andrea J., and Dianne D. Broadhurst. 1996. "The Third National Incidence Study of Child Abuse and Neglect: Final Report." U.S. Department of Health and Human Services, National Center on Child Abuse and Neglect. Washington, D.C. (September).

Smith, Jack C., James A. Mercy, and Judith M. Conn. 1988. "Marital Status and the Risk of Suicide." *American Journal of Public Health* 78(1): 78–80.

Stanley, Scott M., Howard J. Markman, Lydia M. Prado, P. Antonio Olmos-Gallo, Laurie Tonelli, Michelle St. Peters, B. Douglas Leber, Michelle Bobulinski, Allan Cordova, and Sarah W. Whitton. 2001. "Community Based Premarital Prevention: Clergy and Lay Leaders on the Front Lines." *Family Relations* 50(1): 67–76.

Thomas, Adam, and Isabel Sawhill. 2001. "For Richer or Poorer: Marriages as an Anti-Poverty Strategy." Washington, D.C.: Brookings Institution Press.

Turgenev, Ivan. 2000. *Virgin Soil*, translated by Constance Garnett, with introduction by Charlotte Hobson. New York: New York Review Books.

U.S. Department of Health and Human Services. 2002. "Temporary Assistance for Needy Families Program, Fourth Annual Report to Congress." Administration for Children and Families. Washington, D.C. (May).

Ventura, Stephanie J., and Christine Bachrach. 2000. "Nonmarital Childbearing in the United States, 1940–99." *National Vital Statistics Reports,* vol. 48(16) (revised), October 18. Hyattsville, Md.: National Center for Health Statistics.

Waite, Linda J. 2000. *The Case for Marriage: Why Married People are Happier, Healthier, and Better Off Financially* (with Maggie Gallagher). New York: Doubleday.

Wallerstein, Judith S., Julia M. Lewis, and Sandra Blakeslee. 2000. *The Unexpected Legacy of Divorce: A 25-Year Landmark Study*. New York: Hyperion.

Whitehead, Barbara Dafoe, and David Popenoe. 2001. "The Decline of Child-Centered Marriage." *American Experiment Quarterly* 4(2, Summer): 8–16.

CHAPTER TEN

Progressive Family Policy in the Twenty-First Century

Will Marshall and Isabel V. Sawhill

NOT LONG AGO, the family was a prime battleground in America's culture wars. In the last decade, however, the ideological passions unleashed by changes in family structure and social values have subsided. A new center has emerged in the long-running family debate, and with it a chance to build broad political and public support for a progressive, pro-family agenda for the twenty-first century.

We propose a wide-ranging set of policies tailored to the new realities of work, marriage, and family life in America. These ideas aim at promoting stable families by discouraging teen pregnancies, moving more welfare recipients into jobs, making work pay, extending work requirements to absent fathers so they can meet their child support obligations, reforming "no fault" divorce laws to put children's interests ahead of adult convenience, making the tax system more family friendly; and helping harried parents balance the demands of work and family.

More specifically, we would highlight three major priorities:

1. Sharply reduce early childbearing by unwed mothers. We view this as the single most important step we can take to foster family stability and children's well-being, and to reduce welfare dependence and child poverty. It may also be the most practical way to promote

marriage, because young single mothers with children make poor marriage prospects.

2. Establish a universal system of early learning. Every child in America should have access to quality preschool. Not only will this ease a severe child care crunch facing working parents, it will also help us narrow the academic achievement gap between poor and middle-class children. We endorse a proposal from the 2000 campaign to spend $50 billion over ten years to make voluntary preschool available to all four-year-olds and a growing number of three-year-olds. In addition, we support greater funding for child care, especially for low-income working parents.

3. Create a nationwide system of paid parental leave. A growing body of scientific research shows that the early months of a child's life are critical to cognitive and emotional development. Yet until California recently passed the nation's first paid leave law, no U.S. workers could take time off with pay to stay with their children in the first months of life. We propose using the unemployment insurance system to provide new parents with good work histories with up to six months of paid leave, with the federal government picking up the lion's share of the cost.

Before describing these priorities and our other recommendations in greater detail, it is worth examining how we arrived at this moment of possibility for defining a new politics of family after decades of discord.

THE NEW SYNTHESIS ON FAMILY

From the mid-1960s until the early 1990s, the erosion of the traditional family provoked fierce political battles between the right and the left. Conservatives decried rising rates of divorce and out-of-wedlock births as evidence of a breakdown in personal responsibility and general morality. Liberals welcomed women's overdue emancipation from unequal gender roles both at home and in the workplace.

In the early 1990s, a new synthesis began to emerge. Rather than taking sides in the polarized left-right debate, this view embraced both cultural and economic explanations of family change. It acknowledged growing evidence that divorce, teen pregnancy, and out-of-wedlock births were injurious to children and that some public policies unwittingly discouraged parental responsibility and marriage. Yet it also paid equal attention to how economic changes were undermining men's traditional breadwinner role and forcing families to send two parents to work to sustain a middle-class standard of living.

Proponents of the new synthesis took on the relativist myth that "alternative family forms" were the equal of two-parent families, citing a growing body of evidence showing that, in the aggregate, children do best in married, two-parent families. They also confronted the liberal view that government spending could somehow compensate children for the absence of loving, competent adults. "Governments don't raise kids," Bill Clinton said repeatedly during his 1992 campaign, "parents do." His administration subsequently pushed reforms in welfare and other social policies aimed at rolling back the tide of teen pregnancy and unwed parenting, and promoting parental responsibility and family stability.

At the same time, Clinton challenged conservatives to provide new public resources to poor and middle-income working families. He pressed successfully for a big expansion of the Earned Income Tax Credit to "make work pay," increased child care, and other supports for low-income families and, in one of his first acts as president, signed the Family and Medical Leave Act to help families balance work and family. Clinton later turned to parents' cultural anxieties, with proposals for improving children's television programming; enhanced parental control and choice through the television "V-chip," and a program rating system; and reinforced adult authority through curfews and public school uniforms.

Most of these policy initiatives won bipartisan support, suggesting the emergence by the late 1990s of a progressive center in a debate that previously had been dominated by ideological extremes. This doesn't mean, of course, that there are not many serious areas of disagreement between the parties.

Conservatives, for example, have moved promoting marriage to the center of their "family values" agenda. President Bush has promised that his administration "will give unprecedented support to strengthening marriages." In a bid to "restore a marriage culture," the White House has proposed dedicating $200 million in welfare funds to public and private pro-marriage initiatives in the states.

Democrats are mostly skeptical, not about the social value of marriage but about government's ability to promote stable marriages. Liberals suspect religious conservatives of trying to restore the 1950s model of the male-dominated family. If Republicans really wanted to help families, many Congressional Democrats insist, they would support bigger increases in funding for child care, health care for all workers, preschool and after school programs, and more generous leave policies for working parents who need to spend more time with their families.

These differences are important but not fundamental. The truce in the culture war over family appears to be holding. This suggests an opportunity to move the debate beyond partisan paralysis, and to launch a new set of pragmatic initiatives against a stubborn set of problems besetting America's families.

High out-of-wedlock birth rates pose the greatest threat to family stability. The U.S. divorce rate has leveled off, but remains the advanced world's highest. And as marriage declines, there's been a dramatic increase in cohabitation. As a result of these trends, over 30 percent of all U.S. children live apart from their biological fathers, and more than 50 percent can expect to spend some time living in a single-parent household (Ooms 2002b).

"Family relationships today are increasingly complex and unstable," notes social policy analyst Theodora Ooms (2002b). "Parents often have children by more than one partner, and consequently children may have relationships with biological, married, and stepparents (legal and informal), grandparents and stepgrandparents, and half- and stepsiblings."

To researchers Barbara Dafoe Whitehead and David Popenoe, such familial confusion reflects the decline of the "child-centered marriage" celebrated in the TV sitcoms of memory. "Americans today tend to see marriage primarily as a couples relationship, designed to fulfill the emotional needs of adults, rather than as an institution for parenthood and child rearing," they write. "To put it another way, Americans today are increasingly inclined to ask not what they can do for marriage, but what marriage can do for them" (Whitehead and Popenoe 2001).

Meanwhile, U.S. families are struggling to adapt to a sweeping economic transformation. A new economy based on ideas and services rather than producing tangible goods has put a premium on education and social skills and injected a new element of risk and volatility in economic life. These developments have reminded us of the vital economic function of families in equipping their members both to compete and cooperate with others, and in cushioning them against economic reverses.

At a time of accelerated job churning, for example, families with two working parents have added insurance against labor market volatility. Children from intact families tend to have higher education levels and stronger collaborative skills and prove more adept at lifetime learning than children from single-parent families.

"Well-functioning families are needed both to enhance security and reinforce the strengths of character on which lives of self-reliance depend," notes William Galston, a leading family policy analyst. "Success in the new economy means shoring up the oldest of social institutions" (Galston 1997, 152).

Finally, policy makers should be concerned about a strong correlation between the growth in single-parent families and economic inequality. New research by Ellwood and Jencks (2001) shows that most of the increase in single parenthood since 1980 has been among less-educated women. Well-educated women, in contrast, have greater incentives to postpone childbirth as they pursue increasingly rewarding careers. "Over a period when wages became more unequal, changing family structure may be differentially harming children from less advantaged backgrounds and reinforcing inequalities in other domains," Ellwood and Jencks write (2001, 2).

To meet these disparate but related challenges, U.S. policy makers need to forge a progressive family policy for the twenty-first century on the foundations of the new synthesis that emerged in the last decade. It should address the needs not just of poor families, but all families with children. A comprehensive, politically sustainable approach, in our view, would embody these four guiding principles:

1.   A progressive family policy should encourage and reinforce married, two-parent families because they are best for children.

2.   A progressive family policy nonetheless must improve prospects for the millions of children who will grow up in single-parent families.

3.   A progressive family policy must continue reforming policies that unwittingly promote divorce and out-of-wedlock births or discourage marriage in favor of single parenthood or cohabitation.

4.   A progressive family policy must rebalance work and family life in light of two irreversible trends—more egalitarian marriages and the growing link between two-adult households and economic success.

TRENDS IN FAMILY FORMATION AND POLICY PRIORITIES

Because our focus here is policies rather than data, we do not intend to cover trends in family formation in any detail. However, a number of points are worth emphasizing because they inform policies we recommend.

First, the growth of single-parent families has been closely associated with the growth of child poverty and other adverse consequences for children. Specifically, if there had been no increase in single parent families after 1970, there would have been no increase in child poverty.[1] And simulations that marry single mothers to currently unattached men who are good marriage matches for them lead to large drops in child poverty (Thomas and Sawhill 2002). Unmarried men and women were matched on age, education, and race. The marriages formed this way led to closer matching on these and some other characteristics than actual marriages. Among all children, the poverty rate dropped over 3 percentage points when the proportion living in single-parent families was returned to its 1970 level. (We should not assume that it will ever be possible to eliminate all single parenting; some women have no choice.) Among children whose mothers participated in a simulated marriage, the poverty rate dropped by almost 67 percent. However, black single mothers are underrepresented among marriage simulation participants because there are not enough potential black males in some age and education categories.

Second, if our objective is to slow or reverse the growth of single-parent families and ensure that more children have an opportunity to be reared by two married parents, there are two ways to accomplish it. One is to reduce the rate of divorce among families with children. Another is to reduce out-of-wedlock childbearing. Although the divorce rate is twice as high now as it was in 1960, all of the growth in single-parent families over the last two decades has been fueled by an increase in out-of-wedlock childbearing. The divorce rate (per 1,000 women age 15 or older) declined from 22.6 in 1980 to 18.9 in 2000 (National Marriage Project 2002). For this reason, and also because the children of never-married mothers fare more poorly than those in divorced families, we believe that priority should be given to reducing out-of-wedlock births. Such births are especially prevalent within the African American community, where 68 percent of all births are to unmarried women. Although the proportion born outside marriage is lower among whites, the growth rate for whites has been much higher (U.S. Census Bureau 2002). If we want to reduce child poverty, avoiding a situation in which bearing children outside of marriage becomes the norm for the country should be one goal.

Divorce rates have declined since the early 1980s, but births to unmarried mothers have continued to increase, from 18.4 percent of all births in 1980 to 33.2 percent in 2000 (National Marriage Project 2002). This reflects both an increase in births to unmarried women and a decrease among married women—but mostly the latter. Birth rates to unmarried women increased from 29.4 per 1000 women ages 15 to 44 in 1980 to 44.4 in 1999. They have leveled off or declined slightly in the late 1990s (Halle 2002). Of course, we would welcome further declines in the divorce rate as well. And we favor legal changes to ensure that when divorce in unavoidable, children's interests take precedence.

Finally, given the recent emphasis on marriage in so many policy debates, it is worth noting the pitfalls of marrying too early. By the time they are in their early 40s, over 90 percent of all women have been married (U.S. Department of Health and Human Services 2002). Again, there are notable racial differences here. Among black women, the proportion that ever marry is significantly lower than for whites. The problem is the growing gap between age at puberty and age at marriage combined with the failure of women to delay childbearing until after they marry. Average age at puberty is now a little over twelve for girls and average age at marriage is twenty-five (Kirby 2001; The National Marriage Project 2002). This creates a thirteen-year window during which people either need to abstain from sex, use contraception, or rely on abortion to prevent an unwed birth. Current efforts to promote marriage could have the effect of encouraging earlier marriages. The drawback of this solution is that it requires reversing a strong and generally healthy trend toward later age at first marriage. Age at first marriage is one of the strongest predictors of marital stability, thus any success in reducing age at marriage is likely to be accompanied by a higher divorce rate. One recent study found that all of the decline in the divorce rate since 1975 is related to the increase in age at first marriage (Heaton 2002). Not only is this trend good for marriage, it is good for children as well. Younger mothers often lack the maturity, patience, and education that have been shown to produce better outcomes for children. Finally, our economy now demands much more education than in earlier periods, and a social policy that encouraged early marriage would be inconsistent with one that also sees investments in education as beneficial.

Perhaps what is really intended by marriage advocates is not a set of policies that would encourage earlier marriages across the board but only in cases where a woman is already pregnant or has had a child. Such "shotgun" or "after-the-fact" marriages to the biological father were common in the past but have virtually disappeared in recent years. Their modern counterpart is what is often called fragile family initiatives—efforts to work with young couples, many of whom are romantically involved or cohabiting at the time of the baby's birth, to help them form more stable ties and, where appropriate, marry. These efforts often involve education, training, counseling, and peer support for the fathers. An evaluation of one such effort, Parents Fair Share, produced disappointing results (Knox and Redcross 2000), but some researchers believe programs that intervene at the time of birth may be more successful.

About 40 percent of all out-of-wedlock births are to cohabiting couples, and cohabitation seems to be rapidly replacing marriage as a preferred living arrangement among the younger generation. Some believe that the steady rise in cohabitation is the functional equivalent of marriage and is not especially worrisome. But such relationships are far less stable than marriages: less than 50 percent of them last for five years or more (Terry-Humen, Manlove, and Moore 2001). In addition, children do not fare as well in these co-residential families. Acs and Nelson (2002), for example, find that compared to children living with married parents, children living with cohabitors are more likely to be poor, food insecure, read to infrequently, and to exhibit behavioral problems. However, they are somewhat better off than those living with a single parent. For teenagers, living with cohabiting parents is no better than living with a single mother and in most cases is significantly worse (Acs and Nelson 2002; Nelson, Clark, and Acs 2001; also see Cherlin and Fomby 2002; Popenoe and Whitehead 2002).

Whether such cohabiting couples can be persuaded to marry and whether these marriages would endure if they did is not clear. While it is well established that marriages preceded by cohabitation are less stable than those that are not, it is less clear whether this is causal or whether it simply reflects the fact that those who choose to cohabit are less likely to have enduring marriages. Many unwed mothers cohabit not with the biological father of their children but with another man and some of these relationships may also end in marriage. But, surprising as it may seem, in most cases, such stepfamilies seem to be no better for children than being raised in a single-parent home.

Out-of-wedlock births are not just bad for children, they are also bad for the institution of marriage. Once a woman has had a child outside of marriage, her chances of marrying plummet. That chance, Daniel Lichter of the Ohio State University found, is almost 40 percent lower for those who first had a child out of wedlock, and 51 percent if we exclude women who marry the biological father within the first six months after the birth. By age thirty-five, only 70 percent of all unwed mothers are married. In contrast, 88 percent of those who have not had a child are. He compares women who had a premarital pregnancy terminated by a miscarriage to those who carried to term, and finds that these differences in marriage rates persist (Lichter and Graefe 2001). This suggests that out-of-wedlock childbirth, rather than simply reflecting the pre-existing characteristics of this group of women, makes women less likely to marry. Why unwed mothers are less likely to marry is unclear. They may be less desirable marriage partners, may be less likely to spend time at work or in school where they can meet marriageable men, or may simply lose interest in marriage once they have children. Moreover, having had one child out of wedlock, they appear to be relatively uninhibited about having others the same way. In short, early unwed childbearing leads to less marriage and more out-of-wedlock births. Thus, one clear strategy for bringing back marriage is to prevent the initial birth that makes a single woman less marriageable throughout her adult years. Most young women aspire to marry. Publicizing their much reduced chances of marrying once they have a baby might make them think twice about becoming unwed mothers.

Not only are unwed mothers less likely to marry than those without children but when they do marry, they do not marry as well. They are more likely than women who have similarly disadvantaged backgrounds but no children to marry a high school dropout or someone without a job. Although marriage improves on unwed mothers' chances of escaping from poverty, it does not offset the negative effects associated with an unwed birth, according to Daniel Lichter and his colleagues (Lichter, Graefe, and Brown 2001).

Our conclusions based on this evidence can be summarized as follows:

- Changes in the family have produced a substantial increase in child poverty.

- The increase in out-of-wedlock childbearing, not divorce, has been the main driver of these changes.

- Most Americans eventually marry and have children. The problem is timing. Do we want to encourage earlier marriages or later childbearing? Both could lead to a reduction in out-of-wedlock childbearing and slow the growth of single-parent families. But if we care about the well-being of children, the formation of stable marriages, and the education of women, promoting later childbearing rather than earlier marriage is the better strategy.

- Policy makers should refrain from creating programs that provide special supports, such as job training, for cohabiting couples and thereby risk rewarding behavior that society should discourage.

- Finally, as detailed in the next section, we know more about how to reduce early childbearing than we do about encouraging marriage.

INCREASING FAMILY STABILITY

Conservative rhetoric lays the blame for family breakdown squarely on government. Yet this overstates the impact of government policies and overlooks the broader cultural and economic forces that have reshaped the contours of American family life over the last four decades. The sexual revolution, the movement for gender equity, and the emergence of a post-industrial economy based on services and intangible goods—these factors have overwhelmed the effects, for good or ill, of public policy on families.

Yet what government does is important. Social welfare policies over the last generation did penalize work and marriage and foster dependency. The moral premises embedded in public policies (or absent from them) do send signals to citizens about what constitutes socially responsible behavior. And changes in law and regulation can alter culture. Civil rights, environmental protection, and special education laws are all examples of how legal and policy changes not only dealt with discrete public problems but over time transformed broad social attitudes as well.

The 1996 welfare reform signaled a dramatic change in America's social contract. It embodied a consensus that unconditional and permanent entitlement to public assistance discouraged work, weakened marriage, and undermined parental responsibility. The reform made welfare temporary, conditioned assistance on work, expanded child care and other supports for working parents, cracked down on deadbeat dads who do not pay child support, and promoted two-parent families by discouraging out-of-wedlock births. We need to stay the course on welfare reform while rethinking and reforming other policies that have inadvertently contributed to undermining family life.

REDUCING OUT-OF-WEDLOCK CHILDBEARING

Unmarried parents are a diverse group. Increasingly, they are older rather than younger and live in cohabiting relationships. The typical unmarried mother is in her early twenties, does not live with the father of her children, though she may live with another man, and more often than not is poor and depends on welfare.[2]

Unwed parenting often begins during the teenage years. About half of first out-of-wedlock births are to women under twenty (National Center for Health Statistics 2002). This suggests focusing on preventing teen pregnancies and births. Pregnancies among this group are the most likely to be unintended, to interfere with schooling, and to lead to poorer outcomes for the children involved and higher costs for taxpayers.[3] At the same time, greater efforts to provide family planning or reproductive health services to women in their twenties are also needed.

The teen birth rate has declined by 26 percent since 1991. Both increased abstinence and better contraceptive efforts have contributed to this decline (Flanigan 2001). Other likely contributors include the new messages about work and child support embedded in welfare reform, more conservative attitudes among the young, fear of AIDS and other sexually transmitted diseases, the availability of new methods of contraception such as DepoPovera that are less susceptible to user error or inconsistent use, and perhaps the strong economy (Sawhill 2001).[4]

What can be done to reduce teen pregnancy rates still further? One strategy involves preventing a first pregnancy (primary prevention). A second strategy involves reducing subsequent pregnancies to young unwed mothers (secondary prevention). Still, a third strategy involves ensuring that those who experience an unwanted pregnancy have access to abortion and adoption services.

Primary Prevention   Over the past five years, research on teen pregnancy prevention programs has found a number of programs that work. Douglas Kirby's review identifies several rigorously evaluated programs that have reduced teen pregnancy rates by as much as 50 percent (Kirby 2001). Some effective programs involve teens in community service or after-school activities with adult supervision and counseling. Others focus more on sex education but not necessarily just on teaching reproductive biology. The most effective sex education programs provide clear messages about the importance of abstaining from sex or using contraception, teach teens how to deal with peer pressure, and provide practice in communicating and negotiating with partners. The federal government should make sure that this research is widely disseminated and expand funding for state and local investments in proven programs. And because there are a variety of different approaches that can be effective, communities should be allowed to choose from among them based on their own needs and values. In this vein, the 2002 welfare bill passed by the Senate Finance Committee contained a number of worthy proposals including $50 million for "abstinence-first" grants to the states (promoting the value of abstinence but allowing education about birth control), a national resource center, recognizing the value of teen pregnancy prevention as an effective means of promoting healthy marriage, and adopting a national teen pregnancy prevention goal.

Finally, much more emphasis needs to be placed on the potential of sophisticated media campaigns to change the wider culture. Such campaigns have been used to effectively change a variety of health behaviors in the past but their full potential has not been tapped in this arena (Snyder 2001). Some nonprofit groups, such as the National Campaign to Prevent Teen Pregnancy and the National Fatherhood Initiative, are working in partnership with the media to embed new messages into the television shows most often watched by teens. And many states are using the abstinence education funds from the welfare reform bill for media campaigns, but additional resources, including some that could be used to design and implement a national effort, are needed.

Secondary Prevention   Another approach that has been tried is "second-chance homes" aimed at preventing subsequent pregnancies among young unmarried mothers. These homes typically provide housing, supervision, and supportive services for teen mothers and their children. State interest in second chance homes was heightened by the provision in the 1996 welfare bill requiring teen mothers to live with their parents or in another supervised setting. Currently, 132 programs are in operation in twenty-nine states with Massachusetts offering an especially well-established network (Social Policy Action Network 2001; U.S. Department of Health and Human Services 2000). Residents of these homes appear to have lower rates of repeat pregnancies than other teen mothers (Sylvester 1995). However, more rigorous evaluations are needed to confirm this result.[5]

Clearer evidence is available for home visiting programs targeted at disadvantaged young mothers (Olds et al. 1999). Home-visited mothers experienced 43 percent fewer pregnancies than a control group that was not visited. Further replication of this model has continued to produce positive results. Other carefully studied programs aimed at reducing repeat pregnancies among very low-income women, such as New Chance, the Teen Parent Demonstration, and the Comprehensive Child Development Program were not successful. Mothers enrolled in these programs were at least as likely to have a subsequent pregnancy as those who did not receive the services (Besharov and Gardiner 1996).

Abortion and Adoption   Unplanned pregnancies are all too common in the United States. An estimated 60 percent of all pregnancies are unintended, either mistimed or unwanted (Institute of Medicine 1995). Over 50 percent end in abortion. Clearly, better or more accessible contraception that leads to fewer unwanted pregnancies can reduce reliance on abortion. Making adoption easier might also help reduce the number of women who terminate a pregnancy. In the meantime, we believe access to abortion is a fundamental right albeit one that should be used sparingly. To quote former President Clinton, "abortion should be safe, legal, and rare."

WELFARE REFORM: STAYING THE COURSE

The good news is that the rise in the proportion of children born outside of marriage and the simultaneous increase in single-parent families slowed or stabilized in the late 1990s. The proportion of children living with two parents increased slightly, though many if not most of these two-parent families were cohabiting rather than married (Acs and Nelson 2001b; Bavier 2002; Bavier 2001; Cherlin and Fomby 2002; Dupree and Primus 2001). Some of the evidence suggests that welfare reform was at least partially responsible for these developments (Acs and Nelson 2001a; Acs and Nelson 2001b; Bitler, Gelbach, and Hoynes 2002; Fein 1999). And as noted, work requirements and tougher child support enforcement likely discouraged young women from having children outside marriage and young men from fathering them. For these reasons, we favor staying the course on welfare reform in the hopes that it will further reduce out-of-wedlock childbearing and perhaps encourage marriages over the longer term.

It does not seem to be the specific provisions in the 1996 welfare law, such as family caps or abstinence education, that have produced these positive developments. Although there are exceptions, most research finds that these provisions have had little if any effect on behavior.[6] Instead, we believe it is the expectation of work, time limits on the receipt of assistance, and the enforcement of child support that are both most likely to change fertility and marriage behaviors in the future and most probably behind the slight decline in single parenting during the late 1990s. Indeed, we support stronger work participation standards for states combined with a generous credit for those recipients who find employment in the private sector.

A number of studies have found that tougher child support enforcement has deterred out-of-wedlock childbearing (Garfinkle, Heintze, and Huang 2000). Combined with provisions allowing more of the money to be given directly to mothers, better child support enforcement should both reduce single parenting and enhance the incomes of existing single parents and thus be a twofer in terms of improving child well-being.

With respect to who is eligible to receive under the Temporary Assistance to Needy Families Program (TANF), most but not all states now provide benefits to two-parent families on the same basis as they do to single-parent families. Specifically, only sixteen states impose special eligibility requirements on two-parent families, including limits on hours of work, work history requirements, and waiting periods for benefits. Interestingly, once a family is deemed eligible, all states include a new parent, typically the father, in the assistance unit, thereby boosting the monthly grant, if he or she is the biological parent of the child. If the new parent is a stepparent, they may be automatically included, included at the family's discretion, or not included. But the rules are complex.

Federal law also sets higher state work participation standards for two-parent families. The required rate in 2002 was 90 percent. Two-parent families are also expected to engage in work activities for thirty-five hours a week (and even more than this if subsidized child care is provided) though they can achieve this by splitting the hours between them. This compares to twenty hours a week for single parents with no children under 6 and twenty hours for those with younger children (Falk and Tauber 2001).

There is an emerging consensus that all of the rules that discriminate between one- and two-parent families should be eliminated. The bills debated in Congress in 2002 had provisions both to eliminate different eligibility rules and to apply the same work standards.

So-called "marriage plus" policies are worth exploring (Ooms 2002a). Such policies encourage marriage but also try to ensure that families have the economic resources and work supports needed to reduce stress and balance work and family responsibilities. The Minnesota Family Investment Program (MFIP) is a good example. It provided additional income to families that work by boosting basic benefits by 20 percent and disregarding or not counting 38 percent of earned income in calculating benefits, emphasized to families the financial benefits of working, and paid child care costs directly to providers rather than reimbursing for these costs after the fact. It also required longer-term recipients to participate in employment and training services, eased eligibility rules for two-parent families, and combined TANF, food stamp, and state general assistance benefits in a single check. Evaluation of the program showed that MFIP not only reduced poverty and improved child well-being but also reduced domestic violence, stabilized marriages, and modestly increased the likelihood that a single parent on welfare would marry. The program cost between $1,900 and $3,800 more per family than Aid to Families with Dependent Children (AFDC) (Knox, Miller, and Gennetian 2000).

Another option, one that would be still more costly but not discriminate against those who have never entered the welfare system, would be a more generous EITC. To encourage both work and marriage, any expansion of the EITC should be combined with an effort to reduce marriage penalties and work disincentives in the program. A number of specific options that might achieve these objectives are discussed and analyzed by Sawhill and Thomas (2001a), and the marriage penalty in the EITC is discussed in more detail below.

Although we support continued efforts to move from a welfare-based to a work-based set of income supports, there are two areas where welfare appears to have had unintended effects that merit a response. One is some evidence that adolescents are adversely affected when their mothers are required to work (Gennetian et al. 2002; Brooks, Hair, and Zaslow 2001). This finding makes further efforts to develop and evaluate after-school programs for this age group a high priority.

We also need new policies in child welfare. The recent decline in the share of children living in single-parent families is encouraging but a less-publicized trend is also worth noting: the increasing share living with neither parent—that is, in households headed by other relatives, friends, or foster parents. While the share living with neither parent is small, among subgroups most likely to have been affected by welfare reform, such as black children in central cities, the proportion increased much faster than for the population as a whole, reaching 16 percent in the years after TANF was implemented (Bitler, Gelbach, and Hoynes 2002; see also Acs and Nelson 2001a; Bernstein 2002). Some of these children may be better off and some worse than they would be living with their own parents. This should therefore not necessarily be taken as an indictment of welfare reform, but it is a yellow flag that at a minimum raises questions about some of the pressures new welfare rules may have created for these families. Some additional evidence on these issues comes from a rigorous evaluation of Delaware's welfare program, A Better Chance (ABC). The program includes strong work requirements, time limits, and strong sanctions for noncompliance with various requirements. The evaluators found an increase in child neglect among the group exposed to the program (although no increase in abuse or in the use of foster care). They hypothesize that work requirements and tough sanctions may have made it difficult for parents to balance work and family, leaving them unable to provide adequate supervision for their children (Fein and Lee 2000).

DEMANDING RESPONSIBLE FATHERHOOD

The first round of welfare reform required low-income mothers to work rather than make welfare a way of life. The next round should challenge the men who father those children to take responsibility for raising them.

In the last several years there has been a dramatic rise in work partici- pation rates among welfare mothers. But employment rates among non- college-educated men have plummeted. The problem is especially acute among young black men, rates for whom declined even during the boom- ing late 1990s. According to Georgetown University's Paul Offner and Harry Holzer (2002) only about 70 percent of young black men were in the labor market in 1999, despite record low unemployment of 4.2 percent.

Absent fathers who aren't working cannot contribute to the financial needs of the children they help bring into the world. Child support is an important source of income for poor children that—when they actually get it—accounts for over 25 percent of their family's income. But the Urban Institute reports that about 66 percent of the nearly 11 million fathers who do not live with their children fail to pay formal child sup- port.

Fathers must be challenged to go to work, make their child support payments and—because a father should be more than a cash machine— establish an emotional connection to their children where possible. As ar- gued above, Congress should first purge the welfare system of its historic bias against fathers and two-parent families, especially married couples.

Second, Congress should encourage the states to bring men into their job placement and work support systems, boost child support collections, and support proven public and private efforts to connect fathers and their children. Specifically, we propose that Washington and the states act to:

- Put men to work. States now have flexibility to use TANF dollars to fund fatherhood programs. Welfare reform legislation introduced by Senators Bayh, Carper, and Graham would create a powerful new incentive for states to integrate men in their welfare-to-work systems. Their proposal would permit the states to count low-income fathers against their work participation requirements, so long as they are enrolled in TANF-funded employment programs and paying child support.

In addition, the federal government should create a competitive grant program to support such initiatives as the Noncustodial Parent Employment Project in Florida, that give unemployed fathers who owe back child support a clear choice: go to work or go to jail.

In addition to jobs, many absent fathers need help in coping with huge child support arrearages. Combining the carrot and the stick, the state of Maryland provides for the full or partial forgiveness of child support arrearages for absent dads who go through a state-mandated employment program, get a job and get up-to date in their payments.

- Focus on prisoners. Each year, 600,000 people, mostly men, are released from prison. In addition to criminal records that dim their job prospects, they often emerge with poor skills, heavy child support arrearages, and weak links to their families and children. Little wonder, then, that their recidivism rates are so high. What is needed is a new national push aimed at preparing prisoners to reenter the world of work and family responsibility. One idea, for example, is to expand prison labor, allowing private sector companies to employ prisoners in state and federal prisons at least at the minimum wage (Atkinson 2002a). There is clear evidence that prisoner work requirements lead to lower recidivism, and the real-world skills they learn can enhance their job prospects after they're released. A reentry strategy would also encourage states to follow New York's lead in using private firms such as America Works to help find jobs for ex-offenders as well as welfare mothers. And it would include increased federal support for competitive grants to public and private efforts to mentor the children of prisoners. Nearly 1.5 million strong, these children suffer disproportionate rates of substance abuse, gang involvement, early childbearing, and delinquency. Given the scale of the problem, it would make sense to ask the Corporation for National Service to work with faith-based and community groups to organize a nationwide volunteer network of mentors.

REFORM DIVORCE LAW TO PUT CHILDREN FIRST

Divorce disrupts the lives of about one million American children a year. Researchers have linked divorce to poor academic performance, depression, antisocial behavior, and other ills. They have found, moreover, that the damage done by divorce cannot be fully explained by either parental conflict before divorce or declining income after divorce. Divorce itself, often followed by decreasing contact between fathers and children, has an independent negative effect on school performance, emotional development, and long-term psychological well-being (Wallerstein, Lewis, and Blakeslee 2000).

The surge in divorce after 1960 coincided with a dramatic cultural shift in the way Americans view marriage. According to a survey conducted by Whitehead and Popenoe (2001, 8), nearly 70 percent of Americans disagree that "the main purpose of marriage is having children." High divorce rates, the growth in out-of-wedlock births, and a massive increase (800 percent since 1960) in the number of cohabiting couples who live with children are all emblematic of a major cultural shift they call the "decline of child-centered marriage."

Legal changes also have played a key role. The nation's first no-fault divorce statute was signed into law by then-Governor Ronald Reagan of California in 1969. A decade later, every state had followed suit. According to a 1996 study presented to the American Political Science Association, "both no-fault divorce laws and general divorce law permissiveness have a strong positive impact on state divorce rates" (Galston 1997, 156). In work for the Progressive Policy Institute, William A. Galston of the University of Maryland has called for reforming divorce laws to put children first. He has proposed that states take the following steps:

- Make divorce no fault by mutual consent only. States should eliminate easy unilateral no-fault divorce for couples with minor children. As an alternative to fault in unilateral cases, states could establish a waiting period before a nonconsensual no-fault divorce is permitted.

- Institute a braking mechanism even in cases in which both parties consent. For example, states might require a mandatory pause of at least a year for reflection, counseling, and mediation.

- In divorce settlements, put children's interests first. Property division should not even be discussed until adequate provision is made for the economic needs of children. Child support should cover a reasonable share of postsecondary education and training, at least until age twenty-one.

- Create a legal presumption in favor of joint custody whenever feasible. The goal is to mitigate one of the most damaging consequences of divorce: diminished parenting time, both from the noncustodial parent, who is separated from the children, and from the custodial parent, who must combine work inside and outside the home. If joint custody arrangements do not work out, the cost of going to court to change them should be shared by both parents.

The purpose of such reforms is not to make divorce more difficult or trap parents in miserable, conflict-ridden marriages. It is to retain the option of divorce while minimizing harm to children and better preparing divorced couples for the challenges of coparenting their children.

MAKING THE TAX SYSTEM MORE FAMILY FRIENDLY

Marriage can affect people's tax liabilities either positively or negatively. Under current law marriage bonuses are much more prevalent than marriage penalties. However, one of the biggest remaining "marriage penalties" occurs when a low-income working mother marries a low-income man. Before marriage the mother can qualify for as much as $4,000 in an earned income tax credit for herself and her children. If she marries another worker she stands to lose a major portion of this benefit because the EITC phases out at higher incomes.

Concern about marriage penalties in the tax system led Congress to enact major changes in the rules affecting different types of families as part of the Economic Growth and Tax Relief Reconciliation Act (EGTRRA) of 2001. The new law phases in an increase in the standard deduction, and widens the 15-percent rate bracket for married couples. In addition, the law extends the level of income at which the EITC begins to phase down for married couples by $3,000. However, this has only a minor effect on marriage penalties facing low-income couples contemplating marriage. For example, a single mother with two children earning $10,000 a year who married a man earning $15,000 a year lost about $2,500 before this change in the law. After the change, she still loses almost $1,900. Another provision of EGTRRA, the partially refundable child tax credit (CTC), has a bigger impact on marriage penalties because it continues to phase in, or ramp up, over the income range where the EITC is phasing out. Thus, this same couple would qualify for a refundable credit of $2,000 once they married but would receive nothing from the credit while single because families with less than $10,000 of income are not eligible (Sawhill and Thomas 2001b; Carasso and Steuerle 2002).

These two credits are enormously complex, imposing an undue burden on low-income families who often must pay high fees to the professional tax preparers they need to claim their benefits. (Berube et al. 2002). Therefore, we believe that further steps to reduce existing marriage penalties and simplify the tax code are integral to a progressive, pro-family strategy. Marriage penalties will always exist as long as taxes are progressive and government benefits for welfare, Food Stamps, and other programs are income-tested. However, as experience with the new refundable child credit illustrates, it is possible both to provide more income to low-income families and encourage work and marriage at the same time. The refundable child credit not only reduced marriage penalties more than any of the provisions specifically aimed at that problem but provided assistance to more than nine million low- and middle-income working families, including more than eighteen million children. The total amount of assistance they will receive is estimated to be at least $50 billion over the next ten years. Most of the families who will benefit have incomes between $10,000 and about $35,000 per year (Sawhill and Thomas 2001b).

Finally, lawmakers should reform the Child and Dependent Care Credit. This credit, which is estimated to cost $2.4 billion a year, is badly targeted (U.S. Congress 2001a). The nonrefundable credit offers little help to low-income families because most of them pay little or no income tax. It is widely viewed as inequitable because it grants tax relief only to families who purchase child care, thereby discriminating against those who choose either to have a parent stay home or to make informal arrangements, such as leaving the children with relatives or friends. One option for reform would be to eliminate the credit and fold the resulting savings into the Child Tax Credit, which could then be increased for younger children or ramped up more quickly to $1,000 per child.

BALANCING WORK AND FAMILY

As two-worker families have become the norm, harried parents increasingly fret about having less time to spend on their most important job: raising their children. They are acutely aware that neither employer practices nor public policy have kept pace with the dramatic influx of mothers into the workplace. As recently as 1975, less than 40 percent of U.S. women with children under age 6 worked; today, nearly 65 percent do (U.S. Department of Labor 2001). Because mothers remain young children's primary caregivers, the work-family squeeze hits them particularly hard. And for single mothers, the challenge of juggling work, day care, and other daily tasks is even more daunting.

The forces propelling women into the workforce have led to a more equal division of labor between husbands and wives, with the former increasingly sharing in housework and childrearing and the later increasingly pursuing careers. America's social and tax policies, predicated on the old model of male breadwinner and female homemaker, sorely need updating.

What today's working families need are new public supports that enable parents to spend more time with their children and help to protect them when they're not around. There is growing public appetite for more and better child care and for preschool programs that prepare young children to learn; more generous family leave policies, including paid maternity leave; and enriching after-school programs to keep children occupied until their parents get home from work.

Surveys show that parents also yearn for more flexible work arrangements. Parents of newborns, most often mothers, want to stay home without sacrificing their jobs and careers. They want more opportunities to work part-time so they can be home when their children return from school. Above all, working parents want more control over their hours so that they can take off from work to care for sick children, attend important school events or do other parental chores as the need arises. The chief responsibility for creating more family friendly workplaces, of course, lies with employers. But public policy can encourage employers to offer more flexible work arrangements, including part-time jobs with decent pay and benefits, comp time, and telecommuting.

To help our hard-pressed families balance the competitive pressures of work and parental obligations, we propose to increase federal child care support, expand family leave, create a paid leave system, exapnd quality preschool, stimulate after-school programs, promote telework, and allow comp time.

Increase Federal Child Care Support

Since the landmark 1996 welfare reform bill, public support for child care has grown substantially. In 2001, states spent a total of $8 billion on child care, including $4.5 billion in federal funding under TANF and the Child Care Development Block Grant, the principal sources of federal child care funding (U.S. Health and Human Services 2001). Federal spending alone in 2001 was more than four times the amount spent on federally funded, welfare-related child care in 1993 (U.S. House of Representatives 1994). Nevertheless, it is estimated that only 15 to 20 percent of potentially eligible children received subsidized day care (Layzer and Collins 2000). Moreover, demand for child care is likely to rise if Congress, as expected, raises work participation requirements for states from 50 to 70 percent of their welfare caseloads.

And it is becoming more expensive. According to researchers Stephanie Coontz and Nancy Folbre (2002, n.p.), "unless [a poor working mother] is lucky enough to have a family member who can provide free child care, or to find a federally subsidized child care slot, more than 20 percent of her income will go to pay for child care."[7] Access to affordable day care is a huge problem for parents who work untraditional hours: night shifts, weekends, or part-time.

As part of a national commitment to making work pay, Congress should boost child care spending substantially when it reauthorizes the TANF welfare legislation for another five years. Specifically, it should add roughly $8 billion over five years to the Child Care Development Block Grant—a figure that represents the midrange of contending GOP and Democratic proposals. While more money for child care is essential to buttress the states' efforts to move more people from welfare to work, subsidies should be targeted at working poor families generally. National policy should aim at creating a seamless system of child care subsidies that treats all low-income families equally, regardless of whether they have received welfare.

Expand Family Leave

Passed over the vehement opposition of conservatives and employers, the 1993 Family and Medical Leave Act (FMLA) for the first time established a worker's right to take unpaid leave for family or medical emergencies. But the act applies only to firms with more than fifty workers and exempts recently hired employees. "As a result," says Minehan (2000, 40), "the law fails to cover half of employed fathers and 41 percent of employed mothers. Those who are covered by the law are not that much better off—relatively few employees can afford to take twelve weeks off without pay." According to researchers at Harvard, 46 percent of low-wage and low-income parents work at companies too small to be subject to the FMLA (Heymann et al. 2002). Congress should expand the Family and Medical Leave Act to cover more small businesses and give parents unpaid time off for parent-teacher conferences and children's doctor visits. To spare small firms the burden of a twelve-week leave requirement, Congress could build in a second tier of permissible leave time for companies with twenty-five to fifty employees—say, four to six weeks (Heymann et al. 2002).

Create a Paid Leave System

Most advanced countries offer paid leave to new parents. The United States was the conspicuous exception until California instituted the nation's first paid leave policy in October 2002. Prodding lawmakers to action is a growing body of scientific evidence that regards the early months of a child's life as critical to cognitive development. According to the Carnegie Task Force on Meeting the Needs of Young Children

(1994, 44), "experts can now substantiate the benefits of allowing ample time for the mother to recover from childbirth and for parents to be with their new baby during the first months of life."

Under California's new law, most workers will be paid about 55 percent of their salary for six weeks of leave to care for a new child or sick relative. The benefit will be paid out of worker contributions to a state disability fund.

In a variation on the theme, PPI Vice President Rob Atkinson (2002b) has proposed using the Unemployment Insurance (UI) system to provide new parents with paid family leave. Under this approach, the states would pass laws making married parents of newborns eligible for unemployment insurance for up to six months with the period of eligibility starting two months before birth. Either parent, mother or father, could choose to stay at home as the caregiver, though only those who have been employed for at least eighteen months would be eligible for paid leave. To avoid penalizing employers, leave benefits would not be charged to the individual employer's UI account, as they are in cases of layoff, but would be billed against the state's general account paid into by all employers. By confining eligibility to married couples who have been working, a paid leave policy would not destroy incentives for work or create incentives to have children out of wedlock. To give the states a strong incentive to create paid leave, Atkinson proposes that the federal government pay 75 percent of the cost of the new benefits, and the states 25 percent.

Make Quality Preschool Available to All Children

Recent research on the brain has highlighted the advantages of early learning on a child's cognitive development. Moreover, there is growing evidence that high-quality preschool programs can provide a strong foundation for language development, reading skills, and socialization. The RAND Corporation (1998) evaluated eleven different early childhood programs and found that nearly all of them had some positive effect on cognitive development and educational achievement. A growing body of research shows that the best results come from programs that include children from the most disadvantaged homes, employ teachers with a bachelor's degree, provide intensive education and other services, and pursue researched-based strategies to foster development of children's cognitive and language skills. Those results include higher school achievement, less repeating of grades, less need for later remedial education, and less crime.

A growing network of preschool programs can help ease the child care crunch while helping Americans achieve a vital social goal: narrowing the academic achievement gap between poor and middle-class kids. Although many states and localities have launched early learning programs, the movement needs a strong push from above. "Despite the well-documented importance of high quality early-childhood education in how children fare in school, only half of all three- and four-year-olds attend formally early childhood education," a recent report indicates (Heymann et al. 2002, 16).

National policy makers therefore should set an ambitious goal: making high-quality preschool available to every child in America. The federal government can act as a catalyst by providing grants to states to expand access to quality preschool. States would use the money to create preschool programs in public schools, recreation centers, child care centers, and Head Start centers. This approach would offer parents choice while ensuring public oversight to hold providers accountable for results. In exchange for federal money, states would agree to establish preschool readiness standards and ensure that programs have well qualified teachers and use research-based pre-academic curricula. Washington should give the states considerable leeway in setting standards and judge them strictly on results, specifically, progress toward closing the achievement gap between children from low- and middle-income families. Adopting such a pay for performance approach will ensure that federal dollars are targeted on the most disadvantaged students who stand to gain the most from quality preschool. A useful point of departure for this debate is a proposal, made by Al Gore and Joe Lieberman during the 2000 presidential campaign, to spend $50 billion over ten years to make voluntary preschool available to all four-year-olds and a growing number of three-year-olds.

Stimulate the Growth of After-School Programs

With parents caught in a work-family time crunch and educators under mounting pressure to lift academic performance, there is also growing interest in after-school programs. Such programs can give parents peace of mind by providing a safe, supervised place for their adolescent children to spend afternoons—the vulnerable hours when they are susceptible to juvenile crime and teen sex. For educators, after-school programs offer extended learning time to help their students reach the higher performance standards that Washington and the states are putting in place. And there is now evidence that well-designed programs reduce teenage pregnancy and other risky behaviors (Kane and Sawhill 2003).

According to the U.S. Department of Education, nearly 65 percent of all schools offer after-school activities, but they serve on average only about 11 percent of their students. Many of those programs, moreover, are not designed to boost academic achievement for struggling students. School districts increasingly are working with private sector companies, community-based organizations, including faith-based and other partners to create enriching experiences for students in the after-school hours and during summer. To encourage further experimentation, Washington should expand the nearly $1 billion 21st Century Community Learning Centers program and include more money for research into which programs are most effective in promoting student achievement gains and reducing risky behaviors.

Promote Telework

About twenty million Americans are teleworkers. Typically they work nine days per month at home, averaging three hours per week. According to testimony by the International Telework Association and Council (ITAC), American Express teleworkers are 43 percent more productive than their office workers (U.S. Congress 2001b); similarly, JD Edwards, Compaq, Lexus Nexus, and Siemens also report an increase in productivity of their e-workers (Positively Broadband Campaign 2002).

The trend toward telework has accelerated as the cost of outfitting a home-based office has fallen. Yet there are signs that the growth in telecommuting is butting up against a major technical obstacle: the slow speed of transferring data over old-fashioned telephone wires. This suggests that the single most important thing government can do to encourage telework is to spur the build-out of broadband technology.[8]

In the meantime, Congress can offer tax breaks to offer a more direct and immediate stimulus to telecommuting. In 2001, Senator John Kerry, for example, proposed a new tax credit of $500 for workers who work from home, plus 10 percent up to $500 of expenses for telework equipment and internet access, for a total possible credit of $1,000 per teleworker (U.S. Congress 2001b).

Atkinson also argues for exempting home offices from federal and state workplace regulations. It is logistically infeasible, and probably unnecessary, to impose Occupational Safety and Health Administration (OSHA) standards on people whose workplaces are their homes. Government can also lead by example. For example, the Bush administration could encourage telework by federal employees, including reimbursing employee expense for office technology and telecommunications costs (Atkinson, Ham, and Newkirk 2002).

Allow Workers to Take Comp Time

Today's working parents place enormous value on time and the ability to control their work hours because they need to look after aging parents and children, visit doctors and schools, and simply do household chores that cannot be done at night or on weekends. Pollster Mark Penn (2000) reports that 75 percent of Americans, including 83 percent of women with children, say they would like to choose between taking overtime in extra wages or in the form of time off from work. Comp time has been available to public sector employees since 1985. But the Fair Labor Standards Act of 1938 requires that private employers offer only monetary compensation to hourly workers for overtime. Efforts to change this archaic law, unfortunately, have been stymied by unions and their supporters in Congress, who fear that its great achievement—the forty-hour week—could be undermined.

But Congress shouldn't find it hard to create more flexibility for workers without giving employers a green light to work them longer. Specifically, Congress should change the law to offer workers the choice of either one-and-one-half hours of wages or one-and-one-half hours of comp time for each hour of overtime worked. At the same time, it should bar employers from forcing workers into taking time off, protect vulnerable employees, including part-time and seasonal workers; give employees reasonable latitude over when they can take the time off and the ability to cash out their unused comp time.

CONCLUSION

These policy options address what we take to be the central dilemmas facing America's families today: premature, out-of-wedlock childbearing; the failure of too many absent fathers to provide financial or emotional support to their children; divorce laws that put adult convenience over children's interests; public policies that undermine marriage and family; a tax code that gives too much to affluent Americans and takes too much from working parents raising children; and a severe time squeeze on parents trying to juggle the demands of work and family.

The solutions we offer combine important insights from liberals and conservatives in a new synthesis that moves beyond old ideological battles. Our approach acknowledges the cultural as well as economic roots of family instability. It insists on both more personal responsibility from parents and more collective responsibility from government to provide practical supports for parents who work hard and play by the rules. And it recognizes that while top-down bureaucracies cannot substitute for functioning families, neither can voluntary and faith-based organizations fully take government's place.

We offer, instead, a third approach grounded in the values and outlook of the vital center of American politics. It envisions a stronger partnership between government and civil society in fortifying our families. It recognizes that businesses too must change their operations to accommodate the new rhythms of family life in a post-industrial economy. Above all, it seeks to enable families to be strong and self-reliant by equipping them with the tools and resources they need to solve their own problems and perform the vital functions that have always made them the bedrock of healthy societies.

NOTES

1. If the share of children living in female-headed families had remained constant after 1970, the child poverty rate in 1998 would have fallen by 1 percentage point rather than rising by 3.4 relative to the 1970 rate. Thus, the child poverty rate is 4 to 5 percentage points higher than it would be if there had been no change in marriage and child-bearing patterns after 1970. It is a mistake, of course, to assume that single parents who married would look just like currently married parents, but even after adjusting for their poorer marriage prospects, child poverty would fall by over 3 percentage points if marriage were as prevalent now as it was in 1970 (Thomas and Sawhill 2002).

2. According to Ventura and Bachrach (2000), the birth rate for unmarried mothers is highest among the age group twenty to twenty-four, and 55 percent of out-of-wedlock births are to mothers between twenty and twenty-nine years old. In addition, from 1972 to 1999, the percent of unmarried mothers who were cohabiting (with either an unrelated male or the father) increased from 2 to 12 percent (Cancian and Reed 2000). However, 51 percent of unmarried mothers are not living with the father at the time of their child's birth (Fragile Families 2002). Finally, Driscoll et al. (1999) find that women who have children outside of marriage have lower incomes and are more likely to depend on welfare as a source of financial support.

3. Nearly eight out of ten teen pregnancies are not planned or intended (Alan Guttmacher Institute 2002). In addition, teen mothers are less likely to complete their education; among women who have children before age eighteen, only 41 percent ever complete high school, compared to 61 percent of women who postpone childbearing until age 20 or 21 (Hotz, McElroy, and Sanders 1997). Furthermore, children of teen mothers are more likely to repeat a grade, are less likely to complete high school, and achieve lower scores on standardized tests (Maynard 1996; Haveman, Wolfe, and Peterson 1997).

4. For new evidence that welfare reform may have played a role in lowering the teen birth rate, see Kaestner and O'Neill (2002).

5. The Office of the Assistant Secretary for Planning and Evaluation (U.S. Department of Health and Human Services 2000) highlights four methodological shortcomings of the Sylvester (1995) brief. First, the results, which are typically based on self-reported participant information, are not independently verified. Second, the results are based on a relatively small number of mothers. Third, information is gathered only from those who stayed in the programs or who were easily tracked after they left. Fourth, and probably most important, there exists no comparable control group with which to compare the results.

6. See Wertheimer and Moore (1998); Murray (2001); and U.S. General Accounting Office (2001) and Stark and Levin-Epstein (1999) on family caps. For some research that is not consistent with the above statement, see Acs and Nelson (2001b); Fein (1999); Horvath-Rose and Peters (2000); and Knox, Miller, and Gennetian (2000).

7. For more evidence on the child care expenses of working families and how various policies would affect their standard of living, see Sawhill and Thomas (2001a).

8. For more comprehensive recommendations on how government should encourage telework, see Atkinson, Ham, and Newkirk (2002).

REFERENCES

Acs, Gregory, and Sandi Nelson. 2001a. "'Honey, I'm Home.' Changes in the Living Arrangements in the Late 1990s." *New Federalism National Survey of America's Families*, Series B, No. B-38. Washington, D.C.: Urban Institute Press.

———. 2001b. "Changes in Living Arrangements During the Late 1990s: Do Welfare Policies Matter?" Washington, D.C.: Urban Institute Press.

———. 2002. "The Kids are Alright? Children's Well-Being and the Rise in Cohabitation." *New Federalism National Survey of America's Families*, Series B, No. B-48. Washington, D.C.: Urban Institute Press.

Alan Guttmacher Institute. 2002. "Teen Pregnancy: Trends and Lessons Learned." *Issues in Brief 1*. Washington, D.C.: Alan Guttmacher Institute.

Atkinson, Robert D., Shane Ham, and Brian Newkirk. 2002. "Unleashing the Potential of High-Speed Internet: Strategies to Boost Broadband Demand." Washington, D.C.: Progressive Policy Institute.

Atkinson, Robert D. 2002a. "Prison Labor: It's More than Breaking Rocks." Washington, D.C.: Progressive Policy Institute.

―――――. 2002b. "Modernizing Unemployment Insurance for the New Economy and the New Social Policy. Washington, D.C.: Progressive Policy Institute.

Bavier, Richard. 2001. "Recent Increases in the Share of Young Children Living with Married Mothers." Washington: U.S. Government Printing Office for the Office of Management and Budget.

―――――. 2002. "Child-Bearing Outside Marriage and Child-Raising Inside Marriage." Washington, D.C.: Office of Management and Budget.

Bernstein, Nina. 2002. "Side Effect of Welfare Law: The No-Parent Family." *The New York Times* (July 29, 2002): A1, 2.

Berube, Alan, Anne Kim, Benjamin Foreman, and Megan Burns. 2002. "The Price of Paying Taxes: How Tax Preparation and Refund Loan Fees Erode the Benefits of the EITC." Washington, D.C.: Brookings Institution and Progressive Policy Institute.

Besharov, Douglas J., and Karen N. Gardiner. 1996. "Paternalism and Welfare Reform." *Public Interest* (Winter): 70–84.

Bitler, Marianne P., Jonah B. Gelbach, and Hilary W. Hoynes. 2002. "The Impact of Welfare Reform on Living Arrangements." *NBER Working Paper No. W8784.*

Brooks, Jennifer L., Elizabeth C. Hair, and Martha J. Zaslow. 2001. "Welfare Reform's Impact on Adolescents: Early Warning Signs." *Child Trends Research Brief.* Washington, D.C.: Child Trends.

Campbell, Frances A., Craig T. Ramney, Elizabeth P. Pungello, Joseph Sparling, and Shari Miller-Johnson. 2002. "Early Childhood Education: Young Adult Outcomes from the Abecedarian Project." *Applied Development Science* 6(1): 42–57.

Cancian, Maria, and Deborah Reed. 2000. "Trends in Family Structure and Behavior and the Poverty Problem." Paper presented to the Institute for Research on Poverty Conference on "Understanding Poverty in America: Progress and Problems." Madison, Wis. (May 18, 2000).

Carasso, Adam, and Eugene Steuerle. 2002. "How Marriage Penalties Change Under the June 2001 Tax Bill." Washington, D.C.: Urban Institute Press.

Carnegie Task Force on Meeting the Needs of Young Children. 1994 *Starting Points: Meeting the Needs of Our Youngest Children.* New York: Carnegie Corporation.

Cherlin, Andrew, and Paula Fomby. 2002. "A Closer Look at Changes in Children's Living Arrangements in Low-Income Families." In *Welfare, Children, and Families: A Three-City Study.* Baltimore: Johns Hopkins University Press.

Coontz, Stephanie, and Nancy Folbre. 2002. "Marriage, Poverty, and Public Policy: A Discussion Paper from the Council on Contemporary Families." Prepared for the Fifth Annual CCF Conference, April 26–

28. Available at http://www.contemporaryfamilies.org/public/briefing .html (accessed July 20, 2004).

Davis, Donald D., and Karen A. Polonko. 2001. "Telework in the United States: Telework America Survey 2001." Washington, D.C.: International Telework Association and Council.

Driscoll, Anne K., Gesine K. Hearn, V. Jeffrey Evans, Kristin A. Moore, Barbara W. Sugland, and Vaughn Call. 1999. "Nonmarital Childbearing Among Adult Women." *Journal of Marriage and Family* 61(1): 178–87.

Dupree, Allen, and Wendell Primus. 2001. "Declining Share of Children Lived with Single Mothers in the Late 1990s, Substantial Differences by Race and Income." Washington, D.C.: Center on Budget and Policy Priorities.

Ellwood, David, and Christopher Jencks. 2001. "The Growing Difference in Family Structure: What Do We Know? Where Do We Look for Answers?" Unpublished paper. Cambridge, Mass.: John F. Kennedy School of Government, Harvard University.

Falk, Gene, and Jill Tauber. 2001. "Welfare Reform: TANF Provisions Related to Marriage and Two-Parent Families." Washington, D.C.: Congressional Research Service.

Fein, David J. 1999. "Will Welfare Reform Influence Marriage and Fertility? Early Evidence from the ABC Demonstration." Bethesda, Md.: Abt Associates.

Fein, David J., and Wang S. Lee. 2000. "The ABC Evaluation, Impacts of Welfare Reform on Child Maltreatment." Cambridge, Mass.: Abt Associates.

Flanigan, Christine. 2001. "What's Behind the Good News: The Decline in Teen Pregnancy Rates During the 1990s." Washington, D.C.: National Campaign to Prevent Teen Pregnancy.

Fragile Families. 2002. "The Living Arrangements of New Unmarried Mothers." *Fragile Families Research Brief* 7. Princeton University and Columbia University.

Galston, William A. 1997. "A Progressive Family Policy for the Twenty-First Century." In *Building the Bridge, 10 Big Ideas to Transform America,* edited by Will Marshall. Lanham, Md.: Rowman and Littlefield.

Garfinkel, Irwin, Theresa Heintze, and Chien-Chung Huang. 2000. "Child Support Enforcement: Incentives and Well-Being." Paper presented to the Conference on Incentive Effects of Tax and Transfer Policies. Washington, D.C. (December 8, 2000).

Gennetian, Lisa A., Greg J. Duncan, Virginia W. Knox, Wanda G. Vargas, Elizabeth Clark-Kauffman, Andrew S. London. 2002. *How Welfare and Work Policies for Parents Affect Adolescents A Synthesis of Research.* New York: MDRC.

Halle, Tamara. 2002. *Charting Parenthood: A Statistical Portrait of Fathers and Mothers in America*. Washington, D.C.: Child Trends.

Haveman, Robert H., Barbara Wolfe, and Elaine Peterson. 1997. "Children of Early Childbearers as Young Adults." In *Kids Having Kids: A Robin Hood Foundation Special Report on the Costs of Adolescent Childbearing*, edited by Rebecca Maynard. New York: Robin Hood Foundation.

Heaton, Tim B. 2002. "Factors Contributing to Increasing Marital Stability in the United States." *Journal of Family Issues* 23(3): 392–409.

Heymann, Jody, Renee Boynton-Jarrett, Patricia Carter, James T. Bond, and Ellen Galinsky. 2002. "Work-Family Issues and Low-Income Families." Low Income Working Families, The Ford Foundation.

Horvath-Rose, Ann E., and H. Elizabeth Peters. 2000. "Welfare Waivers and Non-Marital Childbearing." *Joint Center on Poverty Research Working Paper No. 128*. Northwestern University and University of Chicago.

Hotz, V. Joseph, Susan W. McElroy, and Seth G. Sanders. 1997. "The Impacts of Teenage Childbearing on the Mothers and the Consequences of Those Impacts for Government." In *Kids Having Kids: Economic Costs and Social Consequences of Teen Pregnancy*, edited by Rebecca Maynard. Washington, D.C.: Urban Institute Press.

Institute of Medicine. 1995. *The Best Intentions, Unintended Pregnancy and the Well-Being of Children and Families*, edited by Sarah S. Brown and Leon Eisenberg. Washington, D.C.: National Academy Press.

Kaestner, Robert, and June O'Neill. 2002. "Has Welfare Reform Changed Teenage Behaviors?" *NBER Working Paper No. W8932*.

Kane, Andrea, and Isabel V. Sawhill. 2003. "Preventing Early Childbearing." In *One Percent for the Kids,* edited by Isabel V. Sawhill. Washington, D.C.: Brookings Institution Press.

Kirby, Douglas. 2001. *Emerging Answers*. Washington, D.C.: National Campaign to Prevent Teen Pregnancy.

Knox, Virginia, Cynthia Miller, and Lisa A. Gennetian. 2000. "Reforming Welfare and Rewarding Work: A Summary of the Final Report on the Minnesota Family Investment Program." New York: MDRC.

Knox, Virginia, and Cindy Redcross. 2000. *Parenting and Providing: The Impact of Parents' Fair Share on Paternal Involvement*. New York: MDRC.

Layzer, Jean I., and Ann Collins. 2000. "National Study of Child Care for Low-Income Families: State and Community Substudy." Washington, D.C.: Abt Associates.

Lichter, Daniel T., and Deborah Roempke Graefe. 2001. "Finding a Mate? The Marital and Cohabitation Histories of Unwed Mothers." In *Out of Wedlock: Trends, Causes and Consequences of Nonmarital Fertility*, edited by Lawrence L. Wu and Barbara Wolfe. New York: Russell Sage Foundation.

Lichter, Daniel T., Deborah Roempke Graefe, and J. Brian Brown. 2001.

"Is Marriage a Panacea? Union Formation Among Economically Disadvantaged Unwed Mothers." Ohio State University.

Maynard, Rebecca A., ed. 1996. *Kids Having Kids: A Robin Hood Foundation Special Report on the Costs of Adolescent Childbearing.* New York: Robin Hood Foundation.

Minehan, Maureen. 2000. "Finding Time for Family." *Blueprint Magazine* (September 1, 2000). Washington, D.C.: Democratic Leadership Council.

Murray, Charles. 2001. "Family Formation." In *The New World of Welfare,* edited by Rebecca Blank and Ron Haskins. Washington, D.C.: Brookings Institution Press.

National Center for Health Statistics. 2002. *National Vital Statistics Report* 50(10). Hyattsville, Md.: National Center for Health Statistics.

The National Marriage Project. 2002. "Social Indicators of Marital Health and Wellbeing." In *The State of Our Unions 2002.* Piscataway, N.J.: Rutgers University.

Nelson, Sandi, Rebecca L. Clark, and Gregory Acs. 2001. "Beyond the Two-Parent Family: How Teenagers Fare in Cohabiting Couple and Blended Families." *New Federalism National Survey of America's Families* Series B, No. B-31. Washington, D.C.: Urban Institute Press.

Offner, Paul, and Harry Holzer. 2002. "Left Behind in the Labor Market: Recent Employment Trends Among Young Black Men." Report. Washington, D.C.: Brookings Institution.

Olds, David L., Charles Henderson, Jr., Harriet J. Kitzman, John J. Eckenrode, Robert E. Cole, and Robert C. Tatelbaum. 1999. "Prenatal and Infancy Home Visitation by Nurses: Recent Findings." *Home Visiting: Recent Program Evaluations* 9(1): 44–65.

Ooms, Theodora. 2002a. "Marriage-Plus." Washington, D.C.: Center for Law and Social Policy.

———. 2002b. "Marriage and Government: Strange Bedfellows?" *Policy Brief, Couples and Marriage Series No. 1.* Washington, D.C.: Center for Law and Social Policy.

Penn, Mark J. 2000. "Why Voters Care About the Quality of Life." *Blueprint Magazine* 8(Fall): 74. Washington, D.C.: Democratic Leadership Council.

Popenoe, David, and Barbara Dafoe Whitehead. 2002. "Should We Live Together? What Young Adults Need to Know Before Living Together." The National Marriage Project. Piscataway, N.J.: Rutgers University.

Positively Broadband Campaign. 2002. "Any Time Any Place Anywhere: Broadband and the Changing Face of Work." Available at: www.positivelybroadband.org/library/downloads/17505_final_whitepaper.pdf (accessed May 24, 2004).

RAND Corporation. 1998. "Early Childhood Interventions: Benefits, Costs, and Savings." RAND Research Brief. Santa Monica, Calif.: RAND Corporation.

Sawhill, Isabel. 2001. "What Can Be Done to Reduce Teen Pregnancy and Out-of-Wedlock Births?" *Welfare Reform and Beyond Policy Brief No. 8.* Washington, D.C.: Brookings Institution Press.

Sawhill, Isabel, and Adam Thomas. 2001a. "A Hand-Up for the Bottom Third: Toward a New Agenda for Low-Income Working Families." Discussion paper. Washington, D.C.: Brookings Institution Press.

————. 2001b. "Summary of the Child Tax Credit Provisions of HR 1836 (The Economic Growth and Tax Relief Reconciliation Act of 2001)." Washington, D.C.: Brookings Institution Press.

Snyder, Leslie B. 2001. "How Effective Are Mediated Health Campaigns?" In *Public Communication Campaign*, edited by Ronald E. Rice and Charles K. Atkin. Thousand Oaks, Calif.: Sage Publications.

Social Policy Action Network. 2001. *Second Chance Homes National Directory.* Washington, D.C.: Social Policy Action Network.

Stark, Shelley, and Jodie Levin-Epstein. 1999. "Excluded Children: Family Cap in a New Era." Unpublished paper. Washington, D.C.: Center for Law and Social Policy.

Sylvester, Kathleen. 1995. "Second Chance Homes, Breaking the Cycle of Teen Pregnancy." *Policy Briefing.* Washington, D.C.: Progressive Policy Institute.

Terry-Humen, Elizabeth, Jennifer Manlove, and Kristin A. Moore. 2001. "Births Outside of Marriage: Perceptions vs. Reality." *Child Trends Research Brief No. 4.* Washington, D.C.: Child Trends.

Thomas, Adam, and Isabel Sawhill. 2002. "For Richer or Poorer: Marriage as an Antipoverty Strategy." *Journal of Policy Analysis and Management* 21(3): 587–599.

U.S. Census Bureau. 2002. *Statistical Abstract of the United States: 2002.* Washington, D.C.: Hoover's Business Press.

U.S. Congress. Joint Committee on Taxation. 2001a. *Estimates of Federal Tax Expenditures for Fiscal Years 2001–2005.* 107th Cong., 1st sess., 2001. Committee Print.

U.S. Congress. Senate. 2001b. *Teleworking Advancement Act.* S 1856. 107th Cong. 1st sess., *Congressional Record* 147, daily ed. (December 19, 2001): S13710–1.

U.S. Department of Health and Human Services. Administration for Children and Families: Child Care Bureau. 2001. *Fiscal Year 2001 Child Care Development Fund Grant Award Summary.*Washington: U.S. Government Printing Office.

U.S. Department of Health and Human Services. Centers for Disease Control and Prevention. 2002. "Cohabitation, Marriage, Divorce, and

Remarriage in the United States." *Vital and Health Statistics,* Series 23, No. 22. Washington: U.S. Government Printing Office.

U.S. Department of Health and Human Services. Office of the Assistant Secretary for Planning and Evaluation. 2000. *Second Chance Homes: Providing Services for Teenage Parents and Their Children.* Washington: U.S. Government Printing Office. Available at http://aspe.hhs.gov/hsp/2ndchancehomes (accessed July 20, 2004).

U.S. Department of Labor, United States Bureau of Labor Statistics. 2001. *Employment Status of Women by Presence and Age of Youngest Child, March 1975–2001.* Washington: U.S. Government Printing Office.

U.S. General Accounting Office. 2001. "Welfare Reform: More Research Needed on TANF Family Caps and Other Policies for Reducing Out-of-Wedlock Births." Washington: U.S. Government Printing Office.

U.S. House of Representatives, Committee on Ways and Means. 1994. *Green Book: 1994.* 14th ed. Washington: U.S. Government Printing Office.

Ventura, Stephanie J. and Christine A. Bachrach. 2000. "Nonmarital Childbearing in the United States, 1940–99." *National Vital Statistics Reports* 48(16). Washington: U.S. Government Printing Office for the Centers for Disease Control and Prevention.

Wallerstein, Judith S., Julia Lewis, and Sandra Blakeslee. 2000. *The Unexpected Legacy of Divorce.* New York: Hyperion.

Wertheimer, Richard, and Kristin Moore. 1998. "Childbearing by Teens: Links to Welfare Reform." *New Federalism: Issues and Options for States* A-24. Washington, D.C.: Urban Institute Press.

Whitehead, Barbara Dafoe, and David Popenoe. 2001. "Introduction: The Decline of Child-Centered Marriage." In *American Experiment Quarterly,* vol. 4, no. 2, edited by Barbara Dafoe Whitehead and David Popenoe. Minneapolis, Minn.: Center of the American Experiment.

CHAPTER ELEVEN

Disincentives to Care:
A Critique of U.S. Family Policy

Nancy Folbre

If American society recognized home making and child rearing as productive work to be included in the national economic accounts . . . the receipt of welfare might not imply dependency. But we don't. It may be hoped the women's movement of the present time will change this. But as of the time I write, it had not.
—Daniel Patrick Moynihan (1973, 17)

IN THE MORE than twenty five years since this observation was made, social scientists have moved toward greater appreciation of the market value of nonmarket work.[1] A number of recent studies focus on the contributions that mothers and fathers make to the next generation of workers and the stock of "human capital" (Haveman and Wolfe 1995; Crittenden 2001). Some economists argue that child rearing offers positive fiscal externalities as well as more general public benefits (Lee and Miller 1990; Folbre 1994). Yet the welfare reform agenda continues to focus on "reducing dependency," interpreted as increasing paid employment and reducing access to welfare, and enforcing "family responsibility," interpreted as confining sex and child rearing to marriage, without much regard for the larger goal of encouraging and supporting commitments to the care of dependents within the family and the community.

Moral values exert a tremendous influence on public policy (see chapter 1). Much depends on whose values we are talking about, and the extent to which they reflect racial or ethnic bias. Conservatives like to use the word immoral to describe out-of-wedlock births. Progressives like to use the word to describe persistently high rates of child poverty.

Social scientists often try to avoid philosophical debate by emphasizing issues of efficiency rather than morality. But whose efficiency? Traditional benchmarks of success are based on the easily quantified output of the market economy. The value of unpaid work devoted to the care of family and community, which includes, but cannot be limited to, investments in our "stock of human capital," is far more difficult to measure. In the long run, however, it may be more important to our collective standard of living. Moral values provide normative incentives to protect long-run gains from short-run temptation. And definitions of efficiency have implications for moral values. An economic system that punishes virtuous behavior on the grounds that it is "unproductive" is likely to see such behavior decline.

I argue that many aspects of U.S. family policy create disincentives for family care. I focus on factors that may directly or indirectly affect the supply of intrinsically motivated labor to activities outside the market economy.[2] Excessive emphasis on reducing "dependency" can punish those committed to caring for the genuinely dependent, including children and disabled family members. Efforts to discourage single-parent families can lead to more "no-parent" families. Incentives to increase hours of paid work can adversely affect parental care and larger participation in community life. Policies designed to reduce the number of people receiving public assistance can hurt the deserving and eligible needy.

Excessive emphasis on family responsibility can also backfire. Conservatives sometimes argue that too much freedom of choice undermines the stability of family life. But traditional breadwinner or homemaker marriages are not best for everyone, and free choice is critical to developing and sustaining intrinsic motivation. External pressures to marry and stay married can lower the quality of personal relationships. Restrictions on women's reproductive choices are not only morally wrong. They can also lead to subsequent resentments and frustrations that impinge on children. Rules designed to strictly enforce child support payments by noncustodial fathers can discourage their active participation and involvement in the children's lives. Such perverse effects are theoretically important and empirically significant.

INCENTIVES TO CARE

Economists have remarkably little to say about factors affecting the supply of intrinsically motivated care for others. Traditional neoclassical economics holds that individual decisions within a competitive market generally lead to efficient social outcomes, treating coordination problems, information problems, and "externalities" or "spillovers" as relatively minor exceptions to the rule. Few economists study the evolution of nonmarket institutions such as the family, charitable institutions, or the welfare state. Those who do tend to assume that individuals make altruistic decisions based on personal preferences. Altruism toward children is generally interpreted as a natural, unchanging instinct or impulse. If it is natural and unchanging, we don't need to worry about it. Its supply—like that of air, or water, or a stable climate—appears costlessly infinite. Gary Becker's famous "rotten kid" theorem simply assumes that the head of a houschold is altruistic enough to effectively represent the interests of all family members (Becker 1991). Even economists who emphasize the public consequences of private investments in human capital tend to point to the unfortunate implications of resource constraints, rather than worrying about possible "disincentives to care" (Haveman and Wolfe 1995).

This traditional approach is increasingly challenged by proponents of the "new institutionalist" and the "new behavioral" economics who focus on coordination problems, the social construction of preferences, and intrinsic motivation (Bowles 2003; Akerlof and Kranton 2000; Frey 1998). Many feminist economists explain how cultural devaluation and market competition can discourage caring for dependents (England and Folbre 1999, 2003; Folbre and Nelson 2001; Himmelweit 1999; Gardiner 1997). Many also argue that the traditional breadwinner-homemaker division of labor imposes higher costs and risks on women than men, and make a case for more sharing of care responsibilities within the family (Appelbaum et al. 2002; Gornick and Meyers 2003).

These arguments suggest new ways of thinking about economic incentives relevant to family life. They also provide a way of translating some familiar criticisms of public policy into the language of economics.

Double-Edged Incentives

Policy makers try to design incentives to good behavior that will lead to efficient outcomes. But the precise effects of incentives can be surprisingly hard to predict, because they often have a double edge, generating both positive and negative effects that vary with specific circumstances. In the 1990s, for instance, many economists agreed that stock options could help align the interests of corporate management and shareholders. With widespread revelations of aggressive accounting procedures, however, it became apparent that stock options could also provide an incentive to misreport profits (Bebchuk, Fried, and Walker 2001).

Statistical analysis can minimize the probability of either accepting a false hypothesis or rejecting a true one. Likewise, institutional design almost always confronts trade-offs. Legal systems can try to minimize the likelihood that an innocent person be found guilty or that a guilty person be set free. Social safety nets risk both denying ssistance to those who need it and providing it to those who might fare perfectly well without it. How should these risks be balanced? Credible answers to this question must confront moral and philosophical concerns (Goodin 1985). They must also address economic outcomes.

Incentives for Paid Versus Unpaid Work

An incentive to engage in one activity is, almost by definition, a disincentive to engage in another. If one activity is always productive, the other always unproductive, and the social goal is to increase productivity, incentive design is relatively easy. Most introductory economics textbooks focus on the tradeoff between two activities, paid employment and leisure. In this context, taxing one person's paid employment income to support another person's leisure creates perverse incentives. If we introduce the possibility that much of what has traditionally been called leisure is actually unpaid work, including the work of caring for family members, the picture becomes considerably more complex. Recent public policies in the United States have intensified existing pressures on individuals to reduce time devoted to family care and community participation. These pressures are particularly hard on low-income families.

Relatively few economists seriously consider the social value of nonmarket work. Standard neoclassical theory associated with Gary Becker (1991) and other economists of the Chicago school points to its economic significance, but minimizes its social implications. A rational utility maximizing individual should allocate time in such a way as to equalize the marginal utility of market and nonmarket work. If private benefits equal social benefits, individual choices will lead to efficient social outcomes. Government interference that distorts individual choices becomes the only source of inefficiency.

But if the social benefits of caring for dependents exceed the personal, individual choices are not necessarily efficient for society. Commitments to the care of others create positive externalities for society as a whole. Not surprisingly, societies generally try to encourage such commitments with public policies such as social safety nets. This type of government "interference" increases rather than decreases overall efficiency because it helps align private and social benefits. Yet this is precisely the type of government interference that has come under attack in recent years as unambiguously and perversely inefficient.

The real story is far more complicated. While it is certainly possible to "oversubsidize" the work of caring for dependents, it is also possible to "undersubsidize" it. The reduction of social safety nets increases the private costs of commitments to dependents. This can lead to a reduction in the supply of family care due to constrainted resources, shifts in relative prices, or changes in social norms and personal preferences. Some caregivers simply do not have enough resources. Others may redefine their commitments and reallocate their time as care becomes more costly. Even if many caregivers are willing to sacrifice their own welfare to meet the needs of dependents at any price, the economic penalties they incur may discourage others from following their example. Both social norms and personal preferences may shift over time in a less altruistic direction.

Critics of current welfare policies argue for more social recognition of nonmarket work (Fraser and Gordon 1994; Mink 1998). The Women's Committee of 100 protests our failure to consider "caring for one's own child as work worthy of support for all families."[3] But most policy makers continue to assume that it is economically desirable to concentrate on incentives to increase the participation of single parents in the marketplace. Many congressmen support a target of forty hours a week.

Incentives to Marry Versus Incentives to Care

Marriage can provide a good institutional framework for the care of family members (Waite and Gallagher 2000). But the legal/demographic status of marriage does not automatically lead to healthy, caring relationships, and not all such relationships are encompassed by marriage. Indeed, current laws in most states prevent gay and lesbian couples who would like to formalize their commitments from doing so (Badgett 2001). The traditional breadwinner-homemaker marriage that many conservatives advocate has some distinct disadvantages for women and children. And efforts to discourage out-of-wedlock births, if taken too far, can have perverse effects.

It is difficult to disentangle the causes of changes in family structure that swept across many countries in the process of economic development. But at least part of the explanation lies in the destabilization of traditional forms of patriarchal control over women (Folbre 1994, 2001). Women have benefited from increased freedom of choice and from additional bargaining power within the family. But they have suffered from a breakdown of institutional structures that once provided them with support for providing care for dependents. The resulting stresses and strains help explain an urge to return to traditional ideals of breadwinner-homemaker marriage. But there are several reasons why we should try to develop new forms of institutional support for care rather than merely trying to reestablish old ones (Goldscheider and Waite 1991).

Traditional marriage urges women toward extreme specialization in care giving, which makes them, as well as the dependents they care for, vulnerable to the withdrawal of support from a husband or father.[4] Even if this does not happen, the threat that it might effectively reduces women's voice in family and community life. Traditional marriage urges men to extreme specialization in earning market income, which discourages them from active participation in care giving (Coltrane 1996; Cherlin 2000). These disadvantages are heightened by high marital instability. Women face poverty in the aftermath of divorce. Many divorced fathers find it difficult to maintain emotional contact with their children.

We are now witnessing a proliferation of new family forms, including married families with stepparents, parents cohabiting with other adults, single parents living alone with their children, and gay and lesbian families. Public policies should seek to promote healthy and stable relationships among adults caring for children. But efforts to stigmatize or punish families who do not conform to any one specific cultural and demographic ideal are both morally questionable and economically unproductive. Making divorce more difficult could further discourage marriage. And moralistic exhortations to traditional marriage may also discourage individuals from marrying by "setting the bar too high."[5]

Current tax and benefit policies impose a steep marginal tax rate on low-income individuals who marry. This policy is unfair and inefficient and should be eliminated. But positive economic incentives to marriage, almost by definition, impose economic penalties on those who are not married. These penalties have a double edge that can lower the welfare of many children living in nontraditional households. Likewise, efforts to reduce sex outside of marriage, such as "abstinence only" sex education, can pose risks to reproductive health and reproductive rights. Likewise, efforts to punish unmarried fathers with harsh child support enforcement policies can discourage low-income fathers' participation in their children's daily lives.

POLICIES RELEVANT TO "DEPENDENCY"

The double-edged effects of incentives to reduce "dependency" can be illustrated through an analysis of specific public policies of relevance to all families as well as more specific features of the Personal Responsibility and Work Opportunity Reconciliation Act of 1996.

Efforts to Decrease Employment-Family Conflicts

The problems posed by rapid increase in mothers' paid employmnt without a concomitant increase in the care provided by fathers have not gone unnoticed. But public policies in the United States aimed to reduce conflicts between paid employment and family work are sorely inadequate. They are also far less generous than in other industrialized countries, contributing to comparatively high rates of poverty among women and children (Christopher et al. 2001). Among the policies designed to help individuals combine paid employment and family work are family leaves from work, child care subsidies, and regulation of employment schedules. In all of these policy areas, low-income families face particularly serious stresses and strains (Albelda 2001).

The Family and Medical Leave Act (FMLA) allows workers to take time away from paid employment to care for newborns and adopted children, for sick children, wives, husbands, or parents. These leaves can last up to twelve weeks, with the right to return to work guaranteed. But only about half of all workers in the private sector are covered by this provision, and FMLA leaves are unpaid. Under these conditions, taking time to take care of families means giving up the means to support them. Many workers use all their personal and vacation time to help cope with children's needs, leaving them with no flexibility when someone in their family falls ill or they become sick themselves. Low-income mothers are less likely than others to enjoy coverage by the FMLA, or employer-provided benefits (Heymann 2000). Two-thirds of workers who need but do not take family leave say they can not afford to take it (Albelda and Manuel 2000). A 2000 survey found that 80 percent of workers earning over $75,000 were paid during their leave, compared to only 26 percent of those earning less than $20,000 (Canter et al. 2001). Increases in maternal participation in paid employment have been associated with an expansion of center-based child care. In 1999, 46 percent of America's three-year-olds, 64 percent of four-year-olds, and 93 percent of five-year-olds were enrolled in center-based care. Participation in such programs tends to increase along with family income and education.[6] Studies show that early childhood education helps improve children's performance in later years. Yet many low-income families are forced to rely on low quality, largely unregulated care providers (Helburn and Bergmann 2002).

The cost of center-based child care in many communities exceeds the cost of tuition at many community colleges and state universities. The Economic Policy Institute estimates that it represents about 30 percent of the total expenses of a family with two children (Boushey et al. 2001). Actual spending on child care tends to be lower, because many families find friends or family members who are willing to provide it for nothing. But families with income under the poverty level who paid for child care spent amounts equivalent to about 20 percent of their earnings in 1997 (Giannarelli and Barsimantov 2000). While public subsidies for child care have increased significantly, only a small percentage of eligible children actually receive it (U.S. Department of Health and Human Services 2000).

Overall, government subsidies account for between 25 percent and 30 percent of all child care expenditures. By comparison, government subsidies cover close to 90 percent of all spending on primary and secondary education, and over 70 percent of the costs of attending a public university, not counting the value of tax breaks (Stoney and Greenberg 1996). Because children from low-income families are less likely to attend colleges or universities, they benefit less from public support for higher education than children from middle-income or affluent families (Ellwood and Kane 2000).

Most employment practices penalize those who take time off from paid responsibilities to provide family care (Williams 2000). The structure of work-related tax and benefit rules forces a choice between poorly paid part-time work with few benefits or career prospects and full-time work with little flexibility for family responsibilities. Many wage earners, including nurses, are required to work extensive overtime. Increased competition for well-paid jobs leads to "squirrel-cage" work regimes and "winner take-all" tournaments that severely penalize those who choose to fulfill obligations to family and community (Schor 1991; Frank and Cook 1995). Increased stresses and strains on family life are compounded by reductions in civic engagement (Putnam 2000).

The double-edged incentive problem here is: how can we encourage men and women to develop their earnings capacity without discouraging them from devoting time to family and community?

Efforts to Encourage Paid Employment

Efforts to encourage paid employment among those receiving public assistance enjoyed enormous success in the late 1990s. Positive incentives, such as expansion of the Earned Income Tax Credit, helped buffer the effect of negative incentives such as work requirements and time limits. Many single mothers who moved into paid employment gained the confidence that comes with earning a wage, as well as important labor force experience. However, the income gains these women enjoyed were modest, particularly when the expenses of paid employment, such as the purchase of child care services, are taken into account (Cancian et al. 2002).

Furthermore, the relative weight of positive and negative incentives varies substantially by race and ethnicity. African American and Hispanic women are less likely than white to receive public subsidies for work-related activities (Delgado and Krajcer 2002). Special restrictions on eligibility apply to legal immigrants, and American Indian populations are underserved by public programs (U.S. Commission on Civil Rights 2002). The larger the percentage of black and Hispanic recipients in individual states at the time welfare reforms were adopted, the more punitive the sanctions (Soss et al. 2001).

Welfare-to-work programs can benefit children if they boost family income (Morris and Gennetian 2002; Morris et al. 2001). Programs that trigger income losses, fail to raise income, or place too little emphasis on child care tend to be associated with negative outcomes for children, such as emotional and behavior problems (Grogger, Karoly, and Klerman 2002; Zaslow et al. 2002).

Those most likely to gain from paid employment were among the first to exit welfare, leaving behind those slowed by more serious obstacles. Studies of TANF recipients reveal significant problems of physical and mental health, domestic violence, lack of transportation and child care (Danziger et al. 2000). Yet proposed legislation would further reduce states' flexibility in dealing with these problems, imposing a higher and more stringent work requirement of forty hours' paid employment per week.

When mothers can choose their hours of paid employment, they tend to avoid significant reductions in the time they devote to activities with children (Bianchi 2000). Indigent single mothers, however, are at the mercy of economic circumstances. Few of the jobs they are able to get are "family friendly" (Albelda 2002). Paid work requirements imposed on mothers of young children have significantly reduced breastfeeding, with negative consequences for children's health (Haider, Jacknowitz, and Schoeni 2003). Experimental studies suggest that increased hours of maternal employment are associated with small but significant reductions in academic performance and increases in grade repetition among teenagers. Mothers may be less able to monitor their teens' behavior, or teens may be asked to supervise their younger siblings to a degree that interferes with their own education (Brooks, Hair, and Zaslow 2001; Gennetian et al. 2002). These findings are reinforced by ethnographic research (Dodson 1998).

The double-edged incentive problem here is: how can we create incentives to paid employment without penalizing individuals who are handicapped by low earnings capabilities and lack of adequate work supports?

Administrative Incentives to Reduce Public Assistance

The transformation of public administration, among many other factors, has contributed to steep declines in welfare rolls. A legal-bureaucratic institution characterized by rules of due process and little concern for administrative efficiency has now swung in the other direction, with administrative efficiency narrowly measured by roll reduction. We have moved from a system in which most recipients were assumed innocent without much examination of possible guilt toward a system in which they are considered guilty unless proven innocent.

In many cases, privatization of welfare services has created direct financial incentives to deny or discourage assistance (Diller 2000). New federal policies under consideration (so-called "superwaivers") create incentives for states to reallocate money appropriated for public assistance, such as food stamps, to other purposes, such as simply balancing their budgets. Research indicates that previous efforts to reduce "overpayment" resulted in significant increases in "underpayment" (Mendeloff 1977). But little effort has been devoted to the analysis of effects of welfare reform on actual service delivery. Small-scale studies reveal serious violations of due process, including evidence that predominantly white case workers may offer less generous treatment to African American recipients (Gooden 1998). The foster care system also shows signs of racial bias (Roberts 2002).

A good service delivery system should discourage shirking and reduce take-up among those who are not genuinely needy. But its success in providing assistance to needy eligibles is also relevant to effectiveness. In this respect, policy effectiveness is declining. The Census Bureau estimates that less than 30 percent of children in poverty in 1998 lived in families who received cash public assistance.[7] Take-up rates for food stamps and Medicaid have declined far more than eligibility in recent years (Ku and Bruen 1999; Zedlewski and Brauner 1999). Although public support for child care increased on both the federal and the state level, most families who made a transition from welfare to work in the late 1990s did not receive a subsidy (Schumacher and Greenberg 1999). If all families with children had participated in the safety net programs for which they qualified in 1998, overall poverty would have been 20 percent lower and extreme poverty 70 percent lower (Zedlewski et al. 2002).

As the welfare rolls decline, their composition changes in ways that change the relative risks of "rewarding shirkers" versus "denying the needy" (Goodin 1985). Analysis of the 1997 Survey of Income and Program Participation shows that nearly half of all single mothers receiving TANF had a disability or a disabled child. While many states exempt disabled welfare recipients or those who care for a disabled child, most do not have policies exempting them from a five-year limit (Lee, Sills, and Oh 2002). Some of these families may be eligible for assistance through Supplemental Security Income, which has experienced increasing enrollment in recent years, but it is unclear how they will fare. The double-edged incentive problem here is: how can we discourage both over- and under-use of public assistance, minimizing both waste and neglect?

POLICIES RELEVANT TO "FAMILY RESPONSIBILITY"

An explicit goal of the Personal Responsibility and Work Opportunity Reconciliation Act of 1996 was the reduction of out-of-wedlock births. This has been pursued at the expense of other goals also relevant to family and social responsibility: promoting healthy outcomes for all children, ensuring reproductive choice, and encouraging fathers' direct involvement in the lives of their children.

Efforts to Discourage Out-of-Wedlock Births and Promote Marriage

Concerns about the growing percentage of children living in single-parent families in the United States have been reinforced by social scientific research documenting the potentially adverse effects of family structures on child outcomes. Strong evidence suggests that children raised with married biological parents fare better than those in single-parent families, even when family income is constant (McLanahan and Sandefur 1994). But for many children in single parent families, the alternative is not living with both biological parents, but one of several less attractive possibilities: living with stepparents or other unrelated adults or living in a "no-parent" family.

The current risks of a marriage ending in divorce are quite high, although they have come down from their 1979 to 1981 peak. It is now estimated that approximately 40 percent of marriages will end in divorce, and the risk of divorce is elevated among people with low income and insecure jobs. Ironically, the greater ease of divorce improves the overall quality of marriages that last. Those who tout the benefits of marriage do not fully account for this selection bias, often implying that the causality works only one way, from more stability to greater benefits. Many people are willing to marry precisely because exit costs are low. Efforts to discourage divorce, whether through cultural stigma or legal restriction, could easily end up discouraging marriage in the first place. Relatively few couples have taken advantage of the "covenant marriages" now available in some states. By encouraging individuals to consider marriage a personal commitment rather than a social obligation, we may actually strengthen intrinsic motivation to succeed (Frey 1998; Deci, Koestner, and Ryan 1999).

Marital distress leads to harsh and inconsistent parenting, regardless of whether parents stay together. Studies show that a high-conflict marriage is often worse for children's well-being than divorce or living from birth in a stable single-parent family (Cherlin 1999). Multiple transitions in and out of marriage can be worse for children psychologically than living in the same kind of family, whatever its form, for a long time. Many low-income parents of newborns already have children from previous relationships. Their marriages thus do not create idealized biological families, but instead more complex blended families in which child support enforcement and stepparenting responsibilities greatly complicate relationships (Mincy and Huang 2001).

Poverty is a cause, as well as an effect, of not marrying. Poor mothers lacking a high school degree and any regular work history are not likely to marry. A study of the National Longitudinal Survey of Youth confirms that poor women, whatever their age, and regardless of whether they are or have ever been on welfare, are less likely to marry than women who are not poor (McLaughlin and Lichter 1997). Their potential spouses have limited economic capabilities. Results from the Fragile Families Survey show that unmarried fathers were twice as likely as married to have a physical or psychological problem that interfered with their ability to find or keep a job, and were several times more likely to abuse drugs or alcohol. More than 25 percent of unmarried fathers were not employed when their child was born, compared to fewer than 10 percent of married fathers (Sigle-Rushton and McLanahan 2001; Edin 2000).

Many aspects of welfare policy, including the "family caps" put into place in many states, are designed to impose negative sanctions on out-of-wedlock births, sanctions that contribute to economic stresses on low-income families. They may push some parents toward marriage or cohabitation, but others toward relinquishment or neglect of their children. No household structure puts children at greater risk than growing up in a "no-parent" family, especially in an institutional care or unstable foster care arrangement. Yet current child welfare policies devote far more resources to foster care than to assistance or support for families encountering difficulties that may result in child neglect. Federal funds to assist states with such services are limited, while expenditures on foster care are open ended (Roberts 2002). In many states the level of payments to foster parents, compared to the level of public assistance, creates incentives to relinquish children to relatives who can obtain foster parent status (Boots and Geen 2000). "Child only" TANF benefits that travel with the child may create incentives for parents to relinquish their children. These benefits are growing as a share of the TANF budget in many states.

Child Protective Service case workers in many states report their perceptions that increased pressure on parents has adverse consequences for children (Geen et al. 2001). Data from the Survey of Income and Program

Participation (SIPP) suggest that economic deprivation leads single-parent families to reduce the number of co-resident children (Brandon and Fisher 2001). Mother-child separations are lower in states with higher welfare benefits (Brandon 2000). Restrictive practices and sanctions help explain variations across states in substantiated cases of maltreatment and increases in foster care placement (Paxson and Waldfogel 2001; Grogger, Karoly, and Klerman 2002). Analysis of the Current Population Survey suggests that TANF implementation was associated with a 7 to 12 percent increase in the fraction of black, central city children living with neither parent (Bitler, Gelbach, and Hoynes 2002). In one random-assignment experiment including strong welfare sanctions and time limits, substantiated child neglect increased substantially (Fein and Lee 2000).

The double-edged incentive problem here is: how can we strengthen married two-parent families without weakening single-parent families?

Reproductive Rights

Current policies in the United States both restrict economic access to abortion and discourage effective forms of sex education, including provision of information regarding abortion, contraception and safe sex. These restrictions provide incentives to conform to moral values held by a substantial subset of the U.S. population. But these restrictions also increase the cost and difficulty of exercising reproductive freedom. If individuals are the best judges of their own willingness and ability to fulfill caring commitments, such restrictions can lead to reduction in the quality of maternal care. Evidence suggests that involuntary motherhood is associated with poor outcomes for children, including a higher likelihood of delinquency and crime (Sampson and Laub 1993). Indeed, econometric analysis of the effects of legalization of abortion across states supports the hypothesis that it led to a significant lagged reduction in crime rates (Donohue and Levitt 2001).

Pregnant women who are young, unmarried, and economically disadvantaged are more likely than others to seek abortions (Levine et al. 1999). This is the group most affected by the Hyde amendment, which prohibits federal funding of all but medically necessary abortions through Medicaid. Many states impose restrictions such as twenty-four-hour waiting periods and parental consent requirements. Right-wing disruption and violence directed at abortion clinics has discouraged medical provision, significantly increasing the transactions costs of securing the procedure. Empirical evidence confirms that decreased access and higher costs lead to lower rates of abortion, and is therefore likely to be associated with a higher frequency of unwanted births (Lundberg and Plotnick 1990; Matthews, Ribar, and Wilhelm 1997). Restrictions on Medicaid funding from

1982 to 1992 had a large positive effect on the fertility of blacks (Klerman 1999).

Social and cultural pressures combine with biological propensities to make it difficult for young men and women to abstain from sexual intercourse or to practice safe sex. The HIV epidemic in the United States, as well as persistently high rates of unintended pregnancies, especially among teenagers, suggest that many lack both the skills and the information they need to protect themselves. Teens in Europe are more likely to use contraception, and teenage pregnancy there is far lower there as a result (Jones et al.1985).

In 2002 the National Campaign to Prevent Teen Pregnancy concluded that sex and HIV education programs that discuss both abstinence and contraception delay the onset of sex, reduce the frequency of sex, and increase contraceptive use. There is no evidence that sexuality and HIV education programs hasten onset of sexual intercourse, increase the frequency of sexual intercourse, or increase the number of sexual partners. However, at least one randomized controlled trial comparing a "safe-sex" and an "abstinence only" program found that those in the latter program reported more unprotected sex (Jemmott, Jemmott, and Fong 1998).

A 2000 report by the Kaiser Family Foundation found that thirty-two states do not even require sex education. One-third of public secondary schools in the United States teach an "abstinence only until marriage" curriculum (Alan Guttmacher Institute 1999). Welfare reform legislation passed in 1996 limited federal expenditures on sex education to "abstinence only." The versions of welfare reform reauthorization currently under consideration in both the House of Representatives and the Senate are similarly limited. "Abstinence-only" is strictly defined to prohibit any discussion of contraception other than reporting of "failure rates."

The double-edged incentive problem is: how do we discourage emotionally and physically risky sexual intercourse and minimize recourse to abortions while ensuring that individuals can fully exercise reproductive choice?

Child Support Enforcement

In recent years, policy makers have made concerted efforts to improve enforcement of the child support responsibilities of noncustodial parents. Despite salutary gains, it seems likely that the inflexible and coercive rules imposed on those who receive public assistance, in particular, have discouraged the emotional connections vital to healthy parental involvement (England and Folbre 2002b).

In most states, father's child support payments go directly into state coffers, rather than family budgets, with no direct benefits for children. Support levels are set in ways that allow fathers, especially those who are unfamiliar with or fearful of the legal system, relatively little voice. Support levels are regressive, representing much larger share of a poor father's than an affluent father's earnings. Support requirements are retroactive, leading to accumulation of huge debt that is virtually impossible for many low-income fathers to pay off. Requirements are also unforgiving of economic circumstances such as unemployment or low earnings (Sorensen 1999). Violators are subject to incarceration, which directly limits paternal involvement with children.

Noncustodial fathers who pay child support usually spend more time with their children than those who do not (Seltzer, McLanahan, and Hanson 1998). But formal support orders can reduce discretionary power to negotiate trade-offs among different kinds of inputs away from the individual parents. By defining the noncustodial parents' responsibility solely in terms of cash support they make it more difficult for that parent to offer inputs of time or emotional effort instead of cash, contributing to paternal disengagement. Noncustodial fathers might be willing to devote more resources to the child if they were allowed to make a larger proportion of their contribution in the form of in-kind transfers or time (Weiss and Willis 1985).

When formal agreements are imposed without any negotiation or voice, noncustodial parents are far less predisposed to cooperate with them. Research shows that voluntary agreements have higher compliance rates and greater flexibility in terms of modifications over time as the child matures (Peters et al. 1993). Voluntary awards are associated with higher contact between fathers and children, as well as better child outcomes (Argys and Peters 1999; Argys et al. 1997). The double-edged incentive problem here is: how do we enforce noncustodial parents' financial responsibilities while encouraging their personal and emotional participation in parenting?

REDESIGNING FAMILY POLICY

Recognition of the value of the care work that takes place outside the market economy calls the traditional distinction between family policy and economic policy into question. The family is part of the economy. It supplies human and social capital that generate a flow of labor services, much as our physical environment supplies natural capital that generates a flow of air, water, raw materials, and ecological services. Many of these input flows are unpriced. This does not mean that they are infinitely available at no cost. Indeed, as the market economy expands it depends increasingly on the development of social institutions that can coordinate its use of these inputs and ensure that they are not depleted or degraded. What economists call "externalities" are not "external" at all.

The supply of unpaid labor to the care of family and community is difficult to pin down in quantitative terms. It has personal and emotional dimensions that distinguish it from other forms of work. But we need only reflect on our daily lives to realize how important it is. Strong cultural values of altruism and social obligation, along with our genetic heritage, buffer us against the effects of changes in relative prices and ensure that the supply of unpaid labor is relatively large and inelastic. But it is not perfectly inelastic. At some point, an increase in the opportunity cost of care for others is likely to reduce the quantity of care services supplied. When economists and policy makers assume this possibility away, they may actually weaken the cultural values of altruism and social obligation on which we almost unthinkingly rely.

Economic Policy IS Family Policy (and Vice Versa)

In some areas of public policy debate, family issues are highly visible. But in other areas, they remain obscured by traditional assumptions that family work has little economic value. Public assistance, child tax benefits, family leaves, child care, and reproductive rights fit comfortably under the family policy rubric. Minimum wage legislation and general tax policies are seldom included, despite their significant implications.

The real value of the minimum wage is low by historical standards. Market-determined wages are often not enough to allow workers with little education and earnings capacity to provide adequate support for their families. The success of local "living wage" campaigns in local areas suggests that there may be broad public support for raising the national minimum (Pollin and Luce 1998). By one estimate, an increase in the minimum wage of $1 per hour would reduce the poverty rate of families headed by a minimum wage earner by nearly 25 percent (Sawhill and Thomas 2001).

Public policies designed to subsidize and supplement low-earnings represent another strategy for reducing poverty (Haveman 2002). The Earned Income Tax Credit (EITC) already in place deserves credit for both reducing poverty and encouraging paid employment. But the effects of this program are blunted by the effect of payroll taxes. Further, this program currently denies extra benefits to families with more than two children and phases out benefits along with income, creating a high marginal tax and a significant marriage penalty (Cherry and Sawicky 2000).

Expansion and revision of the EITC could be accompanied by other measures such as the exemption of poor working families with children from the federal tax rolls.

Targeting further assistance for child rearing only to poor families, however, ignores the issue of "incentives to care" for other families. Relatively affluent families benefit significantly from dependent tax exemptions, child tax credits, and other tax expenditures. Middle-income families fare less well. The graphical relationship between family income and public support for child rearing in the United States shows a distinct dip in the middle (England and Folbre 2002a; Battle and Mendelson 2001; Ellwood and Liebman 2000; Garfinkel 1996). This uneven pattern is unfair and politically divisive. A simpler, more generous universal benefit system for families with children, combined with a means-tested safety net for all individuals, would be more equitable and efficient.

Such a system would of course be quite costly. This is exactly why advocates of more generous support for families with children should think more broadly about economic policy priorities. In particular, they should oppose continued cuts in income taxes, and help articulate the benefits of a more progressive tax policy, including increases in the estate tax.

Progressive tax rates are widely criticized on the grounds that they create disincentives to work. This argument depends entirely on the definition of work. At the margin, progressive tax rates may create disincentives to paid employment because individuals take home a smaller share of their earned income. But a reduction in hours of paid employment can have the effect of increasing time devoted to family and community work, rather than to leisure. Highly paid professionals and managers often put in far more than forty hours a week on the job. This represents an efficient outcome only if one assumes that time they would otherwise have devoted to family, friends, and community offers no benefits beyond the purely personal.[8]

The estate tax also bears both symbolically and practically on issues of family policy. The notion that wealthy individuals should share their accumulated wealth with their fellow-citizens helps enforce norms of social solidarity and obligation.

Economists may argue that such norms are of little value to economic growth measured in terms of market output. But they are of tremendous value to the solution of problems needing social coordination rather than economic competition, problems such as terrorism and global warming, as well as high rates of child poverty. On a practical level, the concept of equality of opportunity for children is a central aspect of an incentive structure that could make social democratic capitalism a better way of organizing economic life.

Public Support and Shared Care

Appreciation of the economic value of care work, combined with analysis of the economic penalties that can be imposed on those who choose to provide it, informs an emerging feminist vision of greater public support combined with restructuring of paid employment, a "universal care giver" model (Fraser 1996). Many of the policies emerging in northwest European countries can be described in terms of "new norms for organizing market work and unpaid care work" (Appelbaum et al. 2002). The most detailed and comprehensive case for developing such policies in the United States is provided by Janet Gornick and Marcia Meyers (2003). Their scenario calls for increases in public child care, paid family leaves from work, and incentives to reduce the length of the work week even while encouraging more steady female participation in the labor force. While these policies have not reached the national political agenda, they are making inroads on the state level, as evidenced by Georgia's impressive early childhood education program and California's recent expansion of gender-neutral paid family leave from work.

This approach could help address each of the six "double-edged" incentive problems outlined earlier in this chapter. Rather than requiring longer hours of market work and lowering benefits for single-parent families, welfare policy could encourage paid employment in more flexible ways. A number of specific suggestions are offered in "An Open Letter from Researchers on Child Reform and Well-Being," signed by more than fifty researchers at major universities.[9] Rather than celebrating shrinking caseloads as an unambiguously good outcome, federal policy could tie state performance incentives to lower poverty rates, establish program participation as a state performance measure, and reward states that implement successful outreach programs (Zedlewski 2002).

A move toward greater universality of benefits could help strengthen and stabilize two-parent families. Provision of in-kind benefits such as flexible, high-quality child care—greater public investments in human capital—would benefit parents and children across virtually all income groups and household structures. Education, counseling, and arbitration services should encourage the development of healthy, committed relationships among adults, including marriage. In the place of current tax policies that penalize marriage among low-income couples and reward breadwinner-homemaker specialization among high-income couples, public policies could provide more generous support for child rearing and the care of sick or disabled family members, including paid leave from employment.

Such policies could encourage marriage and long-term commitments by reducing the stresses associated with child rearing. Young adults today trying to accommodate family life while fulfilling career ambitions face an uncomfortable choice between a "subcontracting" strategy and a "specialization" strategy. Both parents can work forty hours a week or more, and subcontract their care responsibilities to other family members or paid child care workers. Or they can elect for one parent to specialize in child care and suffer a serious reduction in possibilities for career advancement, along with increased economic vulnerability. Offered greater flexibility in employment hours and generous family leaves from work, many potential parents would prefer to share care responsibilities.

The "dual carer" society should include unambiguous commitment to reproductive rights. Isabel Sawhill (1999) argues for a national resource center on teen pregnancy that would support sexuality education programs and ensure access to reproductive health services. These policies could be strengthened by movement towards more consistent and efficient universal health care, including full access to contraception and abortion.

In the area of child support enforcement, "one size fits all" rules could be replaced by policies that encourage parents to reach their own child support agreements by threatening to impose a "fall-back" agreement if they fail. Kathryn Edin (1994) suggests a number of potential guidelines, such as basing father's child support obligations on their current earnings and using a progressive rather than a regressive formula. A number of states are experimenting with arbitration programs designed to help parents come to better agreement (Garfinkel et al. 1998). Public policies should explicitly encourage joint legal custody and active participation of fathers in their children's lives.

CONCLUSION

Double-edged effects make it intrinsically difficult to design efficient incentives. But current social family policies in the United States take familial and social altruism for granted, rather than treating them as precious resources that need to be reinforced and renewed. Efforts to discourage "dependency" and out-of-wedlock births, if carried too far, create "disincentives to care" that are morally troubling as well as economically inefficient. They threaten the welfare of poor children who are disproportionately black and Hispanic. They may also reduce the supply of services that are not currently counted as part of our gross domestic product but are nonetheless crucial to our economic welfare.

Public policy should move towards more explicit efforts to support and reward work devoted to the care of others. This recommendation does not imply a return to policies in place before 1996, which encouraged low-income mothers to provide family care without trying to find employment. Rather this recommendation urges new efforts to help men and women find a better balance between the responsibilities of paid and unpaid work in their families and communities.

I gratefully acknowledge the financial and intellectual support of the MacArthur Foundation Research Network on the Family and the Economy. This chapter draws from previous collaborations with both Paula England and Stephanie Coontz. Kade Finnoff, Tami Ohler, Erika Arthur, and Yifei Wang provided crucial research assistance. Thanks also to Randy Albelda, Robert Goodin, Siobhan Reilly, and Arloc Sherman for important insights and helpful suggestions.

NOTES

1. For instance, the National Academy of Sciences has recently convened a panel of economists to address issues of including valuation of nonmarket work in the national income accounts. Canada, Australia, and the United Kingdom now include imputations of the value of nonmarket work in satellite national accounts, as do most members of the European Economic Community (See also Eisner 1989; Goldschmidt-Clermont 1993; Folbre and Wagman 1993).

2. These activities represent an important subset of a larger universe of caring labor that overlaps the market economy. For a more complete conceptualization of care work see England and Folbre (1999, 2002c) and Folbre and Nelson (2001).

3. See Women's Committee of 100, letter to the U.S. Senate regarding proposed legislation in August 2002. Women's Committee of 100, 400 8th Street NW, room 1107, Washington, D.C., 20004, phone 202-783-3568.

4. Investments in family-related human capital are far less fungible than investments in market-related human capital (England and Farkas 1986; England 2000). Mothers who withdraw from paid employment incur a significant wage penalty over their entire lifetime (Budig and England 2001; Joshi, Paci, and Waldfogel 1999; Joshi 1998; Waldfogel 1997). They also face a higher risk of poverty than fathers in the event of divorce.

5. Kathy Edin's ethnographic research suggests that this counterproduc-

tive "idealization" of marriage may be taking place in many low-income communities (Edin, personal communication).

6. U.S. Department of Education (2000, table 2–1).

7. The Annie E. Casey Foundation (2000).

8. The coordination problems described earlier in this paper (for example, "rat race" and "squirrel cage" effects) call the assumption that individuals equate the marginal personal benefits of their paid and unpaid work into question. Even if they do, however, the social benefits of their unpaid work may exceed the personal benefits they derive from it.

9. A copy of this letter is available from the author on request.

REFERENCES

Akerlof, George, and Rachel Kranton. 2000. "Economics and Identity." *Quarterly Journal of Economics* 115(3): 715–53.

Alan Guttmacher Institute. 1999. *Teen Sex and Pregnancy, Facts in Brief*. New York: Alan Guttmacher Institute.

Albelda, Randy. 2001. "Welfare to Work, Farewell to Families?" *Feminist Economics* 7(1): 119–35.

———. 2002. "Fallacies of Welfare-to-Work Policies." In *Lost Ground: Welfare Reform, Poverty, and Beyond*, edited by Randy Albelda and Ann Withorn. Boston: South End Press.

Albelda, Randy, and Tiffany Manuel. 2000. *Filling the Work and Family Gap: Paid Parental Leave in Massachusetts*. Boston: University of Massachusetts Labor Resource Center. Available at: http://site.www.umb.edu/forum/1/Family_Leave_Report/member/Forums/overviewww.html (accessed May 24, 2004).

The Annie E. Casey Foundation. 2000. *2000 Kids Count Data Online*. Baltimore, Md.: The Annie E. Casey Foundation. Available at: www.aecf.org/kidscount/kc2000/sum_11.htm (accessed May 24, 2004).

Appelbaum, Eileen, Thomas Bailey, Peter Berg, and Arne L. Kalleberg. 2002. *Shared Work, Valued Care. New Norms for Organizing Market Work and Unpaid Care Work*. Washington, D.C.: Economic Policy Institute.

Argys, Laura M., and H. Elizabeth Peters. 1999. "Can Adequate Child Support Be Legislated? A Model of Responses to Child Support Guidelines and Enforcement Efforts." Unpublished paper. Department of Economics, University of Colorado at Denver (February).

Argys, Laura M., H. Elizabeth Peters, Jeanne Brooks-Gunn, and Judith

R. Smith. 1997. "The Impact of Child Support Dollars and Father Child Contact." Paper presented at NICHD Conference on Father Involvement, Bethesda, Md. (October 10–11, 1996).

Badgett, Lee. 2001. *Money, Myths and Change. The Economic Lives of Lesbians and Gay Men*. Chicago: University of Chicago Press.

Battle, Ken, and Michael Mendelson, eds. 2001. *Benefits for Children: A Four Country Study*. Ottawa: Caledon Institute.

Bebchuk, Lucian Arye, Jesse M. Fried, and David I. Walker. 2001. "Executive Compensation in America: Optimal Contracting or Extraction of Rents?" Cambridge, Mass.: National Bureau of Economic Research Working Paper 8661 (December).

Becker, Gary. 1991. *A Treatise on the Family*. Enlarged Edition. Cambridge, Mass.: Harvard University Press.

Bianchi, Suzanne. 2000. "Maternal Employment and Time with Children: Dramatic Change or Surprising Continuity?" *Demography* 37(4): 401–14.

Bitler, Marianne P., Jonah B. Gelbach, and Hilary W. Hoynes. 2002. "The Impact of Welfare Reform on Living Arrangements." Unpublished paper. Davis, Calif: Department of Economics, University of California at Davis.

Boots, Shelly Waters, and Rob Geen. 2000. *Family Care or Foster Care? How State Policies Affect Kinship Caregivers*. Washington, D.C.: Urban Institute Press.

Boushey, Heather, Chauna Brocht, Bethney Gundersen, and Jared Bernstein. 2001. *Hardships in America. The Real Story of Working Families* Washington, D.C.: Economic Policy Institute.

Bowles, Samuel. 2003. *Microeconomics: Behavior, Institutions, and Evolution*. Princeton, N.J.: Princeton University Press.

Brandon, Peter D. 2000. "Did the AFDC Program Succeed in Keeping Mothers and Young Children Living Together?" *Social Service Review* 74(2, June): 214–30.

Brandon, Peter, and Gene A. Fisher. 2001. "The Dissolution of Joint Living Arrangements among Single Parents and Children: Does Welfare Make a Difference?" *Social Science Quarterly* 82(1): 1–19.

Brooks, Jennifer L., Elizabeth C. Hair, and Martha J. Zaslow. 2001. *Welfare Reform's Impact on Adolescents: Early Warning Signs*. Washington, D.C.: Child Trends.

Budig, Michelle, and Paula England. 2001. "The Wage Penalty for Motherhood." *American Sociological Review* 66(2): 204–25.

Cancian, Maria, Robert Haveman, Daniel R. Meyer, and Barbara Wolfe. 2002. "Before and after TANF: The Economic Well-Being of Women Leaving Welfare." *Social Services Review* 76(4): 603–41.

Canter, David, Jane Waldfogel, Jeffery Kerwin, Mareena McKinley Wright, Kerry Levin, John Rauch, Tracey Hagerty, and Martha Stapleton Kudela. 2001. *Balancing the Needs of Families and Employers: Family and Medical Leave Surveys, 2000 Update.* Rockville, Md.: Westat.

Cherlin, Andrew. 1999. "Going to Extremes: Family Structure, Children's Well-Being, and Social Science." *Demography* 36(4): 421–28.

———. 2000. "Toward a New Home Socioeconomics of Union Formation." In *The Ties That Bind: Perspectives on Marriage and Cohabitation,* edited by Linda J. Waite. New York: Aldine de Gruyter.

Cherry, Robert, and Max Sawicky. 2000. "Giving Tax Credit Where Credit is Due." Briefing Paper (April). Washington, D.C.: Economic Policy Institute. Available at: http://www.epinet.org/briefingpapers/eitc.html (accessed May 24, 2004).

Christopher, Karen, Paula England, Sara McLanahan, Katherin Ross, and Timothy Smeeding. 2001. "Gender Inequality and Poverty in Affluent Nations: The Role of Single Motherhood and the State." In *Child Well-being, Child Poverty and Child Policy in Modern Nations,* edited by Koen Vleminckx and Timothy Smeeding. London: Policy Press.

Coltrane, Scott. 1996. *Family Man.* New York: Oxford University Press.

Coontz, Stephanie, and Nancy Folbre. 2002. "Marriage, Poverty, and Public Policy." A Briefing Paper from the Council on Contemporary Families. Available at: http://www.contemporaryfamilies.org/public/briefing.html (accessed May 24, 2004).

Crittenden, Ann. 2001. *The Price of Motherhood. Why the Most Important Job in the World is Still the Least Valued.* New York: Henry Holt.

Danziger, Sandra, Mary Corcoran, Sheldon Danziger, Colleen Heflin, Ariel Kalil, Judith Levine, Daniel Rosen, Kristen Seefeldt, Kristine Siefert, and Richard Tolman. 2000. "Barriers to the Employment of Welfare Recipients." Available at: http://www.ssw.umich.edu/poverty (accessed May 24, 2004).

Deci, Edward L., Richard Koestner, and Richard M. Ryan. 1999. "A Meta-Analytic Review of Experiments Examining the Effects of Extrinsic Rewards on Intrinsic Motivation." *Psychological Bulletin* 125(6): 627–68.

Delgado, Gary and Menachim Krajcer. 2002. "Welfare's True Colors," *The Nation.* October 28, pp. 31–32.

Diller, Matthew. 2000. "The Revolution in Welfare Administration: Rules, Discretion, and Entrepreneurial Government." *New York University Law Review* 75: 1121.

Dodson, Lisa. 1998. *Don't Call Me Out of Name: The Untold Lives of Women and Girls in America.* Boston: Beacon Press.

Donohue, John, and Steven Levitt. 2001. "The Impact of Legalized Abortion on Crime," *The Quarterly Journal of Economics* CXVI(2, May): 379–420.

Edin, Kathryn. 1994. "Single Mothers and Absent Fathers: The Possibilities and Limits of Child Support Policy." Working Paper No. 68. Center for Urban Policy Research, Rutgers University.

Edin, Kathyrn. 2000. "What Do Low-Income Single Mothers Say About Marriage?" *Social Problems* 47(1): 112–33.

Eisner, Robert. 1989. *The Total Incomes System of Accounts*. Chicago: University of Chicago Press.

Ellwood, David T., and Thomas J. Kane. 2000. "Who Is Getting a College Education? Family Background and the Growing Gaps in Enrollment." In *Securing the Future. Investing in Children from Birth to College,* edited by Sheldon Danziger and Jane Waldfogel. New York: Russell Sage Foundation.

Ellwood, David T., and Jeffrey B. Liebman. 2000. The Middle Class Parent Penalty: Child Benefits in the U.S. Tax Code. Unpublished paper. John F. Kennedy School of Government, Harvard University, Boston, Mass.

England, Paula. 2000. "Marriage, The Costs of Children, and Gender Inequality." In *The Ties that Bind: Perspectives on Marriage and Cohabitation*, edited by Linda Waite. New York: Aldine de Gruyter.

England, Paula, and George Farkas. 1986. *Households, Employment, and Gender. A Social, Economic, and Demographic View*. New York: Aldine de Gruyter.

England, Paula, and Nancy Folbre. 1999. "The Cost of Caring." *Annals of the American Academy of Political and Social Science* 561(3, May): 39–51.

———. 2002a. "Reforming the Social Family Contract: Public Support for Child Rearing in the U.S." In *For Better or Worse: The Effects of Welfare Reform on Children*, edited by Greg Duncan and P. Lindsay Chase-Lansdale. New York: Russell Sage Foundation.

———. 2002b. "Involving Dads: Parental Bargaining and Family Well Being." In *Handbook of Father Involvement: Multidisciplinary Perspectives*, edited by Catherine S. Tamis-LeMonda and Natasha Cabrera. Mahwah, N.J.: Lawrence Erlbaum Associates.

———. 2002c. "Care, Inequality, and Public Policy." In *Child Care and Inequality: Re-thinking Carework for Children and Youth,* edited by Francesca Cancian, Demie Kurz, Andrew London, Rebecca Reviere, and Mary Tuominen. New York: Routledge.

———. 2003. "Contracting for Care." In *Feminist Economics Today. Beyond Economics Man*, edited by Marianne Ferber and Julie Nelson. Chicago: University of Chicago Press.

Fein, David J., and Wang S. Lee. 2000. *The ABC Evaluation—Impacts of Welfare Reform on Child Maltreatment*. Washington, D.C.: Abt Associates.

Folbre, Nancy. 1994. "Children as Public Goods." *American Economic Review* 84(2): 86–90.

————. 2001. *The Invisible Heart. Economics and Family Values*. New York: The New Press.

Folbre, Nancy, and Julie Nelson. 2001. "For Love or Money." *The Journal of Economic Perspectives* 14(4): 123–140.

Folbre, Nancy, and Barnet Wagman. 1993. "Counting Housework: New Estimates of Real Product in the U.S., 1800–1860." *The Journal of Economic History* 53(2): 275–88.

Frank, Robert, and Philip J. Cook. 1995. *The Winner-Take-All Society*. New York: Free Press.

Fraser, Nancy. 1996. *Justice Interruptus*. New York: Routledge.

Fraser, Nancy, and Linda Gordon. 1994. "A Genealogy of Dependency." *Signs* 19(2): 309–36.

Frey, Bruno S. 1998. "Institutions and Morale: The Crowding-out Effect." In *Economics, Values and Organization*, edited by Avner Ben-Ner and Louis Putterman. Cambridge: Cambridge University Press.

Gardiner, Jean. 1997. *Gender, Care and Economics*. Basingstoke, UK: Macmillan.

Garfinkel, Irwin. 1996. "Economic Security for Children: From Means Testing and Bifurcation to Universality." In *Social Policies for Children*, edited by Irwin Garfinkel, Sara S. McLanahan, and Jennifer L. Hochschild. Washington, D.C.: Brookings Institute.

Garfinkel, Irwin, Sara S. McLanahan, Daniel R. Meyer, and Judith A. Seltzer. 1998. *Fathers Under Fire. The Revolution in Child Support Enforcement*. New York: Russell Sage Foundation.

Geen, Rob, Lynn Fender, Jacob Leos-Urbel, and Teresa Markowitz. 2001. "Welfare Reform's Effect on Child Welfare Caseloads." Washington, D.C.: Urban Institute Press.

Gennetian, Lisa A., Greg J. Duncan, Virginia W. Knox, Wanda G. Vargas, Elizabeth Clark-Kauffman, and Andrew S. London. 2002. *How Welfare and Work Policies for Parents Affect Adolescents: A Synthesis of Research*. New York: MDRC.

Giannarelli, Linda, and James Barsimantov. 2000. *Child Care Expenses of America's Families*, Occasional Paper No. 40. Washington, D.C.: Urban Institute Press.

Goldscheider, Frances, and Linda J. Waite. 1991. *New Families, No Families?* Berkeley: University of California Press.

Goldschmidt-Clermont, Luisella. 1993. "Monetary Valuation of Non-Market Productive Time: Methodological Considerations." *Review of Income and Wealth* 39(1, March): 419–33.

Gooden, Susan T. 1998. "All Things Not Being Equal: Differences in Caseworker Support Toward Black and White Welfare Clients." *Harvard Journal of African American Public Policy* 23: 23–33.

Goodin, Robert. 1985. "Erring on the Side of Kindness in Social Welfare Policy." *Policy Sciences* 18(2): 141–56.

Gornick, Janet, and Marcia Meyers. 2003. *Families that Work. Policies for Reconciling Parenthood and Employment.* New York: Russell Sage Foundation.

Grogger, Jeffrey, Lynn A. Karoly, and Jacob Alex Klerman. 2002. "Consequences of Welfare Reform: A Research Synthesis." Santa Monica, Calif.: RAND Corporation. Available at: http://www.acf.dhhs.gov/programs/opre/welfare_reform/reform_ch10.html (accessed May 24, 2004).

Haider, Steven J., Alison Jacknowitz, and Robert F. Schoeni. 2003. "Welfare Work Requirements and Child Well-being: Evidence from the Effects on Breast-feeding." *Demography* 40(3): 479–498.

Haveman, Robert. 2002. "When Work Alone is Not Enough." Unpublished paper. Department of Economics, University of Wisconsin-Madison.

Haveman, Robert, and Barbara Wolfe. 1995. "The Determinants of Children's Attainments: A Review of Methods and Findings." *Journal of Economic Literature* XXXIII: 1829–78.

Helburn, Suzanne W., and Barbara R. Bergmann. 2002. *America's Childcare Problem. The Way Out.* New York: Palgrave.

Heymann, Jody. 2000. *The Widening Gap. Why America's Working Families are in Jeopardy—and What Can be Done About It.* New York: Basic Books.

Himmelweit, Susan. 1999. "Caring Labor." In *Emotional Labor in the Service Economy*, edited by Ronnie Steinberg and Deborah Figart. *Annals of the American Academy of Political and Social Science* 561(January): 27–38.

Jemmott, John B., Loretta Sweet Jemmott, and Geoffrey T. Fong. 1998. "Abstinence and Safer Sex HIV Risk-Reduction Interventions for African American Adolescents." *Journal of the American Medical Association* 279(19): 1529–36.

Jones, Elise, Jacqueline Darroch Forrest, Noreen Goldman, Stanley K. Henshaw, Richard Lincoln, Jeanie I. Rosoff, Charles F. Westoff, and Deirdre Wulf. 1985. "Teenage Pregnancy in Developed Countries," *Family Planning Perspectives* 17: 53–63.

Joshi, Heather. 1998. "The Opportunity Costs of Children: More than Mother's Business." *Journal of Population Economics* 11(2): 161–83.

Joshi, Heather, Pierella Paci, and Jane Waldfogel. 1999. "The Wages of Motherhood: Better or Worse." *Cambridge Journal of Economics* 23(5): 543–64.

Klerman, Jacob. 1999. "U.S. Abortion Policy and Fertility." *American Economic Review* 89(2): 261–64.

Ku, Leighton, and Brian Bruen. 1999. "The Continuing Decline in Medicaid Coverage." Series A, No. A-37. Washington, D.C.: Urban Institute Press.

Lee, Ronald, and Tim Miller. 1990. "Population Policy and Externalities to Childbearing." *Annals of the American Academy of Political and Social Science* 510(July): 17–32.

Lee, Sunwha, Melissa Sills, and Gi-Taik Oh. 2002. "Disabilities among Children and Mothers in Low-Income Families." Publication #D449, June 20, 2002. Washington, D.C.: Institute for Women's Policy Research.

Levine, Phillip B., Douglas Staiger, Thomas J. Kane, and David J. Zimmerman. 1999. "*Roe v. Wade* and American Fertility." *American Journal of Public Health* 89(February): 199–203.

Lundberg, Shelly, and Robert D. Plotnick. 1990. "Effects of State Welfare, Abortion and Family Planning Policies on Premarital Childbearing Among White Adolescents." *Family Planning Perspectives* 22(6): 246–63.

Matthews, Stephen, David Ribar, and Mark Wilhelm. 1997. "The Effects of Economic Conditions and Access to Reproductive Health Services on State Abortion Rates and Birthrates." *Family Planning Perspectives* 29(2): 52–60.

McLanahan, Sara, and Gary Sandefur. 1994. *Growing Up with a Single Parent. What Hurts, What Helps.* Cambridge, Mass.: Harvard University Press.

McLaughlin, Diane, and Daniel Lichter. 1997. "Poverty and the Marital Behavior of Young Women." *Journal of Marriage and the Family* 59(3): 582–94.

Mendeloff, John. 1977. "Welfare Procedures and Error Rates: An Alternative Perspective." *Policy Analysis* 3(3, Summer): 357–74.

Mincy, Ron, and Chen-Chung Huang. 2001. "Just Get Me to the Church . . .": Assessing Policies to Promote Marriage among Fragile Families." Prepared for the MacArthur Network on the Family and the Economy Meeting, Evanston, Ill. (November 30, 2001).

Mink, Gwendolyn. 1998. *Welfare's End.* Ithaca, N.Y.: Cornell University Press.

Morris, Pamela A., and Lisa Gennetian. 2002. "Identifying Effects of Income on Children's Development: Integrating an Instrumental Variables Analytic Method with an Experimental Design." Next Generation Working Paper No. 8. New York: MDRC (January 2002). Available at: http://www.mdrc.org (accessed May 24, 2004).

Morris, Pamela A., Aletha C. Huston, Greg J. Duncan, Danielle A. Crosby, and Johannes M. Bos. 2001. "How Welfare and Work Policies Affect Children: A Synthesis of Research." New York: MDRC (March 2001). Available at: http://www.mdrc.org (accessed May 24, 2004).

Moynihan, Daniel P. 1973. *The Politics of a Guaranteed Income. The Nixon Administration and the Family Assistance Plan.* New York: Random House.

Paxson, Christina, and Jane Waldfogel. 2001. "Welfare Reforms, Family Resources, and Child Maltreatment." Paper presented at the Association for Public Policy Analysis and Management 23rd Annual Research Conference (November 1–3, 2001, revised December 19, 2001).

Peters, Elizabeth, Laura M. Argys, Eleanor E. Maccoby, and Robert H. Mnookin. 1993. "Enforcing Divorce Settlements: Evidence from Child Support Compliance and Award Modifications." *Demography* 30(4): 719–735.

Pollin, Robert, and Stephanie Luce. 1998. *The Living Wage: Building a Fair Economy.* New York: The New Press.

Putnam, Robert D. 2000. *Bowling Alone. The Collapse and Revival of American Community.* New York: Simon & Schuster.

Roberts, Dorothy. 2002. *Shattered Bonds: The Color of Child Welfare.* New York: Basic Civitas Books.

Sampson, Robert, and John Laub. 1993. *Crime in the Making: Pathways and Turning Points Through Life.* Cambridge, Mass.: Harvard University Press.

Sawhill, Isabel V. 1999. "Non-Marital Births and Child Poverty in the United States." House Committee on Ways and Means, Subcommittee on Human Resources (June 29, 1999).

Sawhill, Isabel V., and Adam Thomas. 2001. "A Hand Up for the Bottom Third: Toward a New Agenda for Low-Income Working Families." Washington, D.C.: Brookings Institution Press. Available at: http://www.brook.edu/views/papers/sawhill/20010522.htm (accessed May 24, 2004).

Schor, Juliet. 1991. *The Overworked American.* New York: Basic Books.

Schumacher, Rachel, and Mark Greenberg. 1999. *Child Care After Leaving Welfare: Early Evidence from State Studies.* Washington, D.C.: Center for Law and Social Policy.

Seltzer, Judith A., Sara S. McLanahan, and Thomas L. Hanson. 1998. "Will Child Support Enforcement Increase Father-Child Contact and Parental Conflict after Separation?" In *Fathers under Fire*, edited by Irwin Garfinkel, Sara McLanahan, Daniel R. Meyer, and Judith A. Seltzer. New York: Russell Sage Foundation.

Sigle-Rushton, Wendy, and Sara McLanahan. 2001. "For Richer or Poorer?" Unpublished paper. Center for Research on Child Well-being, Princeton University.

Sorensen, Elaine. 1999. "Obligating Dads: Helping Low-Income Noncustodial Fathers Do More for Their Children." Research Brief. Washington, D.C.: Urban Institute Press.

Soss, Joe, Stanford F. Schram, Thomas V. Vartanian, and Erin O'Brien.

2001. "Setting the Terms of Relief: Explaining State Policy Choices in the Devolution Revolution." *American Journal of Political Science* 45(2): 378–95.

Stoney, Louise, and Mark H. Greenberg. 1996. "The Financing of Child Care: Current and Emerging Trends." *Future of Children: Financing Child Care* 6(2): 83–102.

U.S. Commission on Civil Rights. 2002. "A New Paradigm for Welfare Reform: The Need for Civil Rights Enforcement." Available at: http://www.usccr.gov/pubs/prwora/welfare.htm (accessed May 24, 2004).

U.S. Department of Education, National Center for Education Statistics. 2000. *The Condition of Education 2000*. NCES 2000–062. Washington: U.S. Government Printing Office.

U.S. Department of Health and Human Services. 2000. *Access to Child Care for Low Income Working Families*. Washington, D.C.: Administration for Children and Families. Available at: http://www.acf.dhhs.gov/news/press/2000/ccstudy.htm (accessed May 24, 2004).

Waite, Linda, and Maggie Gallagher. 2000. *The Case for Marriage*. New York: Doubleday.

Waldfogel, Jane. 1997. "The Effect of Children on Women's Wages." *American Sociological Review* 62(2): 209–217.

Weiss, Yoram, and Willis, Robert J. 1985. "Children as Collective Goods and Divorce Settlements." *Journal of Labor Economics* 3(3): 268–92.

Williams, Joan. 2000. *Unbending Gender. Why Family and Work Conflict and What to Do About It*. New York: Oxford University Press.

Zaslow, Martha J., Kristin A. Moore, Jennifer L. Brooks, Pamela Morris, Kathryn Tout, Zakia A. Redd, and Carol A. Emig. 2002. "Experimental Studies of Welfare Reform and Children." *The Future of Children* 12(1): 79–95.

Zedlewski, Sheila R. 2002. "Are Shrinking Caseloads Always a Good Thing?" No. 6 in Series, "Short Takes on Welfare Policy." Washington, D.C.: Urban Institute Press.

Zedlewski, Sheila R., and Sarah Brauner. 1999. "Are the Steep Declines in Food Stamp Participation Linked to Falling Welfare Caseloads?" Series B, No. B-3. Washington, D.C.: Urban Institute Press.

Zedlewski, Sheila R., Linda Giannarelli, Joyce Morton, and Laura Wheaton. 2002. "Extreme Poverty Rising, Existing Government Programs Could Do More." Urban Institute New Federalism Series B, No. B-45. Washington, D.C.: Urban Institute Press.

PART IV

Making Sense of Family
Change and Family Policy

CHAPTER TWELVE

The Value of Children

Samuel H. Preston

WILL MARSHALL and Isabel Sawhill say provocatively, "the sexual revolution, the movement for gender equity, and the emergence of a post-
industrial economy based on services and intangible goods—these factors
have overwhelmed the effects, for good or ill, of public policy on families" (see chapter 10). I believe their claim is and will continue to be
accurate. Social change has precluded our return to the family of the
1950s through any device of public design.

The reason is that neither men nor women are willing to accept at the
core of their adult lives an intimate relationship that is not working. The
clearest indication of where we stand in the welfare tradeoffs within a
family is the set of responses to a statement in the 1994 General Social
Survey (1994). The statement was: "When there are children in the family, parents should stay together even if they don't get along." Only 16
percent of the American population agreed with this (Child Trends
2002). People are not going to accept a bad relationship for the sake of
the children, and they are not hypocritical enough to ask others to do so.

The idea that we could make marginal changes in tax laws or in marital
entrance and exit requirements that would turn this ship around seems
fanciful to me. Adults have spoken, not just in the United States but
around the developed world, even in Ireland, where out-of-wedlock
births have risen from 5 percent to 32 percent in two decades, as Kathleen Kiernan and Daniel Moynihan point out. We have selected a family

life cycle that emphasizes the quality of adult relationships relative to the quality of childhood. Because we spend eighteen years or so as a child and sixty years as an adult, this choice would seem to make demographic sense. If children could vote, they might well pull the same lever.

But they cannot vote, and it offends our sense of justice and morality that they are the innocent victims of the choices that adults make. That is the crux of the problem—the principal problem that family policy must confront, in my view. I see no compelling social interest in encouraging childless couples to marry, even if we are assured that they would be happier if they did (see Waite and Gallagher 2000).

Wendy Sigle-Rushton and Sara McLanahan (see chapter 5) review a substantial amount of research that suggests, in the main, that children have better childhoods, and probably better life chances, when their biological parents are married to one another and live together. But, as noted earlier, there is no compelling evidence that social policy can do much to foster marriage. The very useful catalogue and review by Marshall and Sawhill describes programs that might have some positive effects, but it seems likely that those effects would be small, except perhaps in the area of teen pregnancy.

And it is worth noting that saving a relationship through, say, a $500 change in tax benefits sustains a relationship that is worth, at most, $500. This is not like giving farmers a cash incentive to grow more wheat that looks just like the wheat that's already being grown. We're talking about rescuing a relationship that would otherwise have failed. We cannot suppose that the benefits to children at this iffy margin, where there is often a good deal of conflict between spouses, would be the same as in the "average" marriage used to measure these benefits. Perhaps training people to achieve better relationships, as Wade Horn advocates (see chapter 9), is an exception to this pessimistic claim, but the evidence is too scanty to judge.

However, I am not convinced that posing the question the way we have done in much of this conference—contrasting in-wedlock to out-of-wedlock births and childrearing—does justice to the complexity of the issues, even allowing for the complications of cohabitation. It is not the case that the only alternative to an out-of-wedlock birth is an in-wedlock birth. Another alternative, hinted at by Douglas Wolf (see chapter 8), is no birth.

Would we as a society be better off if the children being born and raised out of wedlock were never born? This is a very real alternative. It is pursued, for example, by Italy and Spain, where very low rates of out-of-wedlock childbearing have contributed to the lowest overall fertility levels in the western world. Japan follows a similar pattern in Asia. Without the out-of-wedlock childbearing that occurs in the United States, our fertility rates would be at their approximate level, in a range of 1.4 births per woman, rather than near the replacement level of 2.1 where it currently resides. And these "childless" societies are in a state of near panic. Their low levels of fertility have become a leading social problem, creating a sense of demoralization and decline and making it extraordinarily expensive to maintain programs for the elderly.

Nancy Folbre cites Ron Lee's calculations (see chapter 11) showing the positive economic externalities of a birth in the United States, a benefit that is now worth well over $100,000 to the rest of society. The main reason for this result is an age-pattern of public transfers that is skewed towards older ages and hence that is easier to sustain in a younger, higher fertility population. In a world where over half of federal domestic spending goes to people over age sixty-five, children truly are a precious resource. Although Lee makes no distinction between children raised in and out of wedlock, the volume of age-based transfers is so biased towards the elderly that the result is nearly certain to pertain to both groups.

If children are a national asset, it follows that we should be grateful to, and provide support for, those who make enormous personal sacrifices to feed, clothe, and socialize them. As Nancy Folbre insists, the work may be largely unpaid but it is vital to the future of our society. It should not be taken for granted in formulating government programs because the volume of care depends on the environment in which it is expressed. For evidence, we need look no further than the effect of social changes over the past half century on the volume of care given by fathers. While 92 percent of American children live with their biological mothers over the course of childhood, the figure for fathers is now only about 50 percent (see chapter 2).

We would all agree that society needs to ensure that children are provided with the emotional, moral, and cognitive resources required to become productive adults. As now constructed, most of this massive provisioning is privately accomplished within the home. Public policy can operate indirectly by strengthening the private component, or directly by strengthening public schools, child care facilities, child welfare service, and AFDC (Aid to Families With Dependent Children program).

This conference is focused primarily on the indirect measure of improving a child's life by changing his or her living arrangements. Some may advocate an indirect approach because they are worried that direct approaches may reward mothers for bearing and raising children alone, that is, because it may encourage adverse outcomes. But as argued, we must think very carefully about whether raising children out of wedlock is indeed an adverse outcome.

Were we to decide that the well-being of children is the principal target of family policy, then direct routes to advancing it are demonstrably effective. For example, Lee Rainwater and Timothy Smeeding (see chapter 4) demonstrate that government transfer programs in many societies can be very successful in lifting children out of poverty. And when these are set in reverse, children can be harmed. Marshall and Sawhill and Folbre cite several studies showing a negative impact of welfare reform and related programs on child outcomes, including neglect (see chapters 10 and 11). Direct approaches can be used for good or ill, but there is little evidence that indirect approaches can be used at all.

REFERENCES

Child Trends. 2002. *Annual Report.* Washington, D.C.: Child Trends. Available at: http://www.teachmorelovemore.org/frame.asp?newlink= http://www.childtrends.org&return=/EarlyCareEduDetails.asp (accessed May 21, 2004).

General Social Survey. 1994. *The 1994 General Social Survey, Cycle 9, on Education, Work and Retirement.* Ottawa, Ont.: Statistics Canada. Available at: http://data.library.ubc.ca/datalib/guide/gss.html (accessed May 21, 2004).

Waite, Linda, and Maggie Gallagher. 2000. *The Case for Marriage.* New York: Doubleday Books.

CHAPTER THIRTEEN

Values, Policy, and the Family

Frank F. Furstenberg

THROUGHOUT THE past century, especially in the last few decades, marriage practices have been altered in ways that seem either irrevocable, as many authors suggest, or at least very difficult to reinstate, even if we could agree that it were desirable to do so. Moreover, these changes have been widespread, if not universal, throughout the West and there is growing evidence that the weakening of marriage, as a life-long social form, is occurring throughout much of the world.

It seems there is also agreement that this decline of marriage is exacting a cost for children. Although there is not consensus on its size or how much of it can be attributed to family instability. I think no one would argue that family dissolution enhances children's welfare, unless the parents' marriage is highly dysfunctional, in which case everyone agrees that the child is better with one parent than two.

Where marriage survives as a binding contract between individuals, in countries such as Italy, Greece, or even Japan, it is not necessarily fulfilling its traditional function as the institution of social reproduction because birth rates are so low that they endanger the maintenance of the population. Consequently, one might well argue that where marriage has been resistant to change, the consequences for the population have been more adverse than where it has been altered by common practice. So it seems that contemporary societies are damned either way. A sad state of affairs, indeed.

How then can we imagine the renovation of marriage or marriage-like arrangements that provide the stability, security, and nurture that children need to realize their potential? The central policy question here is how to make marriage more attractive and more viable through shifts in the culture, public policies, or programs designed to shore up marriage. This may not be the right question or at least the most compelling one. Rather, we are likely to address the problem more effectively by addressing the inequities that may be created by growing up in a nonnuclear family than by trying to manufacture more nuclear families as a way of reducing social and economic disadvantage. If this proposition isn't controversial enough, I further claim that we are more likely to improve the state of marriage by adopting the policy of enhancing children's welfare than enhancing marriage directly.

THE PROBLEM OF VALUES

The starting point for this thesis is the long-standing uneasiness that Americans have about adopting policies that might seem to undermine marriage and the family. Historians have pointed out that the nuclear family has been enshrined in American culture from the colonial era onward even though the structure of family was more variable in the eighteenth and nineteenth centuries than even today. Nonetheless, the American family, as one social historian observed, was born modern even if a large proportion of children did grow up in nonnuclear families, thanks to the high rates of mortality and separation throughout much of our early history. Apparently, many children survived, then as now, in single-parent or nonparent households, growing up to function well and productively as adults.

De Tocqueville, among other foreign visitors, observed that marriage and family relations were the seedbed of democracy and thus the essential institution in American society. Throughout much of our history, we have privileged the nuclear family as if it almost single-handedly explains children's success as adults and the success of American society. Americans believe that the nuclear family is, as Wade Horn observes, a natural form despite overwhelming evidence by anthropologists that no human family form is universal much less natural (see chapter 9). Little wonder that we worry more about the impact of family change than any of our European counterparts. By acting as if families are singularly responsible for children, we have placed huge burdens on parents to shoulder the costs of childrearing and accorded parents the responsibility for their children's fate in life.

Paradoxically, despite these beliefs, we have the highest rate of family instability of any nation in the industrial world, though New Zealand, a country that shares our libertarian ideology, runs a close second in divorce, out-of-wedlock childbearing, and single parenthood. Americans have generally steered clear of many of the social welfare policies that could support children and families despite the lip service typically given by politicians and policy makers to child and family friendly policies. When Richard Nixon faced the choice of signing a bill greatly expanding child care services for parents, he couldn't overcome the strong objections of many of his advisors that by doing so, he would create incentives for parents to go to work and hence undermine the family. Similarly, many argue that no-fault divorce ushered in high rates of divorce, that public assistance made out-of-wedlock childbearing more attractive, and that tax policies discourage marriage, and even that marriage among gays will lead to a depreciation of heterosexual marriage. In this triumph of Orwellian logic, policies aimed at supporting the family in fact do just the opposite.

The evidence that family policies have perverse effects on family stability is far from impressive. Few would claim that Nixon's veto of child care legislation kept parents out of the labor force or that promoting contraceptive use increases early and out-of-wedlock parenthood in Europe. Divorce liberalization did not increase divorce beyond a short period of pent-up demand by couples who were already separated or about to separate, and welfare reform has done little if anything to restore marriage. By contrast, there is strong empirical evidence that male joblessness and low earnings produce higher rates of nonmarriage and divorce. Lack of child care forces many parents to stay out of the labor force while its availability seems to reduce stress on marriage. So it seems that many of our objections to supporting the family materially in the form of income supplements and social services have as much to do with our views about the appropriate relationship between the public and private spheres of life as they do with real concerns about undermining marriage and the family.

IMPACT OF FAMILY STRUCTURE ON CHILDREN'S WELL-BEING

Similarly, the evidence on the effects of nonnuclear arrangements on children's well-being is heavily contaminated by an ideological predisposition to believe that parenting is severely compromised when one or both parents are absent from the home. Everyone agrees that children do not fare as well in nonnuclear households, but the explanation for this empirical observation is anything but clear-cut (see chapter 5). Wendy Sigle-Rushton and Sara McLanahan's summary of the most recent literature is somewhat more cautious and circumspect than the message in McLanahan's earlier widely cited collaboration with Gary Sandefur (1994). Researchers have become far more sensitive to the limitations of statistical controls as a means of ruling out unobserved biases than they were a decade or two ago. As Sigle-Rushton and McLanahan observe, the modest to moderate effects attributed to divorce on children's well-being might be greatly attenuated were we able to conduct a random assignment on the impact of marriage and stability (see chapter 5).

It is useful to remember that the period of the 1950s and early 1960s, now regarded with such nostalgia as the heyday of the nuclear family, raised the cohort of children who experienced as teenagers a sharp increase in delinquency, drug use, declining academic scores, and, of course, the spectacular rise in sexual activity and nonmarital, teenage childbearing. Conversely, all these behaviors dropped or leveled off in the late 1990s when close to 50 percent of America's children were growing up in single-parent households. At a macro-level at least, indicators of children's well-being and adult behaviors track changes in the family circumstances very poorly.

Let us suppose, for example, we had a successful way of intervening to promote marriage through family education programs or to deter divorce through counseling unhappily married parents to work through their problems, would we find that the effects of these interventions result in a distinct advantage for children? Probably so, but I am prepared to speculate that the marginal differences of persuading cohabiting parents to wed or discontented couples to remain married might be far less than when parents make these decisions on their own. Many might spend more years in marriage, but would their children be better off as a result? There is no evidence to my knowledge that children spending fifteen years living in a two-biological-parent family fare substantially better than those who spend half or a third of that time doing so. In one English data set parents who delayed divorce until their children had grown up conferred some advantages for their children compared to those who divorced earlier, but the differences were for the most part confined to the timing of sexual activity and family formation rather than school achievement and earnings (Furstenberg and Kiernan 1998). In sum, there is surely something to be gained by increasing the proportion of children growing up in nuclear families, but even if we designed successful policies to achieve that goal, the alteration of children's life course would be far less dramatic than many imagine.

This leads me to consider several alternative models of how we think about the link between children's well-being, the form of the family, and the general welfare of society (see figure 13.1 for a simplified schematic on differing assumptions about these links).

David Ellwood and Christopher Jencks (chapter 2) on the location and

Figure 13.1   Links Between Child, Family, and Social Well-Being

Model 1: Ellwood and Jencks; Kiernan; Moynihan, Rainwater, and Smeeding

Model 2: Sigle-Rushton and McLanahan; Horn

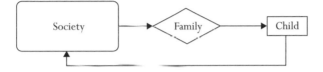

Model 3: Folbre

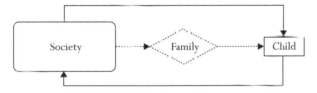

Model 4: Strengthening Marriage Through Family-Neutral Policy

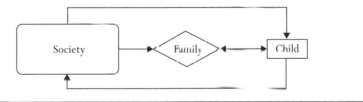

Source: Author's compilation.

sources of marital decline, the comparative perspective on the rise of cohabitation in the West by Kathleen Kiernan (chapter 3), and the summary of marriage and public policies by Daniel Patrick Moynihan, Lee Rainwater, and Timothy Smeeding (chapter 1) are all concerned with the relationship between social and economic change and marriage or its alternatives. Each points to why marriage has become a less obvious choice for young adults. These go a long way towards explaining how younger cohorts have come to think of marriage differently than older and why they may think that it offers fewer advantages to them and their children. The focus is primarily on the changing relationship between society and the family (S → F).

Sigle-Rushton and McLanahan (chapter 5) take up the effects of the family form on children's well-being and social reproduction, showing how and why the offspring of nonnuclear families are disadvantaged and, by implication, the impact reaches the next generation. Their purview is how family forms affect children and the potential problems that form creates for the welfare of society (F → C → S). If this generation of children is less well prepared to enter adulthood, the social costs incurred affect family functioning in the next generation.

This is the starting point for Horn and Nancy Folbre (chapters 9 and 11). Both concern themselves with policy alternatives that might be designed to change the current relationship between family forms and outcomes for children. Horn argues that marriage, if not the only form that promotes children's well-being, is surely the best. He contends that strengthening marriage is the most effective way to improve children's well-being and hence strengthen society (F → C → S). Folbre questions that proposition by posing a series of dilemmas or tradeoffs that might be involved when policy makers address the form of the family. She points to the hidden costs of attempts to restore the institution of marriage, at least as it existed in the heyday of the nuclear family.

Folbre's analysis is provocative, raising as it does interesting questions about the traditional model so widely endorsed by American policy makers: strengthening marriage improves the situation of children and therefore strengthens the larger society. Instead, she points to an alternative model: investing in children directly, in whatever family form they reside, is the best route to effective social reproduction (S → C → S). Her diagnosis of and prescription for managing changes in the institution of marriage, to borrow a phrase from Moynihan, is to adopt a policy of "benign neglect." Focus on supporting the children and their families rather than worrying about what form of family is most efficient and effective. This appears to be the favored strategy of most European countries whose policies do not explicitly favor one form of the family or another.

Folbre's argument for family neutrality might actually work to strengthen marriage rather than undermine it, as is widely believed by many policy makers. Advocates of a pro-marriage approach argue that life-long marriage is the best form of the family for children. They point to the reasons Horn outlines and Sigle-Rushton and McLanahan review on the effects of marital disruption. I do not dispute the evidence but, like Folbre, I do not think that it necessarily follows from this evidence that the best solution is to privilege the nuclear family in our public policies.

My argument goes a bit further than Folbre's. I would argue that by supporting children and parents regardless of the family form is paradoxically the best way of producing more nuclear families. I think the evidence presented here points to reasons why this seemingly improbable scenario is likely to occur.

First, many of the benefits that are family neutral will help make it easier for parents to contemplate marriage and remain in marriage. We cannot disregard the overwhelming evidence from numerous surveys and qualitative studies that the vast majority of low-income and less-educated young people want to get married. In my study of a cohort of teenage mothers and their children in Baltimore, there was widespread wariness about marriage among the women in younger generation, but nearly to a person most wanted and expected to marry someday. Before marrying, they simply wanted to feel more confident about the prospects of the marriage enduring than they did when interviewed in their early twenties. Few felt that the men that they could marry were suitable and reliable partners. They averred that they wanted to wait so that they could have the kind of marriage that their grandparents, rather than their parents, had had. Helping the men whom they might marry return to school, get training, and find and secure remunerative employment would do a lot to make marriage more attractive. So too would efforts to provide support for unmarried couples if they felt that they had access to a range of social services from counseling to child care. Thus there is nothing inconsistent about supporting parents and their children and supporting marriage. Such services could be offered to all low-income parents regardless of their family circumstances; provided with such support, some parents would elect to marry and others might be encouraged to develop more collaborative and mutually supportive care for their children.

A range of economic and social services for low-income married couples might also reduce the incidence of divorce. The vast majority of low-income parents do marry, most often, I suspect, to the father of their first child. But the rates of divorce remain high, as Ellwood and Jencks observe, for this segment of the population and even for those with modest incomes and some college education (see chapter 2). The strains on these families, like those with more resources, are considerable. Bouts of unemployment, financial crises, conflicting job demands, and time pressures on working parents undermine marital solidarity. People can be taught to manage family strains more effectively, but they apply these lessons more successfully if society does more to relieve some of the material stresses on parents. Holding existing marriages together through a combination of material, social, and psychological support makes good policy sense if we believe that children are better off in stable unions.

Even acknowledging that we can greatly improve our efforts to preserve marriage, I argue that we must accept that for the foreseeable future out-of-wedlock childbearing will occur. In the 1950s, at least 25 percent of all first marriages followed a premarital pregnancy. The majority of those marriages did not survive, helping to produce the huge upsurge in divorce in the following decade. In the Baltimore study, close to half of the women married the father of their child. Four out of five of these marriages did not survive. The children of these abortive marriages did not do better than the children whose mothers elected not to marry the father of the child. This finding suggests that we should be very wary of promoting marriages because we think children are better off if their parents marry. They are not unless their parents marry successfully.

The alternative to promoting marriage exclusively is to support low-income parents so long as they are involved in child care and to support children's material, health, educational, and psychological needs directly. Were we to do so, this family neutral approach would likely produce long-term effects that support marriage as much as an explicit marriage-best policy. To the extent that such provisions reduce the proportion of poorly educated and unskilled youth and those with criminal experience, we would surely increase the pool of marriageable young people. While evidence exists that young people are less inclined to marry or marry successfully when they have grown up in a nonnuclear family, most are still committed to the institution of marriage. In other words, their poorer success rates have less to do with their ideals and aspirations than they do with their skills and abilities. Again, drawing on data from the Baltimore study, the overwhelming majority of offspring of teen mothers wanted to marry and many of them, after achieving their educational goals and entering the labor force, were either married or poised to enter marriage.

Referring again to figure 13.1, I advocate a policy approach that supports the child as a means of supporting the family as well as supporting the family as a means of supporting the child ($S \rightarrow C \rightarrow F$ and $S \rightarrow F \rightarrow C \rightarrow F$). Both routes—supporting children through family policies and direct aid for children's educational, health, and social services (such as child care and after school programs) —are likely to produce benefits in the next generation that redound in a favorable way toward strengthening marriage.

While I have not attempted to do so, it is possible to estimate the relative payoff of direct and indirect supports designed to strengthen union stability by examining the intergenerational pattern of marriage practices under different hypothetical policy approaches. Based on my data from Baltimore, I hypothesize that it may actually be more efficient over time to invest in children directly as a means of increasing union stability than to help children by helping their parents stay together. Let me be clear, I do not see these approaches as competing strategies for increasing union stability because most policies that support children ultimately help the parents. Building stronger child care programs, more effective mental health and counseling services, or, for that matter, better schools in disadvantaged communities, are all services for parents, whether married or unmarried.

It is unfortunate that conservatives, who believe in strengthening marriage, and liberals, who want to see family inequality reduced, cannot agree on a set of family friendly policies that achieve both ends. The evidence indicates that helping parents—those who live together in wedlock, those who are previously married, those who might marry, and those who have no prospect of marriage—to support and nurture their children and to manage to do so in a collaborative manner is likely to have the highest payoff in producing stable families in the next generation.

REFERENCES

Furstenberg, Frank, and Kathleen Kiernan. 1998. "Delayed Parental Divorce: How Much Do Children Benefit?" *The Journal of Marriage and the Family* 63(2): 446–57.

McLanahan, Sara, and Gary Sandefur. 1994. *Growing Up with a Single Parent: What Hurts, What Helps.* Cambridge, Mass.: Harvard University Press.

CHAPTER FOURTEEN

Policy and the Family

Irwin Garfinkel

No one has done more than Senator Daniel Patrick Moynihan to call attention to the importance of the question of how public policies affect families. Put simply, the long-term health of the nation depends on the health of its families. All of us share that view.

Through their pioneering work with the Luxembourg Income Study (LIS), Lee Rainwater and Timothy Smeeding have been educating Americans and Europeans about poverty and single-parenthood from a cross-national perspective for two decades (chapters 1 and 4). They use LIS data to demonstrate convincingly that children in single-mother families in the United States fare worse than children in most other western European nations mainly because U.S. policies result in less support for families with children.

David Ellwood and Christopher Jencks document the disconnect between marriage and childbearing and its differential effect by class (chapter 2). For those with a college education, there has been an increase in the age of marriage and the age of childbearing. For those with less than a college education, the age at marriage has increased, but the age at childbearing increased much less. In consequence, out-of-wedlock births are primarily a phenomenon of those who have no more than a high school degree. Although the causes of the huge increase in single parenthood and out-of-wedlock childbearing are not well understood, all the research indicates that a decline in job opportunities and wages for low-skilled males is partly responsible. The effects of women's employment and welfare are less clear. Finally, changes in culture play some role. They recommend better jobs for men and supports for two-parent families.

Kathleen Kiernan (chapter 3) tells us that out-of-wedlock childbearing and cohabitation have increased dramatically in most European nations and are here to stay. The southern European nations are an exception, but in these countries women are having fewer than two children. While cohabitation without children cuts across class lines and is associated with women's independence, unmarried parenthood in Europe, as in the United States, appears to be associated with poverty rather than empowerment.

Ellwood and Jencks distinguish between cultural and economic explanations for the increase in single-parenthood, but Folbre sees the two as interrelated. That strikes me as accurate. Surely, the steady, dramatically large increase in women's participation in the workforce throughout the twentieth century and the accompanying liberation of women is a driving force in the changes in norms regarding marriage and childbearing. A century and a half ago, Marx and Engels predicted in *The Communist Manifesto* (1848) that capitalism would undermine the traditional family by drawing women into the market economy. Their language was colorful. Capitalism, they said, respected nothing and swept all before it. About 100 years later, Nobel Prize winner Gary Becker, using the tools of modern economic analysis, made much the same argument in the *Economics of Discrimination* (1971) with respect to racial discrimination. In the long run, capitalism will undermine both racial and gender discrimination. Why the economic emergence of women (Bergman 1986) has had a more deleterious effect on the family at the bottom of the income distribution needs to be explained.

Sigle-Rushton and McLanahan document big differences in outcomes for children from one- and two-parent families and show that many, but not all, of the differences are due to differences between such families rather than to family structure (chapter 5). Some of the differences are due to differences in the incomes of one- and two-parent families and to differences in parenting practices, and to the absence of a father.

Wade Horn (chapter 9) makes the case for healthy marriages being the best institution for promoting child well-being and recommends funds for experiments to test the effectiveness of PREP (The Prevention and Relationship Enhancement Program) and other marriage training and counseling programs. He recommends reauthorizing (Temporary Assistance for Needy Families) TANF with a forty-hour requirement—only twenty-four of which need be for work, giving a larger percentage of child support collections to TANF recipients, and promoting responsible fatherhood, and improvements in early childhood programs. Horn has done the nation a great service by adding the adjective "healthy" to marriage promotion. Promoting marriage without stigmatizing single parent-hood is quite an accomplishment and the adjective healthy achieves that by recognizing that some marriages are unhealthy. Marriage preparation and training programs may increase marriage rates, are unlikely to cause any harm, and are therefore worth trying. Making serious inroads into nonmarriage at the bottom of the income distribution, however, is likely to require much stronger and more expensive medicine.

Will Marshall and Isabel Sawhill (chapter 10) offer us a smorgasbord of proposals. To prevent teen pregnancy, they advocate sex education (including but broader than abstinence), media campaigns, after-school programs, second chance homes, and assistance with adoption and (as a last resort) abortion. Staying the course on welfare reform, eliminating discrimination against two-parent families, and increasing TANF benefit levels and/or the EITC (Earned Income Tax Credit) are also recommended. To promote responsible fatherhood, they would use TANF funds to put men to work and focus on work after prison. To decrease divorce, they would permit no-fault divorce only with mutual consent, require longer waiting periods to allow couples to rethink decisions, require child support for post-secondary education up to age twenty-one, and make joint legal custody presumptive. To make the tax system more marriage friendly they would reduce marriage penalties by extending the use of refundable tax credits. To balance work and family concerns, they would increase federal child care funding, enact a paid family leave program, and adopt universal pre-kindergarten and after school programs. Most of the money they would spend would be devoted to the final set of child care programs.

Nancy Folbre (chapter 11) urges us to balance incentives for engaging in market work with those for family work. If caring is discouraged, family and ultimately productivity will be undermined. The beauty here lies in the grandness of the vision and the central organizing principle of family care. But Folbre also offers us specific policy recommendations, which overlap to a large degree with Marshall and Sawhill's. She favors sex education (broader than abstinence only) and making abortion more available. More important, she favors universal programs and less reliance on income testing in general and in particular, like Marshall and Sawhill, universal paid family leave and child care.

POLICY CONSIDERATION

A central question that both Folbre and Marshall-Sawhill raise is how to reduce the economic insecurity of single-mother families without unduly increasing their prevalence (Garfinkel and McLanahan 1988). Under the best of circumstances, there will be single-parent families. And they will be poorer than two-parent families because they will have only one wage-earning adult. The answer is to support both one- and two-parent families. Universal provision promotes marriage, first, by raising living standards of low income married couples and helping them balance work and family and, second, by avoiding incentives to become a single-parent family as a way to get benefits limited to single-parent families. The United States is a long way from the ideal of providing benefits to both one- and two-parent families but should move in that direction.

During the 1960s, there was a consensus across the political spectrum about the desirability of eliminating marriage disincentives in welfare—then the Aid to Families With Dependent Children (AFDC) program. The program was criticized for limiting benefits to single-parent families. In 1962, AFDC benefits were extended to families with unemployed fathers, but eligibility for AFDC-UP (Aid to Families with Dependent Children Unemployed Parents) was far more restrictive than AFDC for single mothers. Only about half of the states adopted it. The federal Food Stamps Program in the 1970s and Medicaid eligibility expansions in the 1980s helped put two-parent families on a more equal footing. The Family Support Act of 1988 and the Personal Responsibility and Work Opportunity Reconciliation Act of 1996 also strove to end discrimination against married parents. But in seventeen states TANF and Medicaid still apply rules that make it difficult for two-parent families to receive benefits. Single-parent families continue to get preference indirectly through the priority given to TANF and ex-TANF recipients for underfunded child care subsidy programs. Similarly restrictions against ex-offenders in public housing favor single-parent families. More fundamentally, the steep income testing of TANF benefits combined with the cumulative effects of income testing in Medicaid, food stamps, child care, and housing encourages poor men and women who face risky employment prospects to avoid marriage, associate informally, and depend on welfare.

Discrimination against married couples is not limited to programs for the poor. The EITC contains both marriage bonuses and marriage penalties, as does the broader income tax of which it is a part (Ellwood and Liebman 2001). The biggest EITC marriage penalties are for families in which both low-skilled parents work.

The motivation for categorical discrimination and income testing is, in large part, to target limited public funds on the most needy parents. While understandable in principle, in practice this approach is "penny wise and pound foolish." By placing a wedge between a father's earnings and his children's available resources, these policies reduce children's living standards and create a disincentive for marriage.

Figure 14.1   Universality of Expenditures for the Non-Aged for the
United States and Other Welfare States, Fiscal Year
1997

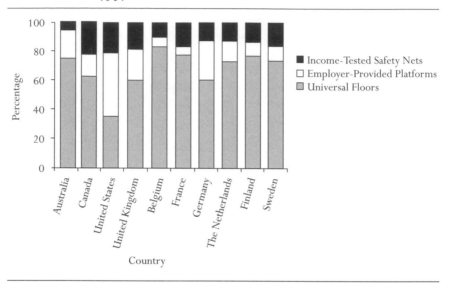

Source: Author's compilation.

Although previous research has shown that the effects of AFDC/TANF on marriage are small, there is no research on the magnitude of the total effects of all the marriage penalties in our income support programs. Taken together, TANF, food stamps, Medicaid, housing subsidies, child care subsidies, and the EITC loom very large in the lives of the poor and near poor. If each program reduced marriage by only 4 percent, the effect would be very small and very difficult to detect. But the sum of the individual program effects could be substantial.

As figure 14.1 indicates, the United States welfare state is unique in the degree to which it relies upon a bifurcated system of income-tested benefits for the poor and employer-provided benefits for the nonpoor for non-aged families. (Garfinkel et al., forthcoming). The other English-speaking countries are the only ones that approach us in this domain. Similarly, though other countries such as Sweden have higher rates of out-of-wedlock births (see table 1.1), the United States also stands out as having far and away the highest proportion of children who live apart from one or both biological parents before reaching adulthood. And though the Andersson table does not reflect this, Kiernan assures me that the other English-speaking countries also have very high rates. It is possible that this relationship between income testing and family breakup is due to cultural differences. The English-speaking peoples do put a premium on individualism and independence. But it is also possible, indeed likely, that some or most of the relationship is causal.

We can reduce marriage penalties by cutting benefits to single-parent families, but that will harm those who are already vulnerable. We can reduce them by increasing benefits to two-parent families. But making public support programs more marriage friendly by making them available to one- and two-parent families is relatively costly because we already provide a relatively generous benefit package to low income single-mother families and very little to two-parent families. We keep the costs of the benefits low by explicitly limiting them to poor families and in some cases to single-parent families, and/or by giving single-parent families priority for scarce services, and/or by structuring the programs such that the government rather than the parents capture any economies of scale.

Undermining marriage at the bottom of the income distribution by over-reliance on income testing is probably undesirable for any nation. For the United States, it is particularly undesirable because it exacerbates racial cleavages. That the proportion of out-of-wedlock black births is almost three times higher than white and that the white proportion is now as high as the black was when Moynihan wrote his *Report on the Negro Family* (1965) are both concerning. That overreliance on income testing may be contributing substantially to both the general increase and the racial differential should be of equal concern.

REFERENCES

Becker, Gary. 1971. *Economics of Discrimination*. Chicago: University of Chicago Press.

Bergman, Barbara. 1986. *The Economic Emergence of Women*. New York: Basic Books.

Ellwood, David, and Jeffrey Liebman. 2001. "The Middle Class Parent Penalty." In *Tax Policy and the Economy Volume 15*, edited by James M. Poterba. Cambridge, Mass.: MIT Press.

Garfinkel, Irwin, Howard Chernick, Marilyn Sinkewicz, and Patrick Villeneuve. Forthcoming. "Social Welfare Expenditures and Beyond." In *New York City and the Welfare State*, edited by Irwin Garfinkel and Marcia Meyers. New York: Russell Sage Foundation.

Garfinkel, Irwin, and Sara McLanahan. 1988. *Single Mothers and Their Children*. Lanham, Md.: University Press of America.

Marx, Karl, and Friedrich Engels. 1848. *The Communist Manifesto*. London, England: League member J. E. Burghard's London Printshop.

Moynihan, Daniel Patrick. 1965. (March) "The Moynihan Report." *The Negro Family: The Case for National Action*. Office of Policy Planning and Research, United States Department of Labor. Washington: U.S. Government Printing Office.

————. 1986. *Family and Nation*. New York: Harcourt Brace Jovanovich.

Myrdal, Alva. 1941. *Nation and Family: The Swedish Experiment in Democratic Family and Population Policy*. Cambridge, Mass.: MIT Press.

INDEX

Numbers in **boldface** refer to figures or tables.